GARVEY
AFRICA, EUROPE,
THE AMERICAS

GARVEY
AFRICA, EUROPE, THE AMERICAS

Edited by
Rupert Lewis & Maureen Warner-Lewis

Africa World Press, Inc.
P.O. Box 1892
Trenton, New Jersey 08607

Africa World Press, Inc.

P.O. Box 1892
Trenton, New Jersey 08607

First Printing

Book design: Jonathan Gullery

Library of Congress Cataloging-in-Publication Data

Garvey : Africa, Europe, the Americas / edited by Rupert Lewis &
  Maureen Warner-Lewis
        p.   cm.
    "Papers . . . originally presented at International Seminar on
Marcus Garvey."
    Includes bibliographical references (p.).
    ISBN 0-86543-415-8. - - ISBN 0-86543-416-6 (pbk.)
    1. Garvey, Marcus, 1887–1940--Congresses. 2. Back to Africa
movement--Congresses. 3. Universal Negro Improvement Association -
-History--Congresses. 4. Afro-Americans--Race identity--Congresses.
I. Lewis, Rupert. II. Lewis, Maureen Warner. III. International
Seminar on Marcus Garvey (1973 : Mona, Jamaica)
E185.97.G3G34   1994
305 . 896 ' 073--dc20
                                        93-43428
                                          CIP

CONTENTS

PREFACE

This collection of essays constitutes a tribute to the 100th anniversary of the birth of Marcus Garvey which will be observed in 1987. The papers were however originally presented at the International Seminar on Marcus Garvey organized by ASAWI, the African Studies Association of the West Indies, Mona, Jamaica, from 2-6 January 1973. But the publication of these papers more than a decade later testifies to the abiding relevance of Garvey's life and work, to the significance of the 1973 congress of Garvey scholars, and to the high quality of the research undertaken by the Seminar presenters.

At that Seminar, Garvey scholars and activists from the Caribbean, North America, Europe and Africa met in Jamaica for a week of papers and discussion. The conference covered many areas of Garvey's work and the papers were written from many differing viewpoints. As Tony Martin has observed, "The papers ... are by persons of widely differing political persuasions and consequently perspectives on Garvey's successes, failures and importance vary somewhat. Among the authors are Black persons writing from Marxist, nationalist and moderate middle-of-the-road positions; and also Whites with socialist and conservative perspectives." As such, these papers evoked lively discussion and comment not only from other scholars but also from Garvey's contemporaries, Rastafarians and young people who were eager to know about Garvey and to examine the many myths that had arisen about him.

For their part, many of the contributors to the conference were already, or were to be, authors and editors of important works on Garvey. They included Amy Jacques Garvey *(Philosophy and Opinions of Marcus Garvey; Garvey and Garveyism);* Tony Martin *(Race First: the ideological and organizational struggles of Marcus Garvey and the Universal Negro Improvement Association, Literary Garveyism,* and other writings); E.U. Essien-Udom (co-editor with Amy Jacques Garvey of *Philosophy and Opinions of Marcus Garvey,* Vol. III); Theodore Vincent

(Black Power and the Garvey Movement); W.F. Elkins, *Black Nationalism in the British West Indies, 1918-1920.* Emory Tolbert was to become one of the editors, along with Robert Hill, of the path-breaking documentary collection *The Marcus Garvey and the Universal Negro Improvement Association Papers* and, for his own part, was to publish *The UNIA and Black Los Angeles.* Rupert Lewis' study entitled *Marcus Garvey Anti-Colonial Champion,* is to be published shortly. Other contributors had published scholarly articles on Garvey.

The Seminar was in large measure a tribute not only to Marcus Garvey but also to Amy Jacques Garvey's own work alongside him during his lifetime, and after his death in 1940. In this post-1940 period, she played an important role as an information co-ordinator and resource person on the movement in which she was such an active participant. No scholar who presented a paper at the Seminar was not indebted to her for help. All had lengthy correspondence with her and most had visited and interviewed her. But little did we know that the Seminar was to be the last major public appearance of Garvey's second wife, who was to live only six months longer. However, at the Opening of the Seminar in January of 1973 she gave an impassioned speech on the life and work of her husband.

Fully aware of Garvey's place in history, she counted him among those "men and women who have emerged from their environment and so far out-distanced their contemporaries in thought and action, that in their day they were apt to be called mad, dangerous or fools ... Heredity and environment seem to influence them ... to carry out a spiritual urge in a given time, an experiment, a mission, or a task." Garvey was obsessed by "the feeling of pity for the underdog," and by the conviction that "Africans at home and abroad" should "be given an opportunity in life to develop themselves to the highest."

Others who spoke at the Seminar Opening were Marcus Garvey Jr. and Michael Manley, then Prime Minister of Jamaica. The Jamaican government had, through the Institute of Jamaica, given welcome material and moral support for the Seminar, thereby enabling this brainchild of ASAWI President, Professor Arthur Drayton, to see the light of day.

In his address, Michael Manley signaled Garvey's intellectual contribution to 20th century national liberation movements which stemmed from his insistence that "the capacity to demand freedom must begin first of all with a process of inner psychological liberation," his "perception of destiny" based on "a spirit of self-reliance," and the continuing validity of his concerns. "Of all our National Heroes, Garvey, who was the first, was the only one whose contribution was genuinely international in its scope and significance," conceded Manley, himself the son of one of Jamaica's National Heroes.

Indeed, as the title of the Seminar as well as of this volume indicates, the essays here have a significant bearing on a new international assessment of Garveyism. They represent an important beginning in re-evaluating this activist and thinker after many years of either neglect or misrepresentation. This collection, it is hoped, will stimulate others in the direction of further research on Garvey, whose activities and writings remain relevant as long as the struggle against racism, colonialism and neo-colonialism continues. The complexity of Garvey's movement for self- and national liberation, and the variety of perspectives offered here bear witness to the significance of such an important early 20th century figure as Marcus Garvey, and to the force of his ideas.

Rupert Lewis
Maureen Warner-Lewis
February 1986

THE AMERICAN ANTECEDENTS OF MARCUS GARVEY

John Henrik Clarke

It is no accident that Marcus Garvey had his greatest success in the United States among Black Americans. There is an historical logic to this occurrence that seems to have escaped most of the interpreters of Garvey's life and the mass movement that he built. For in many ways the scene was being prepared for Marcus Garvey for over one hundred years before he was born. There is no way to understand this without looking at the American antecedents of Marcus Garvey, that is the men, forces and movements that came before him.

West Indians in the Afro-American Struggle

Prior to the Civil War, the West Indian contribution to the progress of Afro-American life was one of the main contributing factors in the fight for freedom and full citizenship in the northern United States. West Indians had come to the United States during the 18th and 19th centuries and the most outstanding of them saw their plight and that of the Afro-American as being one and the same.

In 18th century America, two of the most outstanding fighters for liberty and justice were the West Indians, Prince Hall and John B. Russwurm. When Prince Hall came to the United States the nation was in turmoil. The colonies were ablaze with indignation. Britain, with a series of revenue acts, had stoked the fires of colonial discontent. In Virginia, Patrick Henry was speaking of liberty or death. The cry "No Taxation Without Representation" played on the nerve strings of the nation. Prince Hall, then a delicate-looking teenager, often walked through the turbulent streets of Boston, an observer unobserved. A few months before these hectic scenes, he had arrived in the United States from his home in Barbados, where he had been born about 1748, the son of an Englishman and a free African woman. He was, in theory, a free man, but he knew that neither in Boston nor in Barbados were persons of African descent free in fact. At once, he questioned the sincerity of the vocal white patriots of Boston. It never seemed to have occurred to them that the announced principles motivating their action made stronger argument in favor of destroying the system of slavery. The colonists held in servitude more than a half million human beings, some of them white; yet they engaged in the contradiction of going to war to support the theory that all men were created equal.

When Prince Hall arrived in Boston that city was the center of the American slave trade. Most of the major leaders of the revolutionary movement, in fact, were slave-holders or investors in slave-supported businesses. Hall, like many other Americans, wondered: what did these men mean by freedom? The condition of the free Black men, as Prince Hall found them, was not an enviable one. Emancipation brought neither freedom nor relief from the stigma of color. They were free in name only. They were still included in slave codes with slaves, indentured servants, and Indians. Discriminatory laws severely circumscribed their freedom of movement.

By 1765, through diligence and frugality, Hall became a property owner, thus establishing himself in the eyes of white as well as Black people. But the ownership of property was not enough. He still had to endure sneers and insults. He decided then to prepare himself for a role of leadership among his people. To this end he went to school at night and later became a Methodist preacher. His church became the forum for his people's grievances. Ten years after his arrival in Boston, Massachusetts, he was the accepted leader of the Black community.

In 1788 Hall petitioned the Massachusetts Legislature, protesting the kidnapping of free Negroes. This was a time when American patriots were engaged in a constitutional struggle for freedom. They had proclaimed the inherent rights of all mankind to life, liberty and the pursuit of happiness. Hall dared to remind them that the Black men in the United States were human beings, and as such were entitled to freedom and respect for their human personality.

It was racial prejudice which made Hall the father of African secret societies in the United States, what is now known as the "Negro Masonry." Hall first sought initiation into the white Masonic Lodge in Boston, but was turned down because of his color. He then applied to the Army Lodge of an Irish Regiment. His petition was favorably received. On March 6, 1775, Hall and 14 other Black Americans were initiated in Lodge Number 441. When, on March 17, the British were forced to evacuate Boston, the Army Lodge gave Prince Hall and his colleagues a license to meet and function as a Lodge. Thus, on July 3, 1776, African Lodge No. 1 came into being. This was the first Lodge in Massachusetts established in America for men of African descent. Later, in 1843, a Jamaican, Peter Ogden, organized in New York City the first Odd Fellows Lodge for Negroes.

The founding of the African Lodge was one of Prince Hall's greatest achievements. It afforded Africans in the New England area of the United States a greater sense of security and contributed to a new spirit of unity among them. Hall's interest did not end with the Lodge. He was deeply concerned with improving the lot of his people in other ways. He sought to have schools established for the children of free Africans in Massachusetts. Of prime importance is the fact that Prince Hall worked to secure respect for his people and that he played a significant role in the downfall of the Massachusetts slave trade. He helped to prepare the ground work for those freedom fighters of the 19th and 20th centuries whose continuing efforts have brought the Black American closer to the goal of full citizenship.

In his book *Souls of Black Folk*, Dr. W.E.B. Dubois points to the role of West Indians in the Afro-American struggle. They, he says, were mainly responsible for the manhood program launched by the race in the early decades of the last century. An eminent instance of such drive and self-assurance can be seen in the achievement of John W.A. Shaw of Antigua, who, later in that century, in the early 1890s passed the Civil Service tests and became Deputy Commissioner of Taxes for the County of Queens in New York State.

In his series of articles entitled "Pioneers in Protest," Lerone Bennett, Senior Editor of *Ebony Magazine,* has written a capsule biography of John B. Russwurm, the distinguished Jamaican who was a pioneer in Afro-American journalism. As early as 1827, Russwurm, also one of the founders of Liberia, was the first colored man to graduate from an American college to publish a newspaper in the United States. The following information about Russwurm has been extracted from Bennett's article, "Founders of the Negro Press," *Ebony Magazine,* July 1964.

Day in and day out, the Negroes of New York City were merci-
lessly lampooned in the white press. In the dying days of 1826, the
campaign of vilification and slander reached nauseous heights. The
integrity and courage of Negro men were openly questioned.
Worse, editors invaded Negro homes and impugned the chastity
of Negro women ... This was a time of acute crisis for all Negro
Americans and the New York leaders were agonizingly conscious
of the forces arrayed against them ... More ominous was the creep-
ing power of the American Colonization Society which wanted to
send free Negroes "back" to Africa.

John B. Russwurm and Samuel E. Cornish, two of the youngest
and most promising of the New York leaders, were assigned the
task of inventing a journal that could speak forcibly to both the
enemy and joint friend without and the 'brethren' within the veil.

Samuel E. Cornish, who is virtually unknown today, was born about
1795 in Delaware and raised in the relatively free environments of
Philadelphia and New York. He organized the first Black
Presbyterian Church in New York City. Russwurm was the son of an
Englishman and an African woman. His father neglected to inform
his white wife of "the sins of his youth;" but after his death, the
widow learned of the boy's existence and financed his education at
Bowdoin College where he was graduated in 1826.

Russwurm and Cornish made an excellent team, despite the
proposed paper they idealistically state:

We shall ever regard the constitution of the United States as our
polar star. Pledged to no party, we shall endeavour to urge our
brethren to use their rights to the elective franchise as free citizens.
It shall never be our objective to court controversy though we must
at all times consider ourselves as champions in defense of
oppressed humanity. Daily slandered, we think that there ought to
be some channel of communication between us and the public,
through which a single voice may be heard in defense of five hundred thousand free people of color...

On Friday, March 26, 1827, the first issue of *Freedom's Journal*, the first
"Negro newspaper" in the Western World, appeared on the streets
of New York City. In their ambitious first editorial, Russwurm and
Cornish struck a high note of positiveness that still has something to
say to the Afro-Americans in their present plight. It read in part:

We wish to plead our own cause. Too long have others spoke for us. Too long has the republic been deceived by misrepresentations, in things which concern us dearly, though in the estimation of some mere trifles; for though there are many in society who exercise toward us benevolent feelings; still (with sorrow we confess it) there are others who make it their business to enlarge upon the least trifle, which tends to discredit any person of color; and pronounce anathema and denounce our whole body for the misconduct of this guilty one ... Our vices and our degradation are ever arrayed against us, but our virtues are passed unnoticed...

The timeliness of this editorial, written over a hundred years ago, and the dynamics of its intellectual content, are far ahead of most editorials that appear in present-day AfroAmerican newspapers.

During the later years of his life, John B. Russwurm moved to a position that today would be called Black nationalism. After receiving his master's degree from Bowdoin College in 1829 Russwurm went to Liberia in West Africa, where he established another newspaper, *The Liberia Herald,* and served as a superintendent of schools. After further distinguishing himself as Governor of the Maryland Colony of Cape Palmas, this pioneer editor and freedom fighter died in Liberia in 1851.

Repatriation in Historical Perspective

The back-to-Africa idea has long been a recurring theme in Afro-American life and thought. This Africa consciousness started during the closing years of the 18th century, and was articulated by the first Afro-American writers, thinkers and abolitionists. This agitation was found mainly among groups of 'free Negroes' because of the uncertainty of their position as freed men in slave-holding society. "One can see it late into the eighteenth century," Dr. DuBois explains in his book *Dusk of Dawn,* "when the Negro Union of Newport, Rhode Island, in 1788, proposed to the Free African Society of Philadelphia a general exodus to Africa on the part of at least free Negroes."

DuBois addressed himself to the broader aspects of this situation on the occasion of the celebration of the Second Anniversary of the Asian-African (Bandung) Conference and the rebirth of Ghana on April 30,1957, when he said:

From the fifteenth through the seventeenth centuries, the Africans imported to America regarded themselves as temporary settlers destined to return eventually to Africa. Their increasing revolts against the slave system, which culminated in the eighteenth century, showed a feeling of close kinship to the motherland and even well into the nineteenth century they called their organizations 'African', as witness the 'African Unions' of New York and Newport and the African Churches of Philadelphia and New York. In the West Indies and South America there was even closer indication of feelings of kinship with Africa and the East.

The Planters' excuse for slavery was advertised as conversion of Africa to Christianity; but soon American slavery appeared based on the huge profits of the Sugar Empire and Cotton Kingdom. As plans were laid for the expansion of the slave system, the slaves themselves sought freedom by increasing revolt which culminated in the 18th century. In Haiti they won autonomy; in the United States they fled from the slave states in the South to the free states in the North and to Canada.

Here the Free Negroes helped form the Abolition Movement, and when that seemed to be failing, the Negroes began to plan for migration to Africa, Haiti and South America.

Civil War and emancipation intervened and American Negroes looked forward to becoming free and equal here with no thought of return to Africa or of kinship with the world's darker peoples. However, the rise of the Negro was hindered by disenfranchisement, lynching and caste legislation. There was some recurrence of the 'Back to Africa' idea and increased sympathy for darker folk who suffered the same sort of caste restrictions as American Negroes.

Professor E.U. Essien-Udom of the University of Ibadan, Nigeria, outlined the beginning of this consciousness and how it developed, in three lectures in the C.B.S. Black Heritage T.V. Series, Summer, 1969. In the first lecture on "The Antecedents of Marcus Garvey and His Movement," Professor Essien-Udom gives this analysis:

In the United States it may be said that Garvey's ideas or variants of his ideas, are becoming increasingly relevant for the independent African states in their struggle for real political and economic independence as well as relative cultural autonomy.

A history of the freedom movements of Black Americans is the history of the aspirations for nationality and dignity. The reasons for this are not far to seek. Firstly, the Africans who were forcibly removed from their ancestral homelands to the New World were dramatically alienated from any vital human community, except the community of color, common deprivation and persecution. Because they were drawn from various and distinct African nationality groups and scattered throughout the New World, they lost many vital ingredients as a distinct nationality group, such as a common language, religion, traditions, and more important, the freedom to shape their own destiny.

Secondly, because they were excluded from meaningful participation in the emergent American nationality, they became not only non-citizens, but also, in a sociological sense, non-nationals of the United States throughout most of their history. Early in their history, the Africans were simply an aggregation of persons who were non-citizens and consequently possessed no civic rights in the United States. Such for a long time was their political status.

Similarly, as a group without recognizable nationality, which derives from belonging to a definite and meaningful human community, they could not feel a sense of human dignity. Inevitably, therefore, and from slavery to freedom, the Black freedom movement has had two ambivalent objectives. The first being the aspiration for nationality, a term which I shall use interchangeably with collective identity. And secondly, the aspiration for full citizenship in the United States.

In the past, the history of the Black freedom movement especially in the United States, was interpreted principally in terms of integration or in terms of assimilation into the mainstreams, whatever that is, of American society.

If integration is understood as the enjoyment of full rights of citizenship and full participation in the live activities of the United States, then this has been one of the most important objectives of the Afro-American freedom movement. But to interpret this movement principally in terms of assimilation, is a misrepresentation of historical fact and a negation of the long and tragic history of the struggle for Black identity and dignity. Assimilation necessarily entails the withering away of the distinctly Afro-American nationality which has been forged by the history of the Africans and their descendants in the United States.

The aspiration for Black nationality or a collective identity should not be understood in the narrow political sense, although there have been manifestations of the desire for political nationality; that is, a homeland. Nevertheless, the much-abused term, "Black nationalism," or its recent variant, "Black power," encompasses the various expressions of the need for collective identity. The formation of collective identity has been the result of both history and the conscious activities of Afro-Americans. On occasions, this aspiration for nationality has been expressed in terms of independence from white economic, political and social control. More persistently however, this collective Black identity has been expressed in the assertion of Afro-American cultural autonomy and the dignity of the Black communities in America.

What Professor Essien-Udom is saying is: the Black Americans have been forced by a set of circumstances to walk down several roads simultaneously going to and from America. This seems like a contradiction and maybe it is. The greater contradiction is America itself, and its relationship to Black people. Early in the 19th century some "free" Blacks and escaped slaves began to have second thoughts about the future of African people in this country. These Blacks, in large numbers, responded to the program of the "African Colonization Movement." Superficially, the program was good, but a number of Blacks, mainly, Frederick Douglass and some of the men around him, examined the program and began to have some serious questions about it.

The stated intent of the American Colonization Society was to solve the problems of slavery by advocating the removal of freed slaves to colonies along the west coast of Africa. The founders of the society believed this course would atone for the evil of the African slave trade, help put an end to slavery, restore the "Africans" to their divinely ordained homes, and help "civilize" Africa. By "civilize" the white supporters of the movement really meant "Christianize." Some of the most able Black men and women of the 19th century were attracted to this movement and its concept.

It is generally believed, according to Professor Essien-Udom, that Paul Cuffee set in motion the ideas that led to the founding of the American Colonization Society. Cuffee was one of the most unusual men of his time. He was a rarity, being a Black ship owner in New Bedford, Massachusetts, who made a small fortune hauling cargo to different parts of the world. A free man whose father had been a slave, he founded the Friendly Society for the Emigration of Free Negroes from America. One of his early acts was to change his family name from Slocum to Cuffee (Kofi), a Ghanaian name.

In 1811, Paul Cuffee sailed one of his ships, "The Traveller," to

Sierra Leone on Africa's west coast where he founded "The Friendly Society from America." In 1812, he used his personal funds to take 38 Black emigrants to Sierra Leone. But the most active years of "The American Colonization" came after the death of Paul Cuffee in 1817.

In the middle of the 19th century, while the issue of slavery was being debated in most of the country, the feeling for Africa among American Blacks grew stronger. Publications like *Freedom's Journal and Douglass Monthly*, edited by Frederick Douglass, called attention to the plight of the people of Africa as well as that of Black Americans. With Martin R. Delaney, Douglass was also co-editor of the newspaper, *North Star*.

A Mandingo descendant, Martin Delaney was proud of his African heritage. So much so, that, in a recent book by Dorothy Sterling, he is referred to as "the father of Black Nationalism." Delaney was a multi-talented freedom fighter who seemed to have crammed half a dozen lifetimes into one. Dentist, writer, editor, doctor, explorer, scientist, soldier and politician, he was a Renaissance man of his day. In an article in the supplement to the newspaper *Tuesday*, of November 1971, the writer Phillip St. Laurent has this to say about the present day relevance of Martin R. Delaney:

> Delaney was ... an articulate advocate of ideas that today, 85 years after his death, are topical. Even while the vast majority of his brothers remained in slavery, he was proud of his race and his Blackness, resented his surname as a hand-me down from a slave-holder, advocated Black people's right to self-defense, demanded equal employment opportunities, urged a self-governed state for Blacks in which they could control their own destinies and, yes, argued for women's liberation.

He was one of the leaders of the great debate following the passage of the Fugitive Slave Act in 1850, and as spokesman for Black people who felt that the bitter racial climate in America had made life for them there unbearable, he advocated the establishment of a state by Black Americans in the Niger Valley of present-day Nigeria. Said he of Black Americans at the 1852 Emigration Convention, "Settle them in the land which is ours, and there lies with it inexhaustible resources. Let us go and possess it. We must establish a national position for ourselves and never may we expect to be respected as men and women until we have undertaken some fearless, bold and adventurous deeds of daring, contending against every consequence."

In 1859, he led the first and only exploratory party of American-born Africans to the land of their forefathers. In the region of the

Niger River, in the area that became Nigeria, Delaney's party carried out scientific studies and made agreements with several African kings for the settlement of emigrants from America. He was accompanied on this expedition by Robert Campbell, a Jamaican, who had been Director of the Scientific Department of the Institute for Coloured Youth in Philadelphia, Pennsylvania, and a member of the International Statistical Congress in London, England. His account of the expedition can be found in his book *A Pilgrimage to My Motherland, an account of a journey among the Egbas and Yorubas of Central Africa in 1859-60.*

About his report, Robert Campbell has said, "After what is written in the context, if I am still asked what I think of Africa for a colored man to live and do well in, I simply answer, that with as good prospects in America as colored men generally possess, I have determined with my wife and children, to go to Africa to live, leaving the inquirer to interpret the reply for himself."

What needs to be remembered about this mid-19th century back-to-Africa movement, is that, to a moderate degree, it was successful. There was, of course, no mass exodus to Africa. Individual families did go to Africa at regular intervals for the next 50 years.

However, the emigration movement was not without its opposition. Frederick Douglass and several of his supporters thought that the emigration efforts would divert attention from the more important task of freeing the slaves from the plantations.

General interest in Africa continued though the pre-Civil War emigration efforts to establish an autonomous nation for Black Americans did not succeed. The Civil War and the promises to Black Americans that followed lessened some of the interest in Africa. Pat Singleton started an internal resettlement scheme. His plan was to settle Blacks in free separate communities in the unused areas of America— mainly, at this time, the State of Kansas.

But the betrayal of the Reconstruction and the rise in lynching and other atrocities against Black Americans made a new generation of Black thinkers and freedom fighters turn to Africa again. New men and movements entered the area of struggle. The most notable of the new personalities was Bishop Henry McNeal Turner. In his book, *Black Exodus,* (Yale University Press, 1969) Edwin S. Redkey gives this view of Bishop Turner's importance to the history of this period. He says:

> Bishop Henry McNeal Turner was, without a doubt, the most prominent and outspoken American advocate of Black emigration in the years between the Civil War and First World War. By con-

stant agitation he kept Afro-Americans aware of their African heritage and their disabilities in the United States. Turner possessed a dominating personality, a biting tongue, and a pungent vocabulary which gained him high office and wide audiences, first in Georgia's Reconstruction politics and later in the African Methodist Episcopal (A.M.E.) Church. In his bitter disappointment with the American treatment of Blacks, the Bishop had an all-consuming nationalism which demanded emigration to Africa. To understand his forceful agitation in the years following 1890, one must know Turner's background and the nature of his vision of Africa.

Like most Afro-Americans who can be called Black nationalists, Turner's vision of Africa grew out of his heartbreaking discovery that his love for America was unrequited. Earlier in his life, he thought that the status of a "free" Black man should be no different from that of a white man. His awakening to reality was not long in coming. The new cause that he had found for himself and his energies during the Civil War, and the new hope that he had for the future of Black Americans was consumed in the bitter disappointments that followed the end of that war.

Like Turner, Edward Wilmot Blyden agitated during the latter part of the 19th century, calling attention to the important role that Africa could play in emerging world affairs. Blyden was born in the then Danish West Indian island of St. Thomas in 1832, but reacted against treatment of his people in the New World by migrating to Liberia in 1851. He was convinced that the only way to bring respect and dignity to his people was by building progressive new "empires" in Africa. He was of the opinion that the "New World Negro" had a great future in Africa. He saw Liberia in West Africa as the ideal place where African-Americans could build a great new civilization by making use of the things that they had learned in the West and preserving the best of the African way of life. Because of his, and the work of many others, African consciousness was translated into useful programs of service to Africa. Afro-American institutions of higher learning joined in this service through their training of personnel for churches, as well as their support of Africans studying in their institutions.

The Pan-African Movement

The idea of uniting all Africa had its greatest development early in this century. In 1900 a West Indian lawyer, H. Sylvester Williams, called together the first Pan-African Conference in London. This meeting attracted attention and put the word "Pan-African" in the dictionaries for the first time. The 30 delegates to the Conference came mainly from England, the West Indies and the United States. The small delegation from the latter was led by W.E.B. DuBois.

From the beginning this was a movement that was brought into being by Africans in the Western World. Years would pass before it would have any deep roots in Africa itself. The first Conference was greeted by the Lord Bishop of London, and a promise was obtained from Queen Victoria through Joseph Chamberlain not to "overlook the interests and welfare of the native races." The British were long on politeness and short on commitment.

The aims of the Conference were limited. They were obviously worded in order to appeal, without offending. The aims were:

1. To act as a forum of protest against the aggression of White colonizers.
2. To appeal to the "missionary and abolitionist traditions of the British people to protect Africans from the deprivation of Empire builders."
3. To bring people of African descent throughout the world into closer touch with each other and to establish more friendly relations between the Caucasian and African races.
4. To start a movement looking forward to the securing to all African races living in civilized countries, their full rights and to promote their business interests.

At this conference, there was no demand for self-government for African nations, though the thought pattern was set in motion for later development. In the book, *Africa and Unity: The Evolution of Pan-Africanism,* by the Nigerian writer Vincent Bakpetu Thompson (1969), this observation was made:

> As a forum of protest, the conference showed that Africa had begun jointly, through some of her sons, to make her voice heard against the excesses of western European rule—a sentiment which has been re-echoed in the second half of the twentieth century.

Thompson further observed that, "both protest and fellowship were to re-emerge in the 'African Redemption' movement formed by the Afro-Jamaican, Marcus Garvey, to uplift his down-trodden brethren. Garvey said: ' I know no national boundary where the Negro is concerned. The whole world is my province until Africa is free.'" Assessing the Conference, Thompson further says:

> First, it achieved the idea of oneness in experience and ideal. The spirit of fellowship reaffirmed at this 1900 Conference was never lost. It has reasserted itself again and again. This was demonstrated

when in the post-war period, Afro-Americans and Afro-West Indians joined forces with those who clamored for the dismantling of colonialism in Africa. The spirit lives on, though today the Afro-American interest in the freedom of Africa and the success of Pan-Africanism has three main themes:
1. The continuance of the idea of fellowship which has existed since slavery first took them away from the shores of Africa.
2. Self-interest—a hope for the enhancement of the stature for the Afro-American in the United States. The success of Africa, it is believed, will hasten integration for the Afro-American in American society; whether this is so or not is another matter, but the belief was present in the "back to Africa" fervor of the mid-nineteenth and twentieth centuries.
3. A genuine interest in the study of African history and culture with a view to taking a hand in rehabilitating what they genuinely believe, through "scientific" research, to be the true picture of life in Africa in pre-imperialist days. This is seen in the formation of organizations such as "The American Society of African Culture."

A number of African-oriented cultural and historical societies were formed before and after the active years of the American Society of African Culture (about 1957 through 1968). The long Afro-American interest in Africa is best reflected in publications of the American Society of African Culture, such as: *Africa as seen by American Negroes (1958), and The American Negro Writer and His Roots,* (1959).

In the preface to *Africa as Seen by American Negroes,* Alioune Diop, President of the International Society of African Culture, states: "It is not without emotion that we welcome this evidence of solidarity between Negro intellectuals of America and Africa. What links us first of all is assuredly our common origin.".. Furthermore, he went on to say,

the struggle that African people are waging for their independence and entry upon the scene of international responsibility, is followed with understandable sympathy by Negro Americans. The liberation, unification and development of African countries will be a real contribution to the success of the struggle of Black people in America for their rights as citizens."

Betrayal of the American Reconstruction

In *The American Negro Writer and His Roots* (selected papers from the First Conference of Negro Writers), the historian, novelist and teacher, Saunders Redding, addressed himself to the role of the writer in the self-discovery and the restoration of a people's pride in themselves. He said:

> The human condition, the discovery of self, community identity— surely, this must be achieved before it can be seen that a particular identity has a relation to a common identity, commonly described as human. This is the ultimate that the honest writer seeks. He knows that the dilemmas, the perils, the likelihood of catastrophe in the human situation are real and that they have to do not only with whether men understand each other but with the quality of man himself. The writer's ultimate purpose is to use his gifts to develop man's awareness of himself so that he, man, can become a better instrument for living together with other men. This sense of identity is the root by which all honest creative effort is fed, and the writer's relation to it is the relation of the infant to the breast of the mother.

What we have here is a continuation of the search for identity, definition and direction that started among Black Americans early in the 18th century. This search led to the founding of the first Black societies, publications and institutions in America. In the years following the betrayal of the Reconstruction (1875-1900), these Black societies and institutions were in serious trouble. Most of the white defenders of the Blacks had either died or had given up the fight. Black leadership was in transition. The great Frederick Douglass was losing his effectiveness at the end of the century. A world-wide imperialism, and the acceptance of the Kipling concept of "the white man's burden" gave support to American racism. Like England, France and some other European nations, the United States had now acquired overseas colonies.

A new "leader," approved by the whites, appeared among the Blacks. His name was Booker T. Washington. Washington took no action against the rising tide of Jim Crow, lynching and mass disenfranchisement of Black voters. He advised his people to put their energies into industry, improved farming and the craft trades. He said, "agitation of questions of social equality is the extreme 'folly' because an opportunity to earn a dollar in a factory first, now is worth infinitely more than the opportunity to spend a dollar in an opera house."

White America, mostly editorial writers in white newspapers, responded favorably to the words of Booker T. Washington and made him the leader of Black America. These words, taken from his famous Atlanta Cotton Exposition Speech, were still re-echoing early in this century when an anti-Booker T. Washington school of thought was developed and led by W.E.B. DuBois.

In what can still be referred to as "The Booker T. Washington Era" (1895-1915), new men and movements were emerging. The Niagara Movement, under the leadership of W.E.B. DuBois and Monroe Trotter, was born in 1905. Some of the ideas of the Niagara Movement went into the making of the NAACP in 1909.

During the years leading to the eve of the First World War and those that immediately followed, the flight from the South continued. Over half a million Blacks migrated northward in search of better-paying war-time jobs, better schools for their children and better housing. For a short while, they entertained the illusion that they had improved and that they had escaped from the oppression of the South. The illusion was short-lived. Race riots during wartime (East St. Louis, 1917), and in the post-war period (Chicago, 1919) awakened the new urban settlers to reality. In Washington, D.C., the President, Woodrow Wilson, and the Southern Democrats who had come to power with him, introduced segregation in federal facilities that had long been integrated. Booker T. Washington had died in 1915. An investigation into his last years revealed he had privately battled against disenfranchisement, and had secretly financed law suits against segregation, but publicly he maintained his submissive stance. With Washington gone and the influence of the "Tuskegee Machine" in decline, a new class of Black radicals came forward. For a few years, W.E.B. DuBois was at the center stage of leadership. As founder-editor of the NAACP's *Crisis Magazine*, DuBois urged in 1918, "Let us, while this war lasts, forget our special grievances and close ranks shoulder to shoulder with our fellow citizens..." The continued discrimination against Black Americans, both soldiers and civilians, soon made W.E.B. DuBois regret having made this statement. The end of the war brought no improvement to the lives of Black Americans, and the then prevailing conditions made a large number of them ripe for the militant program of Marcus Garvey.

In his book *New World A-Coming*, Roi Ottley (1943) has observed,

> Garvey leaped into the ocean of Black unhappiness at a most timely moment for a savior. He had witnessed the Negro's disillusionment mount with the progress of the World War. Negro soldiers had suffered all forms of Jim Crow, humiliation, discrimination, slander, and even violence at the hands of a white civilian population. After the war, there was a resurgence of Ku Klux Klan influence; another decade of racial hatred and open lawlessness had set

in, and Negroes again were prominent among the victims.
Meantime, administration leaders were quite pointed in trying to
persuade Negroes that in spite of their full participation in the war
effort they could expect no changes in their traditional status in
America.

This attitude helped to create the atmosphere into which a Marcus
Garvey could emerge.

GARVEYISM IN CALIFORNIA

A CASE STUDY OF

OUTPOST GARVEYISM

Emory Tolbert

There are two vital functions which detailed studies of local Garvey groups should serve: first, to dispel the myth that Garvey's claim to widespread Black support was merely bombast, and that Garvey's only substantial support came from West Indian immigrants in New York City; and secondly, to examine the attitudes and perceptions of rank-and-file Garveyites to determine their understanding of Garveyism. Scholars have too long overlooked the obvious and stressed the insignificant because they failed to consult those persons who participated directly in mass movements. The failure to include oral history, or to use it creatively, has left much of Black history either untold or poorly told.

Scholars who have been investigating Garveyism during the past few decades have, understandably, tended to focus their efforts on the broad outlines of the Garvey Movement: the activities of the UNIA in New York City during its 1920's heyday, the Black Star Line, the trial, and the collective efforts of Garvey's enemies to discredit him. But the story of the UNIA and its founder must also be told at the personal, human level. The notion that Garveyism was an emotional spasm of ignorant urban Blacks, mostly in New York City, has no part in a study of Garveyism that claims to adhere to the facts. The effort to depict Garvey as one of a long line of soothsayers, cultists and spiritualists who were present in all sizable Black communities in the United States during the 1920s and 30s has spawned comparisons with Drew Ali, Father Divine, and others whose programs and methods were decidedly different from Garvey's and whose philosophies were a world removed from his.

Recent interpretations of Garveyism have, it is true, denied the negative picture of Garvey painted by his detractors, but there does in fact exist important but unused evidence against what was once a standard notion of Garveyism among scholars. This evidence is decidedly more difficult to obtain because convenient written records are more often left by leaders than by the rank-and-file. This research takes one to tenth-floor tenement apartments in the Bronx and to nursing homes in Los Angeles. And it is vital, because the accounts of surviving Garveyites add flesh to the skeletal structure which can be built by using written documents alone. Indeed, these interviews are more enlightening than the most thoroughly researched of dissertations on the meaning of Garveyism to the common man.

UNIA Membership

One of the most fascinating questions regarding Garvey and the UNIA has been the question of the size of the UNIA's worldwide membership. A census of the UNIA's membership during the peak years may never be undertaken—and, indeed may not be possible given available records. A close look at Garveyism at the local level, however, may certainly give us some important leads in examining this question. First of all, it is clear that UNIA divisions could be found in virtually every place in North America and the Caribbean area where substantial groups of Blacks were living. In the United States, UNIA divisions defy previous scholarship by appearing in what were previously considered "unlikely" places.[1] Although all of the evidence is not yet accumulated, one would certainly be safe in asserting that the majority of Blacks in the United States' northern communities had some contact with the UNIA during the years of its greatest activities. In short, with evidence of Garvey's considerable following in Africa and among Blacks in Europe, as well as his obviously large constituency in the Caribbean area, those who dismissed his estimates of the UNIA's total membership (which Garvey once claimed to be eleven million) as an empty boast, are becoming more interested in reexamining his claim.

Recently uncovered documents which were preserved by Capt. King's Central Division of the UNIA and later taken from an abandoned building in New York City, are housed at the Schomburg Library in Harlem. Perhaps the most telling evidence of the widespread and persistent support for Garveyism can be found in a listing of the UNIA divisions which were active during the 1925-1927 period. The long list of divisions active in South and Central America as well as Africa (including South Africa) and Europe testifies to the strength of Garvey's support, even during the years in which he was imprisoned in the United States, and to the internationalism in Garvey's program. Scholars have not stressed the long list of divisions in the United States which were located in rural areas. While large cities like New York City, Chicago, Philadelphia, Detroit, Los Angeles and Atlanta certainly had their divisions, Mound Bayou, Mississippi and Waycross, Georgia also had theirs. Indeed, current evidence indicates (for those who still have doubts) that the UNIA was the most pervasive and widely supported mass organization Blacks have ever produced. South Carolina, Mississippi, Florida, Alabama, Louisiana and Georgia, states where Black political organization was an invitation to death, had more UNIA divisions than New York State.[2] Garveyism spread rapidly in the Deep South—as it did among Blacks throughout the United States —prompting Black southerners to make the long trek to New York City at Convention time in the 1920's, not to find a better life in New York, but to see firsthand the workings of Garvey's dynamic movement.

Here the standard interpretations of Garveyism face the necessity of revision. While the social forces of the 1920's in the United States and around the world have been called upon to explain Garveyism in New York City, evidence indicates that Garvey's appeal transcended local considerations and rested on something far more fundamental to Blacks around the world: the desire for what long-time Garveyites call "a place in the sun." This need was as apparent in San Francisco as it was in Kingston. Blacks around the world had witnessed white nations meeting at Versailles to discuss the fate of the entire planet. Where was the Black man's voice? What Black man had power enough to demand the attention of Europe and America?

It was this need for recognition and feeling of "somebodiness" which motivated the founders of the UNIA in California. It is difficult to imagine two more different circumstances than those faced by Blacks in New York City during the 1920s and those facing California Blacks during the same year. Yet their problems corresponded at one vital point: they were Black and living in America.

Garveyism in California

California in the 1920s was still the Golden West to the white Americans. Wrested from the so-called American Indians by the Spanish and then seized by sovereign Mexico only to be again taken by land-hungry Americans in a convenient war, California was a Mecca for asthmatics and movie stars. The railroads had long since spanned the continental United States and, by the '20s, fruit farms and oil wells were commonplace on the U.S. West Coast. Besides, wealthy mid-westerners considered California a novel playground and often went there to escape their hometown climate. But by the '20s the migration westward was intensified and white Americans in hundreds of thousands poured into California.

Although California's largest city, Los Angeles, was founded by a group of settlers which consisted for the most part of people of African and American Indian descent, the Black population of the state during the 1920s never rivaled that of any of the Eastern population centers in the United States.[3] While the Black migration from South to North in the United States swelled New York's Black population from 150,000 to 300,000 between 1920 and 1930 and brought Chicago's African population from 100,000 to 200,000 during that same decade, Los Angeles' 15,000 Blacks in 1920 increased to 38,000 by 1930, while the city's total population was surpassing the one million mark.[4] The question comes: why did Garveyism spread among Blacks who traveled thousands of miles to plunge into a sea of white humanity, which California had become? California Blacks in that era, one could presume, were the ultimate believers in the American dream, since they had traveled miles from their birthplaces to find new homes in the West—a journey very much in the white American tradition. Not only were they not going to Africa; the pattern of their migration shows that they weren't even headed in the proper general direction. But the spread of Garveyism in California belies these assumptions and tells us something of the struggle of Black men wherever they are in the world. While the Black thrust westward included its share of American dreamers, there was among the Black westerners clear evidence of another sentiment, a sentiment which led in many cases to an enthusiastic acceptance of Garveyism.

An ex-slave named Biddy Mason pioneered in the struggle for Black economic power in the far western United States. By the time of her death in the 1880s, she owned much of the land on which the downtown business district of Los Angeles is presently built. When Biddy Mason's heirs refused $200,000 for her land a few years after her death, the city of Los Angeles withdrew its absurd offer and the white business community quietly divested the heirs of their land.[5] Despite its ending, the Biddy Mason story illustrates the fact that Blacks came to California for land, cheap land, on which they could build homes and achieve a measure of independence. Students of Black nationalism in the United States often overlook the fact that the Blacks who rushed into Kansas and Oklahoma after the American Civil War displayed their nationalistic spirit by building all-Black communities there and seeking to become self-sufficient political and economic units. Indeed, Edwin McCabe, an ex-state Auditor of Kansas, led a movement to make Oklahoma an all-Black state, since during the post-war period the majority of the non-Indian inhabitants were Black. Predictably, Mr. McCabe mysteriously disappeared after the American Congress matter-of-factly dismissed this Black attempt to organize the Oklahoma Territory under Black leadership.[6] All-Black communal living was also evident among California Blacks in the 1920s. Shortly after the turn of the century Allensworth had established an all-Black community in the sweltering region near Victorville, California—a community about 100 miles east of Los Angeles.[7] And he among others, confirmed the fact that Blacks in the United States were weary of the starvation and intimidation of share cropping in the South and moved to other parts of the United States not in the sentimental hope of finding more agreeable white people than those they had encountered at home, but to purchase a piece of earth they could call their own and to end their total dependence on the whites who controlled the economy.

So it was with many Black Californians. The Black influx from 1900 to 1922 found most Black immigrants buying stretches of land outside of urban areas; it was their intention to be ranchers, land-owners and producers. Black railroad workers saw California when their Southern Pacific trains stopped at San Bernardino and Los Angeles, and carefully saved their funds to buy the plentiful land they had seen.[8]

By the 1920s Blacks populated scattered areas throughout the state and could be found, interestingly enough, in some areas of California where Blacks today no longer live. By that time Los Angeles' scant 15,000 Blacks had a choice of five Black newspapers, with two more newspapers being published in the San Francisco area and another in San Diego. Whatever else can be said of these Blacks, it is clear that they were a very scattered lot—far away from the large Black communities of the Eastern United States and, except for the embryonic ghettos in the California urban areas, far away from one another. In 1919 news of Garvey's organization reached the West

Coast, as it had most of the world. News of ships and Africa and Black pride reached Blacks who had long since realized that California was no heaven, and was becoming less and less heavenly every day. The newness of California society had temporarily loosened the conventions of white America during the years before 1900 so that Blacks could allow themselves to lapse into periods of forgetfulness about the traditional treatment of Blacks in America. But by 1919 Los Angeles Blacks were being systematically excluded from buying land in nearly all of the city. Employers were turning away Black labor for Mexican and Oriental workers, as local Blacks were being arrested for buying land in "white only" parts of the city.[9]

UNIA divisions could be found in all the widely scattered small Black communities—not only those mentioned above, but in villages and towns where, in some cases, there were only two or three Black families. There is reason to believe that there was no place in California where Blacks were to be found that did not have a UNIA division or chapter nearby. In Los Angeles, the local UNIA sent its choir on tour into the hinterlands to the east and organized divisions there.[10] Garveyism was the Gospel of African redemption, and it had apostles among the common people throughout the west. These Black men and women, perhaps more than those who were surrounded by Black faces in urban ghettos, felt the need for the UNIA. In the arid and dusty farming towns of California in the 1920s as well as in the sprawling city of Los Angeles Black isolation could not have been more stark. Separated by miles from other Black communities and often by hundreds of miles from any large Black settlement, these Blacks had a particular need for the sense of belonging that the UNIA provided. More importantly, California Blacks (as had Southern and West Indian immigrants to New York City) discovered that they had not found the promised land. Indeed, as Blacks were watching the systematic exploitation of Harlemites in New York, they were also witnessing an insidious retrenchment of segregation and white power in the western coast of the United States.

These were the outpost Garveyites of California. They saw Garvey only rarely, when he made one of his tours throughout the nation. They were far from the energy of Liberty Hall, far from the shouts of thousands who proclaimed Black liberation in the meeting halls of the large cities. Theirs was the quiet work of organizing, and of supporting the parent body with their funds. Meetings always included the reading of Mr. Garvey's editorial on the front page of the *Negro World*. Local men and women composed poems and gave addresses on the glory of Africa and the imminence of Black repatriation.

Split in the California UNIA

Before the UNIA was established in Los Angeles, local Blacks had organized a forum to discuss and act against the tightening noose of white oppression. Among its leaders was Hugh Gordon, the brother of Garvey's first Assistant President General.[11] Hugh Gordon had for years led discussions on Africa among local Blacks. When he heard of the Garvey Movement, he hurried east to the small city of Riverside, California, to organize a division there. J.D. Gordon, Hugh's brother, left his congregation at the Tabernacle Baptist Church in Los Angeles, to serve with the parent body in New York. Although J.D. Gordon joined others in a suit against the UNIA in 1921, local Los Angeles Garveyites report that he told them the organization was still a good organization but, to use Gordon's words, "Garvey was somewhat stubborn." Perhaps a local Garveyite's assessment of the events are closer to the mark: "Gordon wanted to be the leader."[12]

The West Coast of the United States becomes a worthwhile locale for a case study of local Garveyism because it became one of the crisis areas for Garvey and the UNIA. The enemies of Garveyism were particularly strong in the West, partly because of the presence of a sizable integrationist element among West Coast Negroes and partly because many of the UNIA leaders in the western United States worked against Garvey and openly sought to undermine the influence of the parent body in California.

When Los Angeles Garveyites organized, they chose as their leader a local newspaper man named Noah Thompson. Thompson was the only Black reporter with the white-owned *Los Angeles Times* and, reportedly, had once been an associate of Booker T. Washington at the Tuskegee Institute. For the purposes of this paper, it should be understood that Noah Thompson was only one of a cadre of young educated men who were caught in a society which seriously limited any attempt to advance. At the *Los Angeles Times* he was essentially a Negro reporter, who, as far as this researcher has been able to determine, never ascribed his name to any article which was published in that journal. With qualifications that far outstripped his duties, he was a West Coast "New Negro" whose view of the Black man's problems led him to seek solace with the UNIA.[13]

At the 1921 Convention of the Universal Negro Improvement Association, Noah Thompson represented the Los Angeles Division as its only delegate. With thousands in attendance, Thompson was only one voice in this gathering of Blacks from around the world. While reading the rather lengthy list of divisions of the UNIA repre-

sented at the Convention, the international organizer allegedly overlooked mentioning division 156 in Los Angeles. This apparently
plummeted Noah Thompson's notion of his own importance to a
new low, and set off a wave of criticism from Mr. Thompson which
had a ferocity only attributable to a man with injured pride.
Thompson demanded to see the "Phyllis Wheatley," one of the ships
purchased by the UNIA, he raised procedural questions, and generally saw to it that anyone who was not previously aware of his presence learned of it quickly.[14]

Thompson, one must understand, was one of many men who
saw themselves as leaders but were unable to collect a following com-
parable to Garvey's. When Booker T. Washington died in 1915, Blacks
in the United States lost a prestigious leader whose mantle remained
unclaimed. W.E.B. DuBois, who had been Washington's chief critic,
was not the sort to attract the mass following of the late Dr.
Washington and, by the 1920s was already in his fifties. The new
(intellectual) Negroes were determined to see to it that Garvey did
not inherit the mantle of leadership that his huge following indicated
he was due. There was the ever present belief on the part of many of
Garvey's enemies that the UNIA could somehow be taken away from
its founder and that these men who saw themselves as more capable
leaders, could take his place. DuBois himself praised the massive
UNIA as a great accomplishment but wished that someone besides
its founder and prime mover, Marcus Garvey, would lead it.[15] At
the bottom of this sentiment seemed to be the steadfast refusal to
believe that Garvey had done what scores of United States born
Negro intellectuals had failed to do. In 1920, during that massive
UNIA convention in New York City, James Weldon Johnson of the
NAACP in an editorial in the *New York Age* expressed the need for
one Negro organization, yet he was unwilling to concede that Garvey
was in the process of doing what Johnson had suggested at that very
moment.[16] The criticism of Garvey became more and more caustic as
it became increasingly clear that millions were accepting his philosophy. From general criticisms of Garvey's plan for African
Redemption and Black liberation the enemies of Garveyism became
more specific and personal, even to the point of criticizing his looks.
The rapid growth of the UNIA simply deepened the already existing
division between the integrationists who saw, or at least thought they
saw, a future for themselves in the United States, and the Garveyites
whose emphasis was on self-reliance and the unity of the Third
World. Garvey's U.S. enemies considered themselves Americans,
although they would concede that daily lynchings and burnings of
Blacks in the South and outside of the South cast considerable doubt

on the contention that they were welcome in America. James Weldon Johnson could describe in lurid detail the sordid murder of a Black man who was cooked to death for hours on a slow-burning coal fire by a white mob.[17] Yet he seemed to see those incidents as part of the hazard of being an American and seriously believed that African repatriation would be more difficult than converting the hearts of the men and women who perpetrated such deeds. Indeed, those who called Garvey a dreamer were themselves vulnerable to a similar indictment. They maintained a hope in the gradual improvement of the Black man's lot in America which, at the time, seemed less plausible to the masses than Garvey's program. Even the most optimistic of integrationists conceded that a Black skin in America was likely to continue to bring abuse. Yet they rejected a plan that sought advancement for Blacks—Black independence in thought and action.

Noah Thompson returned to Los Angeles with scathing criticism for the parent body and its leader, Marcus Garvey. He persuaded some local Garveyites to register a criticism of Garvey in the local press and created a schism in the local UNIA. The result was the Pacific Coast Negro Improvement Association, a group which intended to compete with the local UNIA. The Pacific Coast Negro Improvement Association was so short-lived that very little is known about it, except that it was organized and died.[18] The very substitution of the words "Pacific Coast" for the word "Universal" removed the most important aspect of Marcus Garvey's philosophy from the name of the organization—Black internationalism. Noah Thompson's followers had strayed from the world-wide thrust which distinguished Garveyism from organizations with purely local (United States) goals such as the NAACP and the Urban League. In short, a Pacific Coast Negro Improvement Association was the child of those who rested their hopes on the Pacific Coast, and not the child of Black internationalists. The dissension which arose in Los Angeles was also apparent in Oakland and San Francisco, California, where some local UNIA leaders were criticizing the movement.[19] Of particular significance however is the fact that those Garveyites who founded the UNIA division in Los Angeles remained faithful to the parent body. Noah Thompson was not a founder, but was chosen to lead after J.W. Coleman, a local employment agent, and "Pop" Sanders, another local leader, took action to organize the division. These men remained with the UNIA and helped to build the local organization after Thompson left.

It was after the Noah Thompson defection that Marcus Garvey came to Los Angeles. One must understand that the local UNIA had been undermined with dissension and that the editor of the largest

Los Angeles Black newspaper, the *California Eagle,* as lady president of the local UNIA, had left the organization along with Thompson. Yet, when Garvey arrived 10,000 of Los Angeles' 15,000 Blacks lined the streets to see him. Blacks poured in from small communities in the Southern California hinterlands; tiny communities provided marchers and musicians as the motorcade moved down Central Avenue. Garvey's first speech at Los Angeles' Trinity Auditorium drew a capacity crowd.[20] Arna Bontemps, who was a young man of 20 and who had not yet gone to New York City to join the cadre of young writers there, was in the audience. He described Garvey's oratory as spellbinding as he held the total attention of that vast crowd. Garvey's critics were strangely silent as they watched the charisma of the man who had built the huge Black organization which was the UNIA.[21] Noah Thompson was there. Marcus Garvey reported to the *Negro World* that he had become "as meek as a lamb" and would probably once again become an active member of the UNIA.[22] All talk of the Pacific Coast Negro Improvement Association ceased, as new members joined the UNIA from all over the Southern California area. Garvey journeyed northward from Los Angeles to Oakland where the results were equally devastating for his enemies. In a 1922 cable to New York he wrote:

"Enemies totally defeated. 12,000 members of the UNIA in California send greetings."[23]

Significance of Garveyism for the Rank and File

The musings of the intellectual elite of Garvey's day illustrate the fact that they were clearly out of touch with the men and women to whom Garveyism meant (and means) so much. While Black journalists and integrationist leaders debated the details of African Repatriation and the feasibility of Black self-reliance Garvey appealed to the *commonsense* of *oppressed* Blacks, who were persuaded that action should follow discussion and that the realization of African Redemption would result from deeds, not talk.

The Garveyites who have witnessed both the intense activity of the UNIA during the 1920s and the new burst of Blackness in the present world have a view of Black history which is unmatched by any other observer. To them, the shares they purchased in the Black Star Line were an investment in the future of a people. Here is a key to understanding what motivated millions to sacrifice portions of their meager salaries to help finance the UNIA. To the rank and file Garveyite, debates over details were of little significance. The question, as one Garveyite put it, was "What are you going to leave your children?" Garvey's critics, without ever talking to the men and women whose contributions were financing the UNIA, assumed that physically boarding a ship and sailing to Africa was the total goal of rank-and-file Garveyites. Hence they saw Garveyism as mass hypnotism, and Garveyites as little more than automatons following the lead of their Messiah. Had they bothered to question the masses, they would have found an intelligent people who were perfectly aware of the obstacles to African Repatriation, but who also realized with more immediate evidence, that life in a white-dominated country held little hope for them unless a Black nation could embody the Black man's power and command respect for him around the world. One Garveyite echoed a common sentiment when she declared, "You can't rule in somebody else's house. We must have a house of our own."[24]

The Garveyites of the 1920s were a practical people who fulfilled the UNIA's claim that they were a charitable, friendly and expansive organization. UNIA meeting halls were places where parties were held and the voices of children could be heard. The "Juveniles," as they were called, sat under the instruction of UNIA-appointed teachers where they learned about Africa and the imminent regeneration of Black men. Holidays saw picnics and other family occasions sponsored by the local UNIA divisions both to raise funds and to promote unity among members (and also non-members who chose to attend such functions). One must be careful, however, not to conclude that these were mere social clubs whose aim was local Black fraternity alone. Rather, the interest of the UNIA in the whole man, in every aspect of Black life, emerges from this evidence. Garvey and the millions who followed him realized the need for Black people to appreciate one another and the necessity to refrain from admiring white society and seeking entrance into it. Blacks living in the United States at the time of Garvey's arrival there were at an impasse. President Woodrow Wilson was implementing policies which made even the meekest of Negro leaders shudder with rage. By 1919, when Garveyism had come to national attention among Blacks, the well-known "Red Summer" was in progress and Blacks around the United States were showing their willingness to fight rather than be lynched. There had never been a time when the reality of racism was clearer to the Black masses, and there had never been a time when the need for self-reliance was more forcefully evident. The need for a spiritual self-reliance and a love for the physical presence of other Black people was pointed out by the circumstances of the times and by the astute observer, Marcus Garvey. Hence,

Garvey showed them how to love Black—not just in heated rhetoric at public meetings, but also in quiet family-oriented gatherings where the simple fact of Black people being together was the most potent reality. Whenever the African Legion in Cleveland or Pittsburg or Havana or Kingston marched down streets lined with Black faces, whenever the Black Star Nurses carried their banner through ghetto streets, a revitalization of Black people occurred. And it is this internal story, this personal story which best illustrates the contribution of Garvey the man.

In New York City, Liberty Hall was often a home for the homeless; destitute Blacks found comfort there when the despair of joblessness and hunger left them with no place to go. White men often cruised uptown in search of Black prostitutes, since Harlem of the 1920s was considered a playground by many downtown whites. On more than one occasion African Legioneers sent white male pleasure-seekers speeding back downtown, unsatisfied and often glad they had escaped to see a new day.[25] The UNIA loaned money to Blacks which was to be repaid in installments. Plans to cover funeral expenses for deceased members, and a court to settle disputes among members were only part of the numerous UNIA services.[26] It is important to remember that Garvey's idea was that of a Black government, with all of the functions and services of a government. It was Garvey who originated the notion that Black people are a nation, and that that fact only needs to be given substance by a growth in Black consciousness.

The Los Angeles Division, as well as those in Oakland and San Francisco remained active into the 1930s when the devastating Depression ended the formal activities of UNIA divisions there. But to attempt to draw the curtain on Garveyism and the UNIA in California or elsewhere in the 1930's is to underestimate the persistence of the Black man's need for "a place in the sun."

In present-day Harlem, for instance, the Vanguard Local Division of the Universal Negro Improvement Association meets in a small upstairs auditorium on Eighth Avenue. Each Sunday night, meetings are held under the red, Black and green, with a large full-length portrait of Marcus Garvey gazing purposefully into the audience from the front of the room. A mixture of young and old attend; some have been Garveyites for 50 years, others are products of the new birth of Black nationalism whose recent martyr is Malcolm X, but whose patron saint is Marcus Garvey.

Mr. Thornhill, after 50 years of adherence to Garveyism, still attends UNIA meetings in the full uniform of the Universal African Legion. His fruit wagon traverses 125th Street, as he daily preaches

Black self-reliance and pride to passers-by, much as Garvey did in his early days in New York City. Colonel Von Dinzey, Mr. Sewell, Mr. and Mrs. Stephens and others continue to nurture this direct descendant of the UNIA of the 1920s. Mr. Benjamin Samuel plays the piano when this mixture of old and new Garveyites opens each meeting with the Anthem which brought millions a new appreciation of themselves and a new evaluation of the Black man worldwide.

In Los Angeles, Samuel Marlowe and James McGann, both in their 80s, recall Garvey's visit there in 1922, and contend in voices weakened by age that Garvey's prophecies are coming true at this moment and, indeed, have been coming true since the years in which they were spoken.

The echoes of Garvey's call still ring in the ears of those who heard him. The young lad who carried a ladder from street-corner to street corner during Garvey's early appeals to teeming Harlem still recalls his dynamic personality, and still firmly believes his teachings. Some of the young men who experienced a birth of pride in the African Legion still remember with pleasure marching in formation during the big convention. But Garveyism is not nostalgia; it is alive and well throughout the Black world. Indeed, wherever Black expressions of pride are heard, Garvey's whirlwind has done its work. "Look for me in the whirlwind," were Garvey's words to his followers when he was to be taken to Atlanta prison. And the whirlwind has continued through the years since Garvey's death. The whirlwind moved through California in the 1940s when young Blacks and Mexicans revolted against police humiliation in the so-called "zoot suit riots." It came again with devastating force in 1965 when flaming Watts became a monument of Black discontent and the beginning of a new birth of nationalism among the Blacks of that region. The whirlwind touched Meritt College in Oakland, California where Black students first demanded that they learn of themselves in a Black Studies program and eventually became the genesis of the Black Panther Party, which once again raised the issue of Black manhood and self-defense before the world. The whirlwind is the Watts Festival and the Congress of African Peoples.

Succinct testimony of the force of Garvey's movement has been offered by an 86-year-old Garveyite. In answer to the question: What had Garvey done for the Blacks both in the 1920s and today, he simply stared this researcher in the eye and replied, "The UNIA was more than a religion to the people."[27]

Notes

1. Central Division UNIA Papers, Schomburg Library, Reel 1, Box l;
    Records from the 1926-27 period indicate that there were at least 989
    divisions and chapters of the UNIA scattered throughout 42 nations.
    The United States led all nations with over 700 divisions and chapters.
    Cuba was second with 50, and Panama was third with 45.
2. Central Division UNIA Papers, Schomburg Library, Reel 1, Box 2;
    There were UNIA divisions in 38 of the 48 states that comprised the
    United States. The states with the largest numbers of UNIA divisions
    were as follows:

Louisiana	75
Virginia	50
North Carolina	48
West Virginia	45
Pennsylvania	45
Mississippi	41

    The States which are generally considered the "American South" are
    the 11 states which comprised the Confederacy during the American
    Civil War (1861–1965). According to Central Division data, 362 of the
    727 divisions and chapters in the United States were in the South.
3. Charlotta Bass, *Forty Years: Memoirs From the Pages of a News-paper* (Los
    Angeles: Charlotta Bass, 1961) p. 200; J. Max Bond, "The Negro in Los
    Angeles" (Unpublished Doctoral Dissertation, University of Southern
    California, 1934) p. 44. Both sources indicate that the City of Los
    Angeles had among its 22 original settlers "9 Negroes and Mulattoes"
    and "9 Indians."
4. United States Census, 1920 and 1930.
5. Charlotta Bass, pp. 9-10.
6. Mozell C. Hill, "The All-Negro Communities of Oklahoma: The
    Natural History of a Social Movement," *The Journal of Negro History,*
    Vol. XXXI, No. 3, July, 1946, pp. 254-268.
7. *Los Angeles Times,* Feb. 12, 1909, Sec. III, p. 2; *California Eagle,* May 6,
    1914, p. 16.
8. Charles S. Johnson, "Industrial Survey of the Negro Population of Los
    Angeles" (Unpublished Survey, National Urban League Department
    of Research and Investigation, 1926) p. 10.
9. Charlotta Bass, pp. 50-65. Lawrence DeGraaf, "Negro Migration to Los
    Angeles: 1930-1950" (Unpublished Doctoral Dissertation, University
    of California, Los Angeles, 1962) p. 35.
10. *California Eagle,* July 2, 1921 and July 23, 1921.
11. Hugh Gordon was the most important Black nationalist in Southern
    California before the arrival of the UNIA. His brother, John D.
    Gordon, was the pastor of the Tabernacle Baptist Church, one of the
    largest Black churches in Los Angeles. John Gordon was one of the
    charter members of the UNIA in Los Angeles. Later, he became an
    Assistant President General of the UNIA.

12. Interview with Garveyite, February, 1971.
13. Delilah Beasley, *Negro Trail Blazers of California* (Los Angeles: Delilah Beasley, 1919) p. 137.
14. *Negro World,* August 27, 1921, p. 7. *California Eagle,* October 29, 1921, p. 1.
15. *Crisis,* January 1921, pp. 112-115.
16. James Weldon Johnson, "Crime Against Nature," *New York Age,* August 1920, p. 8.
17. *Ibid.*
18. The PCNIA membership briefly outnumbered the Garveyite loyalists. Plans were made by this dissident group to purchase a "big business block" in the Los Angeles Black community. There were also plans to expand throughout the state. After Garvey's visit to California in 1921, the PCNIA disbanded without carrying out its original plans. The most influential members of the PCNIA formed an investment company which sought to exploit land development opportunities in Southern California and Mexico.
19. *Negro World,* June 10, 1922, p. 7.
20. *California Eagle,* June 10, 1922, p. 1.
21. *Negro World,* July 15, 1922, p. 3.
22. *Ibid.*
23. *Negro World,* June 10, 1922, p. 7.
24. Interview with Garveyite, February 1971.
25. Interview with Garveyite, Los Angeles, California, January 1972.
26. Interviews with Garveyites, New York City, January 1972.
27. Interview with Garveyite, Los Angeles, California, February 1971.

The author gives special thanks to the Garveyites who consented to be interviewed for the research involved in this article. Those who were quoted directly were:

Mr. and Mrs. Daniel Kemp of Los Angeles, California
Reverend Briggs Williams of Perris, California
Mr. Benjamin Samuel of New York City
Mr. Samuel Marlowe of Los Angeles, California
Mr. James McGann of Los Angeles, California

MARCUS GARVEY, THE NEGRO WORLD, AND THE BRITISH WEST INDIES: 1919-1920

W. F. Elkins

"The capitalists realized that the movement led by Garvey, the movement for Negro independence, ... contained the embryo of the future revolutionary movement ... And the American Government decided to smash Garvey's organization by killing him politically as a leader..."

— Presidium of the International Peasants Council,
August 21, 1925

Black workers and petty bourgeoisie in the British West Indies united against the colonial structure immediately after the First World War — Black solidarity challenged white supremacy. The binding agent for the common front consisted of a new awareness of the conditions of oppression, an awakening most notably stimulated by Marcus Garvey through the columns of the *Negro World*, the organ of the Universal Negro Improvement Association published in New York City.

The new spirit of Blacks in the United States caused agitation that went "far beyond the redress of grievances," the British Directorate of Intelligence warned; it assumed the form of "Pan-

Negroism and a combination with other coloured races..."[1] In Berne, Switzerland, a military attaché reported Black agitation to be "international in its proportions." Great quantities of propagandist literature, such as the *Negro World*, had been shipped from the United States to the West Indies and Africa.[2]

The British rulers feared, with cause, that Black nationalism and socialism, radiating from the United States, might infect and inflame their Black subjects in the Caribbean. Most of the British colonies in the West Indies banned the *Negro World*. A brief survey of events connected with the suppression of the paper in the various colonies will suggest the potency of the new national and social consciousness. The response of the American government to the growth of Garveyism in the Panama Canal Zone, where thousands of British Afro-West Indians worked, will also be delineated. This response led to a successful campaign initiated by J. Edgar Hoover in the Department of Justice to have Garvey deported from the United States.

British Honduras

The acting governor of British Honduras, R. Walter, in January of 1919 prohibited the importation of the *Negro World* to the colony after he read an article in which Marcus Garvey declared that the former German colonies in Africa should not be given to England nor returned to Germany. Garvey claimed they rightfully belonged to the Blacks, who would get them sooner or later, even if it meant a bloody fight. Through the auspices of the British ambassador in Washington, Walter also sought to have the paper suppressed in the United States.

The prohibition of the *Negro World* did not succeed: several sources indicated that more copies of the paper were smuggled into the colony after the ban than had previously entered legally. More important, the ban created a definite grievance among the Black population. On July 16,1919, the Belize *Independent*, in the introduction to a story about the recent mob attacks upon Blacks in Cardiff and Liverpool, implied that a double standard existed: Walter had suppressed the *Negro World* in the colony supposedly to prevent racial antagonism, but British authorities had not as yet combated the growing prejudice against Blacks in the United Kingdom.

On the night of July 22, 1919, a group of returned soldiers of the British West Indies Regiment, armed with sticks, marched through the streets of Belize, breaking windows, inaugurating an uprising in which an estimated four thousand Blacks vented their anger against colonial oppression by looting the stores. Two days later a British gunboat, the "Constance," arrived and landed an armed naval party. Subsequently, a combined force of seamen and local police attempted to arrest a "notorious agitator," Claude Smith, while he addressed a labour meeting. The Black leader escaped, and the crowd retaliated against the seamen by throwing bottles and various missiles. Thereupon the seamen attacked the Blacks, "shooting a couple of them and running the bayonets through a couple more."[3] Apparently none died, but one man had to have his foot amputated. The next day the governor proclaimed martial law.

According to the District Attorney of British Honduras the riot in Belize on July 22nd "was of a character which savoured of a rebellion...."[4] The local volunteer force and the police, both consisting mainly of men of African descent, proved unreliable to the colonial administration during the outbreak. F.R. Dragten, a well-informed coloured barrister, told Eyre Hutson, the governor of the colony, that the uprising had started with the Blacks resentful at profiteering by merchants, and that after it began, cries were heard that the whites should be treated the way the Blacks had been treated in Liverpool. Dragten stated that prior to the revolt the Blacks had been suffering from three primary grievances: the censorship exercised on criticism of local military authorities during the war, the racial discrimination encountered by Black soldiers abroad, and the suppression of the *Negro World* by Walter.

The Black nationalistic upsurge continued in 1920. T.D.W. Napier, the commander in chief of the British fleet in North America and the West Indies, warned in May that "British Honduras is much open to and influenced by propaganda of the '*NEGRO WORLD*' style." He considered the Blacks in the colony "more inflammable" because they had "already tasted blood, beaten white men, looted stores...."[5]

Governor Eyre Hutson, too, found the Blacks unrepentant. He had received a petition from a "troublesome agitator," S.A. Haynes, the general secretary of the local branch of the Universal Negro Improvement Association and a veteran of the British West Indies Regiment, asking for the release of all soldiers imprisoned for riot. (Later Haynes went to the United States where he headed the Pittsburgh division of the U.N.I.A.) On May 10th 1920, Hutson wrote Viscount Milner, the Colonial Secretary, that if approached about the ban on the *Negro World*, he intended to say that the prohibition had lapsed, since any other course of action might give important publicity to the Black movement in the colony, "which would do more harm than good at the present moment."[6]

British Guiana

The acting governor of British Guiana, C. Clementi, in May of 1919 asked the American Consul in Georgetown to make confidential inquiries to the United States government about the *Negro World* and other Afro-American publications. It is likely that Clementi hoped the publications might be suppressed at their source, since the consul informed the State Department that the British Guiana government hesitated to forbid circulation of the publications because the Black population in the colony outnumbered the white several times and it included prominent persons. Nevertheless, on June 20, 1919, the Executive Council of British Guiana proscribed the *Crusader*, the *Monitor*, and the *Recorder*, as well as the *Negro World*, which it singled out for special treatment as a publication of "grossly offensive character."

The legal basis for the prohibition of the newspapers, a censorship ordinance, had a limited duration, so in early September, upon the advice of the Colonial Secretary, the British Guiana government introduced a seditious publications bill, a measure which made anyone possessing seditious reading matter liable to penal servitude for life. The bill prompted mass protest meetings by the newly-formed British Guiana Labour Union, an association which had drawn inspiration for its organizing activities from the *Negro World* and similar Afro-American papers. If deprived of these publications the working-class of the colony would be unable to learn about the methods of self-betterment adopted by labourers in the United States, a deputation from the Labour Union informed Clementi in a written statement. Furthermore, there would be no way to gauge the progress of Black people in the United States.

At the meeting of the Court of Policy on September 26, 1919, the British Guiana government, obviously reacting to public pressure, amended the seditious publications bill, modifying its scope and limiting the maximum period of imprisonment under it to two years. In a speech to the legislative body Clementi produced a copy of the *Negro World* and called attention to one of its headlines: "British Colonials the most prejudiced beasts in the world." He considered it very dangerous that "half-educated people" should read such a publication. A gentleman might read it at his breakfast table without causing any harm, "but in the hands of the people it might create race and class hatred."[7]

The amended version of the seditious publications bill passed the second reading, but the government did not move for a final reading which would have enacted it. The protests against the original bill had been so strong that a local naval officer had been frightened into sending an S.O.S. message, with the result that the British gunboat "Yarmouth" arrived on the day that the Court of Policy considered the measure. However, apparently something besides the fear of the people kept the bill from being passed. According to the Georgetown *Daily Argosy*, A.A. Thorne, the leader and acknowledged mentor of the Labour Union, made a tacit agreement with Clementi that the legislation would be put aside, in return for a promise that the Union would no longer import the *Negro World*. [8]

The British Guiana government presented a new seditious publications bill to the Court of Policy in February of 1920. By then Thorne had left the Labour Union, and Hubert Critchlow, the father of Guyanese unionism, had predominant control of the organization. Again the Labour Union protested the bill, again a warship (the "Calcutta") appeared on the scene, again the measure passed the second reading, and again the highest official in the government postponed final enactment. Governor Wilfred Collet held off on the bill at the request of the elective members of the Court of Policy, who feared strife if the people got the impression that the warship had come to force the measure through the legislature. Besides, Collet saw no immediate necessity to bring the bill into force. He wrote Viscount Milner that some people had the mistaken idea that "when Black people make complaints, this is seditious, but it is not if complaints are made by Europeans." [9]

The Windward Islands

The governor of the Windward Islands, G.B. Haddon-Smith in August of 1919 reported to the Colonial Secretary that the *Negro World* had openly counseled Blacks to "turn to Lenin and the Bolshevists for assistance against their real oppressors, such as Lloyd George, Wilson. and Clemenceau." Haddon-Smith advocated drastic legislation against the paper "without delay." [10]

A few months later Haddon-Smith banned the *Negro World* from St. Vincent when he discovered that its circulation caused a "grave danger" on the island. He instructed the police to keep a close watch on the local agent of the paper, R.E.M. Jack, and if possible to prosecute him. In response 375 Black people from the Stubbs District sent a petition to Haddon-Smith, informing him that any outrages upon Jack by the government would "not be tolerated by the true and new Negroes of St. Vincent." [11] The Blacks asked that Jack be recognized as their spokesman and that their wages be raised. The government did increase the minimum pay of its labourers, but refused to give Jack any special recognition.

In a letter published in the Bridgetown, Barbados, *Weekly Illustrated Paper* of October 18, 1919, Jack revealed that there were 475 members of the Universal Negro Improvement Association in St. Vincent, of whom 275 were from the Stubbs District. The Association had started the St. Vincent Trading Company and had planned a parade to Stubbs later in the month to celebrate the launching of the Black Star Line Steamship, a business venture of the U.N.I.A. in New York. Jack said that although the *Negro World* had been suppressed, he hoped to communicate with Marcus Garvey by mail. He knew that the government would try to stop the progress of the poor and innocent Blacks, but he believed that "the day is not very far distant when the right of the Negroes will overcome the might of the whites."

On February 16, 1920, a large number of labourers and 22 policemen in Castries, St. Lucia, stopped work, demanding higher pay. It appeared "not unlikely that the whole community would go on strike," reported the *Voice of St. Lucia.* Officials attributed the instigation of the trouble to the local branch of the Universal Negro Improvement Association, headed by a man named Norville. The Black agitation included an attempt to bring about a strike of domestic servants in order to make "the white and coloured people do their own work."

With the support of marines from the warship "Constance," which arrived the following night, authorities dismissed the striking policemen, and the labourers returned to work, but in a truculent and resentful mood. A few days later, the chief of police of St. Lucia, in a report on the local U.N.I.A., stated that many labourers were giving three pence a week toward support of the Black Star Line and, if required, as a future strike fund. The organization, he said, held secret meetings regularly "at which sedition is preached...." As long as the Association continued its operations in the United States, the administrator of St. Lucia wrote, "there will always be discontent among the natives here, and antagonism on the part of the Black to the Coloured and White populations."[12]

Meanwhile, in St. George's, Grenada, the outbreak of many incendiary fires caused officials to enroll sixty special constables to patrol the town at night. We find no evidence in government documents of any involvement by the U.N.I.A. in the incendiarism, although it is possible that the *Negro World* provided partial inspiration. In *The Hero and the Crowd in a Colonial Polity,* A.W. Singham mentions attempts to burn down St. George's in 1920 being attributed to the influence of returning soldiers and "inflammatory literature from abroad." Whatever the case, Grenada, St. Lucia, and St. Vincent all enacted seditious publications ordinances in 1920. The Grenada law elicited much protest, including an emergency resolution passed against it by the Labour Party of Great Britain.

The Other Colonies

Although extra-legally banned from Trinidad in February of 1919, copies of the *Negro World* were smuggled into the colony from North American steamers.[13] And Black soldiers of the British West Indies Regiment brought the paper home with them. The paper indirectly influenced the militant longshoremen's strike of December 1919 in Port-of-Spain. After the strike the government of Trinidad enacted a sedition ordinance and officially proscribed the *Negro World.* Nevertheless, the paper still circulated in the colony: at meetings of the Trinidad Workingmen's Association Black speakers used "verbatim quotations from the 'Negro World' and the writings of Marcus Garvey . . ."[14]

In Jamaica, the birth-place of Marcus Garvey, the colonial government never officially banned the *Negro World.* But the American Consul in Kingston wrote home in September of 1920 that the police authorities "do not permit the introduction of Garvey's periodicals into the Island."[15] The Consul referred to local press reports about the convention of the U.N.I.A. recently held in New York where discussions took place about an alliance of the world's Blacks "with Hindus working for independence from British rule, with Japan and China and with the Russian Bolsheviki...." The agitation of the U.N.I.A., he said, had been treated with a "certain amount of seriousness in Jamaica...."

The governor of Barbados wrote the Colonial Secretary in October of 1919 that the introduction of legislation to control the press "would only stir up trouble without any chance of becoming law."[16] He did not think the *Negro World* precipitated wrongdoing among the population in general, even if inflammatory headlines might cause excitement. In the opinion of the coloured Solicitor General of the colony the *Negro World* provided a useful service: it was good for "the Barbadian Coloured Man to see the disabilities of the Negro in America as he should be better contented with his position here."[17] Nevertheless, for some reason the government of Barbados apparently did introduce a seditious publications ordinance in 1920. We can find no indication in colonial correspondence that the legislature enacted the measure, but it might have—in later years Marcus Garvey stated that the *Negro World* had been suppressed in the colony.

Bermuda's governor, James Willcocks, in April of 1920 characterized the *Negro World* as "violent and inflammatory." But he did not think that it should be officially suppressed, as this would give it undue importance and drive it underground where it would circulate anyway. Willcocks' attitude toward Black nationalism is illustrated by his treatment of Reverend R.H. Tobitt, who had been elected 'Leader of the West Indies (Eastern Province)' at the U.N.I.A. convention of 1920 in New York. Upon Tobitt's return to Bermuda, Willcocks caused the government to withdraw its financial assistance from a school which the Black clergyman presided over. In New York Tobitt had signed the Declaration of the Rights of the Negro People of the World, and he supported its principles. This, Willcocks believed, made Tobitt "no longer a fit person to be entrusted with the education of children..."[18] (The African Methodist Episcopal Church dismissed Tobitt from its ranks for the same heresy.)

Seditious publications ordinances aimed at the *Negro World* were enacted in the Bahamas and the Leeward Islands, in 1919 and 1920 respectively. These laws, like many of the same kind in other colonies, had been instigated by the Colonial Secretary, who in September of 1919 had assured the West Indian governors that because of the unrest among Blacks, he would be prepared to approve of legislation which would allow stricter control of the press.

Panama Canal Zone

The national and social awakening among British Afro-West Indians who worked in the Panama Canal Zone paralleled that of their comrades in the Caribbean colonies. They, too, suffered under stultifying conditions forced upon them by their rulers. Official discrimination in the Canal Zone between Black alien workers, who were paid in silver, and white American workers, who were paid in gold, caused much bitterness. The "Silver Employees" got less than one third as much pay as the "Gold Employees"; they were debarred from the white unions; and they had to work ten hours before daily overtime commenced.

The only things that Blacks on the Isthmus were accustomed to receive from the whites, an organizer for the Industrial Workers of the World declared in an article published in a Finnish-language newspaper, were "scorn, growl, and abuse." The only things cheap were "the sun, liquor and women." To show the militant mood of Black consciousness in 1919 he quoted a verse by Claude McKay:

Think ye I am not friend and savage too,
Think ye I could not arm me with a gun
and shoot down ten of you for every one
of my Black brethren murdered, burned by you.
Be not deceived, for every deed you do,
I could match, outmatch:
Am I not Africa's son,
Black of that Black land, where Black deeds
are done.[19]

The activities of two representatives of the United Brotherhood of Maintenance of Way Employees and Railway Shop Labourers, with headquarters in Detroit, Michigan, gave impetus to the development of Black solidarity in the Canal Zone. In March of 1919, J.L. Allen, a one-armed man, began organizing a branch of the Brotherhood on the Atlantic side of the Canal, promising to secure an increase in the wages of common labour to forty cents an hour, while his comrade, C.H. Severs, undertook the same task on the Pacific side, In their meetings, complained Chester Harding, governor of the Canal Zone, they denigrated the Gold Employees, "stating Americans on the Isthmus are hogs doing no work and getting all the pay while negroes are doing all the work and getting nothing."[20]

Unorganized Black dock workers in Cristobal went on strike during the first week of May, demanding forty cents an hour. Allen and Severs had no direct connection with the walkout; they publicly disassociated themselves from it. The British *chargé d'affaires* at Panama City noted that the strike had been "preceded by agitation of the usual kind, all of which aimed at the regeneration of the Black man."[21]

When workers at the coaling plant quit too, a general strike of the entire Black labour force threatened the Panama Canal. As a conciliatory measure Canal officials slightly raised the pay of the class of workers who were on strike and convened the Silver Wage Board in order to consider a general increase for all workers. This move, plus opposition to the work stoppage by the conservative Silver Employees' Association, broke the strike.

In conference with officers of the Silver Employees' Association the representative of Governor Harding agreed upon a general increase of eight cents an hour for all classes of workers. Yet when the Silver Wage Board published the new silver rates of pay on July 16th, the increase amounted to only two cents per hour for common labour and less for other categories. Because of the duplicity of Canal officials, the Silver Employees' Association warned President Woodrow

Wilson in a memorial, the masses were in a "seething condition of discontent."

Governor Harding, in a letter of August 21, 1919 to A.L. Flint, Chief of Office of the Panama Canal in Washington, D.C., attributed the unrest among silver employees to the influence of labour conflicts throughout the world, the visit of Allen and Severs, the activities of "professional negro agitators," and the propaganda of two local Black newspapers modeled after the *Negro World*. Harding supplied Flint with a copy of one of the papers, the *Despatch*, in which "A True Negro" called upon his brethren to beat their ploughshares into swords and to heed the bugle call of Marcus Garvey, the "Modern Moses."

In September Harding heard a rumour that Marcus Garvey planned to visit the Canal Zone within a few weeks. To corroborate his opinion that Garvey should be excluded from the Canal Zone, Harding cabled Flint, asking for information on the Black nationalist from the Department of Justice.

Flint contacted the Department of Justice and the Military Intelligence Division of the War Department. Frank Burke, the Assistant Director and Chief of the Bureau of Investigation in the Justice Department, informed Flint that Garvey edited *The Crisis*—a journal in fact edited by W.E.B. DuBois. Burke revealed that many complaints had been made about Garvey's radical activities, but nothing definite had been ascertained. Garvey had been "very discreet in his remarks;" his speeches had been "somewhat of a general nature."[22]

In contrast, Military Intelligence, in a memorandum submitted to Flint, maintained that in a speech in Harlem Garvey had advocated reprisals against whites in the north for lynchings of Blacks in the south. Garvey appealed to the "racial instinct" of Negroes, Military Intelligence reasoned, "by urging them to do like the Irish." As an example Military Intelligence quoted circulars written by Garvey which stated:

> The Irish, the Jews and East Indians and all other oppressed peoples are getting together to demand from their oppressors Liberty, Justice, Equality, and we now call upon the four hundred millions of Negro people of the World to do likewise.[23]

The American Response

Upon receipt of the information from Military Intelligence Governor Harding definitely determined to keep Garvey out of the

Canal Zone. Flint wrote to Passport Control in the State Department, seeking the appropriate action. He thought that relatively it would do more harm "to allow Garvey to go to the Canal Zone than to allow him to remain in the United States in view of the preponderant coloured element in the Canal Zone, the stirring up of which would have a serious effect on the operation of the Panama Canal."[24]

On September 27, 1919, Governor Harding wrote to Flint, enclosing two newspaper clippings from the Panama *Star Herald* about the imminent sailing from New York of the first ship of the Black Star Line, the company which Garvey headed. Harding believed the stories in the clippings to be the propaganda of Garvey, designed to promote the sale of stock of the Black Star Line in Panama and the West Indies. He felt it "unfortunate that means cannot be found to put a stop to such a palpable fraud." "However," acknowledged Harding, "it seems that Garvey has managed, so far, to keep within the law."[25] A copy of Harding's letter and the two clippings were forwarded by Flint to the Bureau of Investigation in the Department of Justice on October 9, 1919.[26]

Two days later at the Bureau of Investigation J. Edgar Hoover used the Harding letter and at least one of the clippings as the basis of a memorandum on Garvey for Hoover's colleague, Harry S. Ridgely. Hoover wrote in the memo that Garvey had been "particularly active among the radical elements in New York City in agitating the negro movement." "Unfortunately, however," observed Hoover, "he has not as yet violated any federal law whereby he could be proceeded against on the grounds of being an undesirable alien, from the point of view of deportation. It occurs to me, however, from the attached clipping that there might be some proceeding against him for fraud in connection with his Black Star Line propaganda...." Therefore, Hoover was sending the communication received from the Washington office of the Panama Canal to Ridgely for his "appropriate attention." Hoover ended the memorandum by noting that Garvey's paper the *Negro World* had upheld "Soviet Russian Rule" and had openly advocated Bolshevism.[27]

On October 15, 1919, R.P. Stewart, the Assistant Attorney General, conveyed to the Labour Department the Harding correspondence and clippings, along with Flint's cover letter. Stewart advised the Labour Department that if no action could be taken against Garvey under the immigration laws, they should refer all their records to the Postmaster General so that an investigation could be made to find out if Garvey had used the mails to defraud.[28]

Subsequently, the government prepared a case against Garvey and brought him to trial. Found guilty of using the mails to defraud stockholders of the Black Star Line Corporation, he received a sentence on June 21,1923, of five years in prison and a fine of $1,000. The Justice Department immediately started proceedings for his deportation. When he entered Atlanta Penitentiary in February of 1925, following an unsuccessful appeal of his conviction, immigration authorities lodged a warrant of deportation with the warden.

Less than a year later, in January of 1926, the British Consul in Atlanta reported that a local immigration officer had informed him that the Department of Justice "is now considering the question of commuting Garvey's sentence of imprisonment into a sentence of deportation."[29] The immigration officer applied for a passport for Garvey.

On November 18, 1927, President Coolidge commuted the sentence of Marcus Garvey to expire at once. Although the commutation did not contain a word about deportation, immigration officials insisted that it had been made only on condition of immediate deportation. Conviction of fraud automatically had made Garvey an "undesirable alien." The officials put Garvey aboard a ship bound for the West Indies.

The evidence indicates that the deportation of Marcus Garvey cannot be considered simply as the outcome of his conviction for fraud. On the contrary, his conviction for fraud must be considered as the outcome of the intention of govemment officials to effect his deportation. Likewise, it is evident that the Justice Department initiated efforts to convict Garvey for fraud not because of any wrongdoing on his part, but because of his radical ideology.

In the national and class struggles of 1919 and 1920 the *Negro World* was clearly the revolutionary paper of the Black workers and petty bourgeoisie. Marcus Garvey believed that the suppression of the paper by white colonial governments revealed the real significance of the doctrine of Black racial inferiority. "Superior beings do not go out of even the ordinary way to mingle into the affairs of lesser creatures," he stated, "but we find that the whites lose no opportunity to suppress the intelligence of 'native races.' "[30]

Notes

1   "A Weekly Review of the Progress of Revolutionary Movements Abroad," Secret Report No. 4, May 21,1919, PRO, CAB 24/80/7306. (PRO: Public Record Office, London.)
2.   "Negro Agitation," Report No. 232 (M), Military Intelligence, New York, January 6,1920, PRO, FO 371/4567.
3.   J. Biddle, American Vice Consul, Belize, to I.T. Williams & Sons, New York, July 28, 1919, NA, RG 69, 844a.00/3. (NA: National Archives,

Washington, D.C.)

4. "Report on the cases tried at the October Sessions arising out of the Riots of the 22nd July," January 30, 1920, PRO, CO 123/299.
5. General Letter No. 4, Admiralty House, Bermuda, May 8, 1920, PRO, CO 318/358.
6. PRO, FO 115/2619.
7. Paraphrased in the Georgetown *Daily Argosy*, September 27, 1919.
8. See the issues of February 7th and 10th, 1920.
9. April 14,1920, PRO, CO 111/630.
10. August 19,1919, PRO, CO 321/304.
11. October 10, 1919, reprinted in the Bridgetown (Barbados) *Weekly Illustrated Paper*, November 8,1919.
12. February 23,1920, PRO, CO 321/310.
13. "I have the honour to state that ... the 'Negro World' has been stopped in this colony ... I may add that the proclamation required ... has not been issued and that ... the action taken by this Government is not strictly covered by law." W.M. Gordon to the Governor of British Guiana, June 10,1919, PRO, CO 295/521.
14. J.R. Chancellor, Governor of Trinidad, to Milner, November 30, 1920, PRO, CO 318/356.
15. C. Latham to the Secretary of State, Washington, D.C., September 12,1920, NA, RG 59, 811.108gl91/11.
16. 0'Brien to Milner, October 13,1919, PRO, CO 318/349.
17. Quoted by O'Brien in a letter to Milner, June 24, 1920, PRO, CO 318/355.
18. J Willcocks to Milner, November 2, 1920, PRO, CO 318/356.
19. Translation from article by Paul Miner (alias Paavo Mylleri) in the *Industrialists* of October 28, 1919, quoted in a report made by Special Agent F. Pelto of the Department of Justice, NA, RG 185, 91-C, 220. The article does not attribute the verse to McKay, but see his *Selected Poems* (New York, 1953), p. 38.
20. C. Harding, Balboa Heights, Canal Zone, to Panama Canal Office, Washington, D.C., March 31,1919, NA, RG 185, 91-C, 176.
21. British Charge d'Affaires, Panama City, to Earl Curzon of Kedleston, May 10,1919, PRO, CO 318/350.
22. F. Burke to A.L. Flint, September 23, 1919, NA, RG 185, 91-E, 209.
23. See "Memorandum—RE: Marcus Garvey," NA, RG 185, 91-E, 210.
24. A.L. Flint to R.W. Flournoy, Chief, Division of Passport Control, September 29,1919, NA, RG 185, 91-E, 211.
25. NA, RG 185, 91-E, 212. The almost identical clippings were from the issues of September 16th and 27th. The clipping from the 16th read: "New York, Sept. 15.—Yesterday was a red letter day in the history of the negroes of the United States. The first ship of the Black Star Line Steamship Corporation, of which Marcus Garvey is president, was inspected by thousands of negroes in New York harbor. The vessel will make her maiden voyage on October 31." See RG 185, 91-E, 213.
26. A.L. Flint to The Chief, Bureau of Investigation, October 9, 1919, NA,

RG 185, 91-E, 213.

27. J.E. Hoover, "Memorandum for Mr. Ridgely," October 11,1919, NA, RG 60, 198940/1-293. Items 2-4 and 291-293 in this file of the Department of Justice on Marcus Garvey are in the National Archives. The "Memorandum for Mr. Ridgely" is not numbered but is located next to item 4. On November 12,1970, the Director of the Legislative, Judicial and Diplomatic Records Division, National Archives and Records Service, reported that items 5-290 "are missing from the file, ...and we regret that we do not have any information concerning them." In 1919 Hoover had not yet become the Director of the Federal Bureau of Investigation.

28. R.P. Stewart to the Secretary of Labor, October 15, 1919, NA, RG 60, 198940/4.

29. British Consul, Atlanta, Georgia, to the British Ambassador, Washington, D.C., January 8,1926, PRO, FO 115/3120.

30. *Philosophy and Opinions of Marcus Garvey* II, 2nd ed. (London, 1967), p. 358.

MARCUS GARVEY AND TRINIDAD, 1912–1947

Tony Martin

Marcus Mosiah Garvey was born in 1887 in rural Jamaica. By the end of World War I he was well on the way to becoming the most loved, most feared and most hated Black man in the world. The years of his greatest triumph (1916 through 1927) were spent in the United States. That he organized the largest Black mass movement in the history of that country is well known. That he was the most potent force in his time for the forging of a spirit of Pan-African oneness among Black people everywhere, is widely acknowledged. What is yet to be fully appreciated is the tremendous influence exerted by Garvey on the development of working class militancy and Black nationalism in the West Indies. Garvey's organization, the Universal Negro Improvement Association (UNIA), was formed in Jamaica in 1914. By the early 1920s it existed all over the Caribbean—in Jamaica, Cuba, Santo Domingo, the U.S. Virgin Islands, Trinidad, British Honduras, Grenada, British Guiana, Surinam, St. Lucia, Barbados—these were but some of the places which boasted UNIA branches. In addition, some of the most loyal units of Garvey's worldwide organization were to be found among the many groups of West Indian exiles and immigrants in such greater Caribbean territories as Costa Rica, Honduras, Guatemala, Nicaragua, and Panama. In the United States, substantial numbers of UNIA members in such places as New York City and Florida were from the islands, and in other areas, though less numerous, they were often prominent.[1] Garvey's followers were everywhere composed overwhelmingly of proletarians and peasants. And among his followers and those influenced one way or another by the UNIA there appear some of the most important labour leaders in the West Indies in the period from World War I through World War II. Among these are Captain A.A. Cipriani of Trinidad, A. Bain Alves of Jamaica, D. Hamilton Jackson of the U.S. Virgin Islands, and Hubert Critchlow of what was then British Guiana. One longstanding participant in the West Indian labour leadership has suggested that most of the major labour leaders who came to prominence in the British West Indies as late as the 1930s were profoundly influenced by Garvey.[2] This paper will confine itself to a demonstration of some of the often intimate links which developed between Garvey and large numbers of Black people in and from Trinidad. On occasion, as will be seen, the radical nature of Garvey's program of African liberation, economic emancipation, race pride and anti-colonialism, could also lead to collaboration with radical representatives of Trinidad's Indian, Chinese and white communities.

It is impossible to pinpoint Garvey's first contact with Trinidadians. Certainly, by the time of his wanderings through Central America (1910-1912) there were emigrants from Trinidad among the communities of West Indian labourers he worked amongst. It was during this sojourn, round about 1912 in Panama, that he met J. Charles Zampty. Zampty, a native of Belmont,[3] Port-of-Spain, had recently come to Panama in search of work on the Panama Canal. This brief meeting took place, significantly, in the context of a labour union, for the occasion was an address by Garvey to the Colon Federal Labour Union, composed mostly of Black workers. Zampty migrated to New York in 1918 and immediately became a member of the one-year-old New York UNIA. In 1919 he moved to Detroit in the hope of finding work with the Ford Motor Company and shortly afterwards became one of the founders of the Detroit UNIA. In 1922 he accompanied Garvey all over the United States, acting as UNIA auditor. In 1977, two generations later, he is still a member of the Detroit UNIA and Auditor-General of the organization on the international level.

By the time that Zampty was joining the New York UNIA late in 1918, Garvey was already in the process of disseminating his propaganda throughout the Caribbean. Zampty himself had read copies of Garvey's paper, the *Negro World,* on the Panama Canal, where they were distributed by Japanese sailors. By late 1918 and early 1919, the paper was being circulated in Trinidad. "NEGROES GET READY," its masthead proclaimed, in huge letters which dwarfed the headlines. Among the Trinidadians who were most ready were the militant members of the Trinidad Workingmen's Association.

UNIA and Trinidad Workingmen's Association

Formed by Alfred Richards in 1897, the Workingmen's Association could already boast a respectable record of agitation on behalf of Black workers. But its major exploits were still to come. And the propaganda of Marcus Garvey was to play an intimate role in the organization's development from this period on. Within a remarkably short space of time the top leadership of the Association would largely overlap with the top leadership of the UNIA in Trinidad, and members of the Association would play important roles at the UNIA headquarters in Harlem.

One of the main figures behind the resurgence of the Association in 1919 was W. Howard Bishop.[4] He later edited the Association's organ, the *Labour Leader*, and was for long a major figure in Trinidad Garveyite circles. Articles from his *Labour Leader* were sometimes reprinted in the *Negro World*.[5] He may have been responsible for the appearance in the *Negro World* as early as June 15,1919, of the text of a memorial from the Workingmen's Association to the British government. When he died in 1930 the Trinidad UNIA was represented at his funeral by its president E. J. Louis, and Garvey's Jamaican *Blackman* newspaper (by this time Garvey had been deported from the United States) lamented the loss of a friend. At his death he was general secretary of the Workingmen's Association.[6]

The activities of Bishop and his colleagues in 1919 centered around several strike actions which involved workers in a variety of occupations. This trade union type activity was enacted, however, against a context of agitation for representative government and social justice for the oppressed Black masses. In all of these areas Garvey's *Negro World* provided powerful supportive propaganda.

The colonial authorities first became aware of Garvey's efforts in the island in February 1919. Then it was discovered that UNIA agents were soliciting membership and selling the *Negro World*.[7] The government immediately declared war on the publication. Copies of the paper shipped as freight were seized under the provisions of an Ordinance No. 25 of 1909, while those entering through the mails were confiscated under a War Censorship Ordinance No. 38 of 1914. Seizure under the 1909 ordinance was illegal, a fact readily admitted by the acting governor, since the proclamation required by the ordinance had not been issued.[8] The Colonial Office was quite happy to condone the suppression of "publications inciting to race hatred," as one official put it, provided they were "likely to lead to violence."[9] The *Negro World* was obviously considered within this category.

Sharing this view of the *Negro World* was the American Consul in Port-of-Spain, Henry D. Baker. Baker, an energetic and apparently efficient character, dabbled incessantly in the internal affairs of Trinidad, and on occasion gave the appearance more of an unofficial governor of the island than a mere diplomat. The British governor held him in enough deference to pass over to him confidential documents in which he might be interested, and Baker did not hesitate to directly request confidential information from the British police authorities in the island when he felt like it. He also belonged to the White Union Club, a favorite haunt of the local white overlords. From this informal perch he could observe intimately the attitudes and intentions of a powerful section of the Trinidad community. Baker repeatedly suggested to the U.S. State Department that they attack the *Negro World* at its source. The *Negro World,* he fumed after the riots of December 1919, was "responsible for the rapid growth of class and race feeling, and of anarchistic and Bolshevist ideas among the ignorant population here."[10] In October 1919 he went so far as to return to the Post Office Department in Washington wrappers in which Garvey had posted copies of the paper to individuals in the island. He claimed that thousands of copies were arriving in Trinidad with every mail.[11] Despite the efforts of the British authorities and of Baker himself, a large number of copies continued to circulate through the island, a fact which Baker admitted. And it would appear that they were on occasion sold quite openly.[12]

Baker's reference to the *Negro World* link with socialism in Trinidad was corroborated by W.A. Domingo, editor for a few months in 1919 of Garvey's paper and himself a socialist. In an article published in July 1919 while he was editor, he had deplored the ignorance of socialism manifested by New World Black people. The only exceptions of which he was aware were some small groups in the United States, and "a relatively well-organized group in the island of Trinidad, British West Indies."[13] This may well have been a reference to the Trinidad Workingmen's Association, some of whose material had already appeared in the *Negro World.* For the Association maintained close ties with the British Labour Party, which considered itself socialist.[14] Garvey himself, though eschewing socialistic doctrines concerning the primacy of class over race, nevertheless remained a lifelong admirer of both the British Labour

Party and Lenin, so the Association's simultaneous espousal of social-ism after a fashion and Garveyism was in no way incompatible with the tendencies of Garvey himself.[15]

Garvey's links with the Trinidad populace in 1919 were not confined to the Workingmen's Association. Other persons obviously read his paper, and Black soldiers returning from the war, some of whom undoubtedly found their way into the ranks of the Association, were said to be bringing back copies picked up while on duty overseas. The *Argos,* a local paper owned by a Chinese immi-grant (Mr. Lee Lum) but edited by Black radicals, was also a potent vehicle for the spread of Garvey's ideas. Their espousal of represen-tative government for the Black race was a cause of some concern alike to the British authorities and the local white elite. One *Argos* reporter, Charles A. Petioni, moved to the United States, and partic-ipated actively in the New York UNIA. He was a signatory to Garvey's important Declaration of Rights of the Negro People of the World in 1920.[16]

1919 was a year of continuous labour and racial unrest in Trinidad, marked by, among other things, anti-white feeling, assaults on white people, bitterness among returned much-discriminated-against Black soldiers, and the dissemination of Garveyite and other Afro-American ideas. All of this culminated in serious riots early in December of that year. The rioting grew out of a strike by stevedores in Port-of-Spain and spread to other parts of the island and to Tobago.

Many of the workers involved, the stevedores especially, were represented by the Workingmen's Association, which succeeded in obtaining a 25 per cent wage increase.[17] Consul Baker placed much of the blame for these events on Garvey.[18]

If Baker and the British administration needed any corrobora-tion for Garvey's connection with the 1919 unrest it came shortly after the December riots in the form of a letter from Samuel Augustus Duncan. Duncan, a naturalized American from St. Kitts, had been the president in 1918 of the newly formed New York branch of the UNIA. From this position he was ousted by Garvey, who objected to the nascent organization being used as a party-affiliated club by New York Republicans and Socialists. Duncan's response was to write a large number of British governors of West Indian and African colonies charging Garvey's "subtle and underhand propaganda" with responsibility for, among other things, "the recent bloody strikes in Trinidad."[19] The Governor of Trinidad, Sir John Chancellor, received a copy of Duncan's letter and passed it on to Baker, who advised his superiors in the State Department that "this propaganda from New York should not be tolerated by our government."[20]

The Trinidad government meanwhile embarked on a campaign of repression against Garvey and his associates in the Workingmen's Association. James Braithwaite, secretary of the Workingmen's Association, sometime president of the Port-of-Spain UNIA,[21] and a leader of the December strike, was fined, together with his principal aides, five pounds with an alternative of thirty days in jail, for calling the strike. On appeal to a higher court the latter not only agreed with the original verdict but took away the option of a fine and made the jail sentence mandatory. An ordinance was also introduced making striking illegal.[22]

But imprisonment was not the most serious sanction employed against the Garveyite leaders of the Workingmen's Association. Some were deported. Among these was an assistant secretary of the Workingmen's Association, Ven Edward Seiler Salmon. Salmon's interesting career in the Black struggle included labour agitation against the United Fruit Company in British Honduras and membership in the African Orthodox Church, which was closely related to the UNIA.[23]

Of the deportees, one John Sydney de Bourg, went on to become a member of the UNIA hierarchy in the United States. Born in Grenada, de Bourg came to Trinidad at the age of thirty and had lived there for thirty-seven years at the time of his expulsion by the British.[24] He had held various high positions in the Workingmen's Association, having been a member of the executive committee since at least 1906. In 1914 he had led a radical coup within the organization which resulted in the eventual ouster of Alfred Richards, the more moderate incumbent president.[25]

Following his deportation from Trinidad, de Bourg sojourned briefly in Grenada and proceeded to New York where he arrived on July 28, 1920. The purpose of his visit was to attend Garvey's First International Convention of the Negro Peoples of the World, where he was part of the Trinidad delegation. De Bourg's entry into the United States represented a victory, unwitting or otherwise, over Consul Baker. For Baker, early in 1919, had begun selectively refusing visas for entry into the U.S. to Trinidadians he considered undesirable. The action was condoned by the State Department which advised him to obtain the co-operation of neighboring consuls. In December, following the riots, Baker had reaffirmed his position, informing the State Department that he would refuse a visa to any of those who might be deported from Trinidad.[26]

Having successfully negotiated the visa hurdle, de Bourg and his colleagues proceeded to make a favorable impression on the convention. De Bourg's name appears among the signatories to the celebrated Declaration of Rights of the Negro Peoples of the World adopted by the conference, and, with the backing of Garvey himself, he was elected leader of the Negroes of the Western Provinces of the West Indies and South and Central America, with an annual salary of $6,000.[27] An official at the British Colonial Office, examining the UNIA Declaration of Rights a few months after the conference, expressed some alarm at the role of the Trinidad delegation. He wrote, "I recognize such old friends from Trinidad as de Bourg, McConney and Braithwaite among the signatories. It's the signatories rather than their publications which are dangerous."[28]

De Bourg spent most of the next two years traveling widely on behalf of the UNIA. He delivered speeches, helped resuscitate failing branches, sold stock in Garvey's Black Star Line Steamship Corporation and negotiated with governmental authorities on behalf of UNIA members. These activities covered places as far afield as Brooklyn, New York; Louisville, Kentucky; Camaguey, Cuba; Jamaica; and San Juan, Puerto Rico.[29] In 1921 he toured the West Indies with Garvey. Of great assistance to de Bourg in his UNIA work was his experience in the leadership of the Workingmen's Association. For in 1922 we find him negotiating on behalf of the UNIA members in San Pedro de Macoris, Santo Domingo, with plantation owners and officials of the U.S. military administration which was then occupying the island. With the former he negotiated for a schoolroom and other fringe benefits for UNIA use, and from the latter he recovered confiscated UNIA property.[30] For his UNIA work de Bourg was elevated to the UNIA aristocracy of merit. He was made a Knight Commander of the Nile and Duke of Nigeria and Uganda, and received the Gold Cross of African Redemption.[31]

De Bourg eventually fell out with Garvey, testified against him during his celebrated 1923 trial, and was awarded $9,781 in a suit for back pay against the UNIA.[32] Garvey lamented de Bourg's treachery, claiming that de Bourg had proved a failure as a fund-raiser, an important part of his job, having raised only $200.00 in sixteen months of active UNIA employment.[33] Garvey wrote,

There was one old man from Trinidad, over sixty years of age, who came to the convention with tears in his eyes. He made a pitiful plea to the convention for help. He stated that he was once a man of means in the Island of Trinidad, but that he fought the battles of the poor Blacks and was hounded by the British, who impoverished him and drove him out of the country. His story was plausible. He appeared poorly attired and suggested that he was really in need of help. I, myself, suggested this man for the position of leader of one of the Provinces of the West Indies at a salary of $6,000 per annum. I personally did everything to help the old man, yet he was the principal enemy witness against me for the Government in 1923 ...[34]

The presence of de Bourg and his colleague at Garvey's 1920 convention was evidence of what had by this time become a fairly widespread adherence to Garvey's ideas by the Black masses in and out of the Workingmen's Association. Governor Chancellor reported during the year that "at the meetings of the 'Workingmen's Association', and elsewhere, verbatim quotations from the 'Negro World' and the writings of Marcus Garvey are used by negro speakers." He mentioned also that shares in Garvey's Black Star Line were held in Trinidad.[35] Earlier in the year Baker had requested confidential information from the local police on two young Trinidadians who were planning to work for the line. One, Randolph Flanner, an ex-employee of the Trinidad Government Foundry, was already in New York and expected to be shortly appointed third engineer on the line's *Phyllis Wheatley*. The other, Allan Berridge, son of a Town Hall clerk and also a foundry employee, was about to leave for New York where he hoped to study mechanical engineering with a view to also joining the Black Star Line. The police authorities assured Baker that they were both of good character.[36] This attraction of the Black Star Line for Trinidadians, as for Black people elsewhere, was enhanced by the discriminations which Black passengers were forced to endure on white-owned ships. In a typical account a writer to the *Negro World* in 1920 catalogued the racist practices of the Trinidad Shipping and Trading Company Ltd. and the British ship *Maraval* plying between Trinidad, Grenada and New York. Among other things Black first class passengers were required to eat after the white passengers.[37]

The Negro World

In order to further try and stem the onrush of Garveyite influence the Trinidad government in April 1920, in concert with several other West Indian governments, passed a Seditious Publications Ordinance, aimed especially against the *Negro World* and *Crusader* (yet another New York publication published by yet another West Indian-American, Cyril Briggs). The Colonial Office had authorized the passage of this bill in 1919, with a view, at that time, to dealing in a legitimate fashion with the *Argos* and the *Negro World*.[38] (The latter, as already mentioned, was being illegally destroyed since early 1919.) The procedure both before and after the Seditious Publications

Ordinance was to search Black crews as well as the ships themselves if they came from New York. A police inspector checked the mails for those entering by that route.[39] In a typical operation the police in August 6, 1920 discovered a large cache of the *Negro World* hidden in between a cargo from New York. Among the find (and confiscated in the mail also at about the same time) was a large number of leaflets, including a pamphlet specially addressed by Garvey to the people of Trinidad.[40] With the passage of the new ordinance the authorities also intensified their efforts against those papers which still eluded the police net and found their way into the island. Houses were searched by detectives. Indeed as late as 1931 Albert Gomes, then editor of the radical *Beacon* magazine, was visited by a detective with "an apologetic mien, a roving eye, [and] a notebook" who was searching for Communist and more especially for Garvey's papers.[41]

Consul Baker, of course, applauded the action of the British overlords, and the *Argos*, not surprisingly, protested the Seditious Publications Ordinance.[42] A wide cross section of opinion in fact opposed the ordinance, but not always because of any love for Garvey. Thus the *Port-of-Spain Gazette* argued that the bill was worded so broadly as to make any criticism of government vulnerable. Also opposing the measure was the *Teacher's Journal*.[43] And in England at the annual conference of the Labour Party Mr. Ben Spoor, a member of parliament from Durham, introduced a resolution against restrictive legislation in the colonies in general and requesting the withdrawal of this ordinance in particular. Spoor and others pointed out that the "so-called negro population" (as one delegate put it), were still treated like slaves and subjected to tyrannical government, and that if labour was to advance in England it would have to advance in the colonies too. One delegate, presumably expressing the sentiment of many present, feared the effect the ordinance would have on the English labour paper, the *Daily Herald*.[44] And a popular calypsonian denounced the blatant class nature of this legislation and the tyranny of British rule. He sang,

> Class legislation is the order of this land;
> We are ruled with the iron hand.
> Class legislation is the order of the land;
> We are ruled with the iron hand.
> Britain boasts of equality,
> Brotherly love and fraternity,
> But British colours have put we,
> In perpetual misery in this colony.[45]

The sentiments of the masses, as expressed in this calypso, contrast with those of the local white businessmen, whose organ, the *Trinidad Guardian*, applauded the measure, arguing that the only persons with any cause for objection ought already to have been in jail.[46]

Therefore 1920, was a year of advance and consolidation for Garvey's ideas among Trinidadians at home and abroad. One discordant note was provided, however, by a Trinidadian in New York who fell in among Garvey's enemies, and who for a while tried to operate a rival organization under Garvey's nose in Harlem. The person in question was F.E.M. Hercules, whose history of participation in race struggles certainly rivaled Garvey's. His record included formation of a Young Men's Coloured Association while still a schoolboy in Trinidad, and important roles in the Society of Peoples of African Origin and the African Progress Union in England around the period 1918-1919. In 1919 he had toured the West Indies propagandizing Black people to an awareness of their oppressed condition and doing what he could to encourage self-reliance and resistance.[47]

In Harlem early in 1920 Hercules began holding weekly meetings of his newly-formed African International League. The League's program did not look too different from Garvey's, featuring as it did economic self-reliance and PanAfrican cooperation. His meetings were well attended by Garvey's Black enemies and were regularly and favorably reported in the *Emancipator* of W.A. Domingo, Jamaican ex-editor of the *Negro World*, now turned anti-Garvey propagandist. In March the *Emancipator* published a thinly veiled Hercules criticism of "a certain would-be imperialist organization" (undoubtedly the UNIA) which wrongly, in his opinion, wished to set up its headquarters in Liberia.[48] Hercules, however, slid into relative oblivion, while Garvey proceeded from strength to strength.

Early 1921 saw a further deepening of the links between Trinidad and Garvey. Eugene Corbie, a Trinidad student at the City College of New York and a UNIA member, early in 1921 attempted to set up a music bureau in connection with the UNIA. The bureau would encourage and consolidate the efforts of Black artists.[49] Corbie had a brilliant academic career at City College and won wide acclaim for his prize-winning performances in inter-collegiate oratorical contests. Trinidadian George Padmore considered Corbie one of the "two most outstanding coloured youth leaders in college circles" in the United States, the other being Padmore himself.[50]

But perhaps the most noteworthy, and certainly the most colorful link between Garvey and Trinidad in 1921 came in the person of Hubert Fauntleroy Julian, or, as he quickly became known, the Black Eagle. Julian, an intrepid and flamboyant immigrant from

Trinidad, is reputed to have been the first Black person to qualify as a pilot in North America. He entered the United States from Canada in March 1921, headed for Harlem and soon met Garvey. According to Julian they "quickly became close friends." For Garvey's 1922 convention they secretly agreed upon a publicity stunt which would both advertise the UNIA and gain Julian the entree into influential circles which he desired. He flew a Curtis biplane back and forth over the convention parade. Due to the absence of restrictions against low-flying at that time he could get near enough to the marchers to create considerable interest. To heighten the effect, the plane was inscribed with UNIA slogans. Later that night Garvey introduced Julian to a mass meeting as the mystery pilot, taking the opportunity to hold up Julian as an example of what the Black man could achieve, given an equal opportunity.[51]

By June 1921 the Black Star Line was announcing that its ship, the *Phyllis Wheatley*, would call at Trinidad on its way to its maiden West African voyage,[52] and on the line's *S.S. Kanawha* transporting Garvey's party in the West Indies there was at least one crew member from Trinidad, namely Joshua Parris, a fireman. Parris had previously been fourth engineer on the line's *Yarmouth*.[53]

Also 1921 was the year in which Garvey, as a preliminary step to moving his headquarters to Liberia, set up a legation there. As resident secretary of the legation he named Cyril A. Crichlow, a naturalized American citizen from Trinidad. The post carried a salary of $2,500 per annum. Crichlow was co-proprietor of the Crichlow-Braithwaite Shorthand School in Harlem, apparently the leading Black business school in New York City. He himself had for some time been the UNIA's "official reporter," which post involved taking down verbatim shorthand notes at UNIA meetings. In 1920 he had been among the signatories to the Declaration of Rights of the Negro Peoples of the World. In Liberia Crichlow soon ran afoul of the Liberian UNIA potentate, Gabriel Johnson, who saw Crichlow's position as an attempt to usurp his own power. In his conflict with Johnson, Crichlow took the extraordinarily asinine step of turning to the U.S. minister in Monrovia for support. In the process he turned over confidential UNIA documents to this representative of the U.S. government and thereby contributed more than his share to the downfall of Garvey's Liberian plans. To add to his discomfiture he fell ill. His stay in Liberia lasted from March 18 to August 6, 1921. He sued Garvey on his return for $1,237.99, claiming arrears of pay. A court awarded him $700.00 since he had not fully performed his contract.[54]

The British Colonialists React

Meanwhile in Trinidad in 1921 the British colonialists continued to do what they could to humbug the UNIA. Their big achievement for the year consisted in denying entry to the Rev. Richard Hilton Tobitt, a UNIA commissioner who was visiting branches in the Caribbean area. Tobitt was nonetheless allowed into places such as Barbados and British Guiana, and a few years later while again on UNIA business, was received by the governor of Surinam and given the freedom of that country.[55] Tobitt's exclusion from Trinidad was also an oblique attack by the government on the Workingmen's Association whose "leading members," the *Port-of-Spain Gazette* reported, had arranged a "sumptuous breakfast" for him.[56] Tobitt complained to Winston Churchill at the Colonial Office about the arbitrary action of the Trinidad government. Churchill refused to intervene.[57] Local UNIA members remained undaunted. Robert E.R. Fletcher, assistant secretary of the Port-of-Spain division, condemned the British authorities for inciting racial hatred and declared that the Black masses would not be intimidated, for "We feel that the same vision that the other Negro peoples of the world have caught sight of, we too, have caught sight of. . ."[58]

The government's exclusion of Tobitt served only to confirm what was by this time a fairly obvious fact, namely that Trinidad, of all the British possessions, seemed to be the most repressive against the UNIA. The exclusions, jailings, shootings, deportations, initial illegal burnings of the *Negro World,* house searches, ordinance against striking, prompt passage of the Seditious Publications Ordinance, and other similar measures all added up to an extremely regressive package. None of these measures taken individually was of course peculiar to Trinidad, but Trinidad has a good claim for first place for the comprehensiveness of its hostility to the UNIA. Of the British possessions and dominions, Bermuda, with its large and proverbially reactionary white population, came closest to Trinidad in anti-UNIA endeavor. South Africa, which possessed the largest number of UNIA branches on the African continent, is not exempted from these comparisons.[59] The infamy of Trinidad's government had by 1922 become so notorious that a West African newspaper, the *Gold Coast Leader,* could editorially speak of "the obstructionist parts of the West Indian Colonies, such as Trinidad." [60]

That Trinidad's reputation was well-merited was further evidenced by two events in 1922 and 1923. The first involved a projected world tour by Garvey. Garvey's announcement threw the British Colonial Office into a dither. A flurry of correspondence ensued between London and all British governors in Africa and the West Indies. The Colonial Office wanted, if possible, to agree on some pre-arranged strategy for dealing with the visit if it materialized. Of the British West Indian colonies, British Honduras, the Leeward Islands, Grenada, Jamaica, British Guiana and initially Barbados, all accepted the Colonial Office suggestion that it would be preferable to let Garvey in and then try and treat him as of no consequence, rather than risk unrest by refusing him entry. Trinidad and Bermuda insisted on prohibiting his entry.[61]

The second event concerned the ban on the *Negro World*. By 1922-1923 some West Indian governments had lifted the ban on the paper due to a combination of public protests and the belief in some gubernatorial quarters that the tone of the paper had mellowed since 1919. Jamaica and Barbados were among the areas now admitting the paper.[62] In this situation the governor of British Guiana communi-cated his desire to lift the ban to the Secretary of State for the Colonies, Winston Churchill. He however expressed reservations about admit-ting it into British Guiana while it was still seditious in nearby Trinidad.[63] The governor of Trinidad, in response to an inquiry from Churchill, declared it his intention to keep the ban in Trinidad. He added that he had recently refused a petition from the Trinidad UNIA to repeal the Seditious Publications Ordinance and withdraw the proclamation prohibiting entry to the paper, "owing to the objec-tionable character of the matter" still appearing in it.[64]

The extreme anti-UNIA stance of the Trinidad government can no doubt in large part be explained by the presence there of one of the more rabidly obscurantist white minorities in the islands. And their reaction was matched by their influence and vocality. They ran the Chamber of Commerce, selected candidates during the war for their white Merchants and Planters Contingent, controlled their own newspaper, and were in no way awed by British governors. During the 1919 unrest, for example, they bombarded the governor, the pub-lic and the Colonial Office with alarmist and sometimes openly racist petitions and statements of all kinds. And when the governor at one point capitulated to the strikers they threatened to report him to the Colonial Office and exacted an apology from him.[65]

The attitude of the government can also be explained in part by the simple fact that the Trinidad UNIA, with its large membership, and its intimate link with one of the most powerful working class organizations in the British islands at the time, was a force not to be taken lightly. By the early 1920s Trinidad was the most thoroughly organized UNIA stronghold in the British West Indies, and of the non-British islands only Cuba had a larger number of UNIA

branches. De Bourg at the 1922 convention in New York gave a figure of 33 for the association's branches in the island.[66]

The following year UNIA commissioner Tobitt gave the number as 32 and testified to the continued circulation there of the *Negro
World* despite the opposition.[67] A UNIA headquarters compilation of
1927 named 30 divisions. They were spread all over the island, in
large towns and rural areas alike. Branches were listed for Balandra
Bay, Carapichaima, Caroni, Cedros, Chaguanas, Couva, D'Abadie,
Enterprise, Gasparillo, Guaico, Iere Village, La Brea, Lily of the Nile
(the headquarters division in Port-of-Spain), Los Bajos, Mucurapo
(St. James), Marabella, Matura, Morne Diablo, Palmyra, Penal, Port-
of-Spain, Princes Town, Rio Claro, St. Mary (Moruga), St. Madeleine,
San Fernando, Siparia, Tableland, Victoria Village and Williamsville.
Cuba, according to the same compilation, had fifty-two branches and
Jamaica ten.[68] Apart from the areas listed above this author has come
across references to divisions in Brother's Road, New Grant, Cumana,
Tabaquite and St. Joseph. And the absence of a division in an area did
not necessarily imply an absence of UNIA members. Thus persons
from Toco belonged to the division in nearby Cumana[69] and there
were Garveyites in Mt. Stewart Village, Pointe-a-Pierre and
Vistabella,[70] which places may or may not have had divisions of their
own.

The Trinidad UNIA

The Trinidad UNIA enjoyed a very active existence and minis-
tered to many of the needs of its members. In addition to its obvious
function of stimulating race pride and Black self-reliance, its effectiveness as a workers' organization was enhanced by the close association with the Workingmen's Association. And both the workers
and peasants within it benefited from the fact that, like UNIA
branches everywhere, they also doubled as friendly societies, paying
death and other benefits to members.

Activities revolved here, as elsewhere, around the regular meetings of the association. The Lily of the Nile (headquarters) division
possessed its own Liberty Hall[71] (as all UNIA meeting places the
world over were called). Some divisions had to make do with the use
of halls belonging to other institutions. Thus we find the St.
Madeleine division using the Be of Good Cheer Friendly Society Hall,
the Port-of-Spain division using the Ideal Hall on Tragarete Rd., and
so on.[72] Many of the UNIA auxiliaries familiar to branches elsewhere
also existed in Trinidad. These included the Black Cross Nurses, the
Universal African Legions, Boy Scouts, Scout Girls, and UNIA choirs.

Sometimes, instead of a lay chaplain, clergymen from the African Methodist Episcopal (A.M.E.) Church handled the religious aspects of meetings.[73] There was considerable interaction between members of different divisions. It was quite common for members to travel long distances by train to attend meetings of far away divisions. This would be especially true for a special event, such as the unveiling of a new charter or the dedication of a new Liberty Hall. Such interaction also existed between members from various countries in the area. Trinidad Garveyites crop up addressing UNIA gatherings in St. Kitts, British Guiana and Barbados, among other places.[74] Members from other islands also turned up at meetings in Trinidad.

This interaction extended also to the parent body in Harlem, U.S.A., and took many forms. A large number of Trinidad members, for example, contributed to various funds being raised by the parent body in Harlem. Throughout the pages of the *Negro World* for 1922 there appear a fairly large number of Trinidadians among contributors to the convention fund and the Marcus Garvey defense fund. These persons represented divisions in St. Joseph, Princes Town, Port-of-Spain and La Brea, among other places. In one edition of the paper no less than 55 names from Palmyra, Mt. Stewart Village, San Fernando, Pointe-a-Pierre and Vistabella were listed as contributors to the defense fund.[75] In 1924 one Jonathan C. Watts of Princes Town donated $120 to Harlem headquarters.[76]

Close contact with the Harlem headquarters was also maintained by the sending of delegates to Garvey's international conventions. Their presence at the 1920 convention has already been noted. At the 1922 convention, apart from Trinidadians living in New York, Fitz Aaron Braithwaite was sent as a Trinidad representative, and returned home immediately after the event.[77] At the 1924 convention (there was none in 1923) a Trinidad delegate, I. Cipriani, was mentioned several times in reports of the deliberations.[78] The next convention at which Garvey presided was in 1929 in Jamaica. Here Miss Edith Devonshire, lady president of the Trinidad headquarters (Lily of the Nile) division, played an active part, being elected to the convention's Social and Political Committee.[79]

For those who could not make it to Harlem, the Trinidad branches sometimes held a convention of their own to coincide with Garvey's. In 1921 the Carapichaima division hosted such a convention.[80] And in 1922 the Lily of the Nile division held a 31 day convention, coinciding exactly with that in Harlem. Over a thousand people attended the opening night festivities, during which a picture of Garvey was unveiled. Among the speakers was a lady president from Barbados and a Mr. Cyrus (possibly himself a Trinidadian) who was described as a founder of the New York division and on a visit to the island. Four hundred and sixty new members were added to the organization during this convention.[81]

Other special meetings celebrated such events as Ethiopia's admission into the League of Nations, Emancipation Day, and the expected visit of Garvey's representative, Mme. M.L.T. de Mena.[82] There is no better way to capture the everyday flavor of the organization than by a brief description of an important, but fairly typical meeting. This particular meeting celebrated the unveiling of the charter for the Port-of-Spain division and was held at the Ideal Hall in Tragarete Road, Port-of-Spain, in March 1922. The huge, standing-room-only crowd included several members from country districts. The meeting started at 3 p.m. with a procession led by the UNIA Juveniles (both girls and boys) and the choir, under choirmaster Reginald Solomon. Next came the officers, including president Stanley Jones, vice-president Thomas O'Neale, chaplain Reginald Perpignac, the director of the Black Cross Nurses in Trinidad and Tobago, Mrs. Louise Crichlow, and Percival Burrows, commissioner for Trinidad. They were followed by a detachment of Black Cross Nurses.

Commissioner Burrows then presided over the unveiling, which was performed by little Miss Nauma Braithwaite, dressed as an Ethiopian queen. Burrows next presented each officer with his emblem of office, a gavel to the president, Bible to the chaplain, and so on. The recipients included officers of the choir, nurses, Motor Corps, juveniles and the African Legion. A number of speeches followed, delivered by Mrs. Crichlow, Mrs. Isaac Hector, lady president of Chaguanas, Joshua Douglas, president of La Brea, who had traveled by boat and train to be present, and Joseph Charles, also of La Brea, who urged Black-owned businesses. These last three then left to catch a train back home. At least eight speeches followed, interspersed with a violin solo and a song. The feature address was by W. Howard Bishop of the Workingmen's Association, who spoke on the need for Black unity. This presentation was much applauded. The recessional hymn was sung as the procession made its way to the robing room, and the meeting ended with the singing of the Universal Ethiopian anthem (adopted in the 1920 Declaration of Rights as the anthem of the Black race).[83]

The presence of W. Howard Bishop at this meeting is evidence of the continuing close relationship between the two associations. Meetings of the Workingmen's Association were regularly held at Liberty Hall in downtown Port-of-Spain. When in 1924 the British Guiana Labour Union leader Hubert Critchlow visited Trinidad on his way to a labour conference in England, he addressed a meeting sponsored by the Workingmen's Association at Liberty Hall. Critchlow's union not only enjoyed cordial fraternal relations with the Trinidad Workingmen's Association, but also maintained links with the UNIA in British Guiana.[84] At this 1924 meeting in Port-of-Spain's Liberty Hall Critchlow was given a mandate by the Workingmen's Association to lobby in England for trade union laws for Trinidad. The close association between organized labour and the UNIA is further evidenced by the fact that most of the Workingmen's Association dignitaries on the platform for the Critchlow speech were also high ranking Garveyites. These included W. Howard Bishop, general secretary of the Workingmen's Association; James Braithwaite, its ex-secretary and sometime president of the Port-of-Spain UNIA; and Fitz Aaron Braithwaite who, apart from being sometimes treasurer and pianist of the Port-of-Spain division,[85] had represented Trinidad at Garvey's 1922 convention.[86] Captain A.A. Cipriani, the president of the Workingmen's Association and chairman of the meeting, also, as will be seen, maintained close ties with Garvey.

This Liberty Hall, at 28 Prince Street, Port-of-Spain, was the seat of the Trinidad headquarters division, the Lily of the Nile (not to be confused with the Port-of-Spain division).[87]

That there may, however, have been an occasional reservation about the Workingmen's Association connection is suggested in a very valuable account of five UNIA branches appearing in the *Negro World* of November 19, 1921. The account was written by J.R. Ralph Casimir, head of the Dominica UNIA and one of the most influential and hardworking UNIA figures in the West Indies, after a trip to Trinidad.

Casimir first visited Guaico, where the charter was unveiled during his stay on June 25, 1921. This branch had about a hundred members of whom only about twenty were financial. At Casimir's urging a unit of the Universal African Legions was formed here with four recruits under Mr. Elbert Morancie, an ex-corporal in the British West Indies Regiment.

Casimir next proceeded to the Tabaquite division, where he arrived on July 2nd. Here he was distressed to find that some of the officers had sent for Mr. Bishop and Mrs. Raviak of the Workingmen's Association for guidance in UNIA affairs. Mrs. Raviak informed Casimir that Bishop was a personal friend of Garvey, who had personally authorized him to propagate the UNIA message in Trinidad. The Garveyites in Tabaquite had also sent about $40.00 to James Braithwaite in Port-of-Spain, believing (wrongly, in Casimir's opinion) that he was head of the Trinidad UNIA.

On July 3rd, Casimir visited Brother's Road, where he found a well-organized division containing about 75 members, despite being less than a month old. Casimir addressed them for three hours on organizational matters.

Penal was next, with a visit on July 10th. Here he reported 150 members and was peeved at the Rev. A.E. Taylor of the A.M.E. Church for representing to the people that his was the church of the UNIA.

Casimir was most impressed by the La Brea division which he visited on August 7th. This division dated from around January 1921.

In his general remarks Casimir again criticized James Braithwaite, this time for collecting money allegedly for the Black Star Line without accounting for how it was spent. He was equally hostile to the "so-called" UNIA organizer Herman D. Thompson of St. Joseph who ordered UNIA supplies from New York and resold them at exorbitant profits. Thompson, he thought, belonged to the "old type of Negroes and is too bombastic." So it would appear that Trinidad, like the parent body in New York itself, was not without those who were willing to capitalize on the Black struggle for personal gain.

Presiding as UNIA commissioner over District No. 5 of the Foreign Fields, which included Trinidad, Grenada, St. Vincent, Brazil, Colombia and Venezuela, was Percival Leon Burrows.[88] As in the case of all UNIA commissioners, his job involved traveling to and overseeing the work of branches in the district, as well as acting as an ambassador on behalf of Black people. The document appointing him in 1922 read:

> Mr. Burrowes (sic.) is authorized to supervise the various branches, divisions and chapters of the Universal Negro Improvement Association and African Communities League. He is commissioned to represent the interest of all Negroes domiciled in the countries. In the matter of trouble and disturbances, he is authorized to take up the matter with the respective governments in protecting the interest of all Negroes.
>
> The Universal Negro Improvement Association represents the interest of 400,000,000 negroes the world over, and lends its moral, financial and political support to the actions of Commissioner Burrowes in the performance of his duties in connection with the Negro race.
>
> We ask that all with whom he comes in contact exchange with him the courtesies due to a representative of a sovereign race.[89]

Burrows, like Zampty, de Bourg and Cyril Critchlow before him, moved on to occupy a top position in the UNIA international hierarchy. By August 1923 we find him presiding at Liberty Hall in Harlem (Garvey was in jail following his trial) and he shortly thereafter became secretary general of the association.[90]

Burrows by no means completes the list of persons connected with the Trinidad UNIA members who achieved high office at the Harlem headquarters. The *Negro World* in 1925 reported that one Francis X. Quattell had been transferred from the Port-of-Spain division to Harlem, where he addressed a Liberty Hall meeting, but little is heard of him thereafter.[91] Much more important was Hucheshwar G. Mudgal, editor of the *Negro World* during some of its later years after Garvey's expulsion from the United States. Mudgal was born in India and emigrated to Trinidad before moving on to the United States. His connection with Garvey's publications began in 1922 when he took over the *Negro World* foreign affairs column vacated by Garvey's mentor, Duse Mohamed Ali. At this time he was also a foreign affairs columnist for Garvey's *Daily Negro Times*. After a period of apparent inactivity his foreign affairs articles reappeared on a regular basis in 1929 and he thereafter became the paper's editor. He busied himself debating the ideological correctness of Garveyism against Communists, and in 1932 produced a pamphlet, *Marcus Garvey—Is He the True Redeemer of the Negro?*

In 1929 Mudgal was described as having an M.A. from Columbia University and being a Ph.D. candidate.[92]

But one of the most important United States based Trinidadians influenced by Garvey was George Padmore, who was never, as far as is known, a member of the UNIA. In 1928, about a year after Garvey's deportation, Padmore was responsible for a protest at the Howard University campus against a visit by the British ambassador to Washington, Sir Esme Howard. Lengthy mimeographed documents signed by Padmore as secretary of the International Anti-Imperialistic Youths' League accused the ambassador of complicity in Garvey's deportations from the U.S. in 1927 and Canada in 1928. Padmore was assisted in this endeavor by another Trinidadian student, Cyril Ollivierre.[93]

During the same year that Padmore was accusing the British ambassador of engineering Garvey's deportation from the U.S. and Canada, the British authorities in Trinidad were busy making plans to prevent Garvey's entry into Trinidad or expel him if he should somehow manage to land. Their plans had in fact started almost as soon as Garvey arrived back in Jamaica in December 1927. The governor, on hearing that "the notorious Marcus Garvey," as he put it, was contemplating a West Indian tour, immediately called together his executive council. This colonialist conclave unanimously agreed to prohibit Garvey's entry and the governor, again in his own words, "signed an order for use in case of need."[94] This was followed up with a law drafted especially for Garvey, empowering the governor in executive council to prevent the landing of, or engineer the expulsion of a person convicted anywhere of a crime for which sentence of imprisonment was passed, that person's British nationality notwith-standing.[95] Garvey addressed himself to this law some months later. He berated "the minority white colonists and the non-racial coloured class who have jointly lived off the ignorance and unfortunate con-dition of the Black masses" and charged, correctly, that the law was passed for his benefit when it appeared that he might visit and con-fer with Black Trinidadians in an effort to better their condition.[96] Garvey was equally peeved by the fact that a section of the Black teachers came out against his visit on the ground that it might cause misunderstanding between the races. Garvey pointed out that the teachers themselves had lamented the poor economic situation of the Black section of the population, which made ludicrous their concern for understanding when other races were rich and happy. "In Trinidad," he declared, "the Negro teachers have openly declared themselves the enemy of the Black masses." And from this circum-stance he drew the important lesson that "We must adopt the inter-nal boycott against traitorous Negroes as we shall do against our enemies of other races."[97]

Cipriani Supports Garvey

Nine years later, in 1937, another projected Garvey visit to the West Indies found Trinidad still outdoing the other colonies in anti-Garvey hostility, as had usually been the case since 1919. This time Garvey obtained the support of Captain A.A. Cipriani. Cipriani, as the white leader of the Trinidad Workingmen's Association (in 1934 it became the Trinidad Labour Party), occupied a situation which was immensely unusual for one of his race in the island. During World War I, he had been a captain in the British West Indies Regiment and apparently much disturbed by the multitudinous dis-criminations meted out to the Black rank and file. Back home from the war in 1919 he accepted leadership of the Workingmen's Association which was by this time, as has been seen, a Garveyite stronghold. His record of struggle on behalf of Black soldiers, the fact that his whiteness may have caused him to be perceived as less vulnerable to official harassment, and the fact that the largely non-

Trinidad born leadership of the association not infrequently found itself the victims of deportation, may all have contributed to the choice of Cipriani as leader.

Cipriani thus found himself in control of a largely Garveyite organization in which a large number of his fellow leaders doubled as major UNIA figures. In this situation, then, it is not surprising that Cipriani and Garvey developed a mutual admiration for each other's political position. Garvey's *New Jamaican* newspaper, for example, went on record in September 1932 in praise of Cipriani. Apart from the obvious UNIA connection, the political ideas and careers of both men reveal many similarities. Cipriani served for many years on the Port-of-Spain City Council, Garvey on the Kingston and St. Andrew Corporation Council. Cipriani served in the Legislative Council, Garvey attempted unsuccessfully to do the same. Cipriani, as leader of the Trinidad Labour Party, pioneered modern party politics in Trinidad. Garvey did the same in Jamaica with his Peoples' Political Party. Both men campaigned for trade union legislation and such related measures as the eight-hour day. Both had a peculiar fascination with the British Labour Party. And both were the targets of Communist attacks, so that George Padmore, during his Moscow years, could in the same paragraph attack "Negro capitalist misleaders, like Marcus Garvey" and "the white trade union faker, Captain Cipriani, in the West Indies" as "agents of imperialism."[98] Similarly, when in 1930 Otto Huiswoud of the American Negro Labor Congress was expelled from Trinidad by the government, he accused Cipriani, a "faker" and member of the "treacherous Amsterdam International," of being behind it.[99] Huiswoud was a Communist and long-standing foe of Garvey.

When Garvey decided, therefore, to include Trinidad on his West Indian itinerary for 1937 he immediately obtained Cipriani's assistance, since experience made him anticipate trouble from the Trinidad government. Cipriani conferred with the governor on July 5 and wrote Garvey (now living in London) on the same day conveying assurances that he would be allowed to land. Garvey's precautions were well advised, for officials at the Colonial Office, when they became aware of his intentions, did indeed suggest that he should be allowed into the other islands but kept out of Trinidad.[100] The reason for this attitude was that in 1937 Trinidad was in the throes of labour riots and unrest similar to that of 1919. The governor, Sir Murchison Fletcher, apparently unaware of Garvey's illustrious past, claimed to have heard Garvey's name for the first time at the outbreak of the 1937 unrest, when there was a rumour that he and Cipriani would appear in Trinidad together on July 3rd. Governor

Fletcher nevertheless preferred to let Garvey in, lest making him a martyr at that particular time might turn out to be the greater of the two possible evils.[101]

On July 21 Garvey called on the Colonial Office. He showed officials Cipriani's letter and claimed that he would not stir up any trouble in Trinidad since in the present world conditions (presumably a reference to his fear of the greater evils of Nazism and fascism) he supported Britain. He went so far, according to the Colonial Office, as to deplore the recent outbreaks in Trinidad. He also agreed to a Colonial Office suggestion that he write to the West Indian governors concerning his good intentions. The Colonial Office expressed a belief in Garvey's sincerity.[102]

Garvey's unusual tractability here was in marked contrast to his earlier attitudes. By 1937 his organization was but a shadow of its former self and he had not only been deported from the U.S. but hounded out of Jamaica as well. In his time he had been kept out of the United States for five months (in 1921), practically deported from Canada (1928) and denied entry into Bermuda (1928) when he refused to give written assurances that he would not speak there. He had been jailed several times in the United States and Jamaica on palpably unfair grounds.[103] Now with his financial resources at a minimum and UNIA ranks across the world substantially reduced, Garvey may have considered it wiser to compromise in order to gain entry into Trinidad where he could perhaps rally his members and raise some money from public meetings. The Colonial Office statement that he deplored the Trinidad strikes was strange in the light of several articles of his in his *Black Man* magazine in 1938 in which he supported the strikers and rioters in Jamaica in particular and the West Indies in general. In similar vein with the Colonial Office remarks was a news release put out by the anti-Garvey Crusader News Agency in October 1937 accusing Garvey of attacking the strikers in the Trinidad press. According to this news release the local UNIA president, E.M. Mitchell, promised a cool reception for Garvey unless he could come up with "some satisfactory explanation of the remarks attributed to him."[104] Both the Crusader release and the Colonial Office remarks are further seemingly contradicted by the *Black Man* for August 1937 which reprinted an article in which Cipriani praised the governor for denouncing the "economic slavery" to which Trinidad's sugar workers were subjected.

In any event Garvey arrived in Trinidad on October 20 and was given a big welcome by the local UNIA who arranged a morning meeting for him at the Globe Theatre in Port-of-Spain. In the afternoon a concert was held at the same venue, followed by a Garvey speech. Garvey sailed the same night for British Guiana. He returned on October 26 and addressed UNIA meetings at the Gaiety Theatre in San Fernando, and in La Brea and Port-of-Spain. This very full day included a civic reception in his honor by the Port-of-Spain City Council, no doubt due to the efforts of Cipriani's Trinidad Labour Party which controlled this body. Less than a year previous to this the Labour Party's mayor, Alfred Richards (the same one who founded the Workingmen's Association in 1897), had arranged a similar civic reception on the Lighthouse Jetty for President Roosevelt of the United States who was in transit from a Pan-American Peace Conference.[105]

Despite Garvey's willingness to comply with all the Colonial Office stipulations concerning his visit, the governor of Trinidad still would take no chances. He was allowed to land only upon acceptance of the following written conditions:

a) that he would not hold any public meetings in any open space or park in this Colony;
b) that he would on no occasion or in any public utterance make any reference to or comment on recent disturbances in this Colony;
c) that he would not make any political speech or make any utterance which was calculated to cause disaffection among the people of the Colony or to promote ill will between the different races and classes resident in the Colony.[106]

One immediate casualty of these stringent conditions was an open air welcome meeting which Garvey's supporters had originally planned for a city park.[107] In the *Black Man* Garvey referred to his pleasant two days in Trinidad but said nothing of the restrictions placed on him.

During Garvey's last few years in London (he died there in 1940) the occasional contribution from such places as Belmont, La Brea and Port-of-Spain continued to trickle into his London headquarters.[108] He regularly indulged his love of public speaking at "Speaker's Corner" in Hyde Park at this time, where one of his most illustrious hecklers was Trinidadian Trotskyist C.L.R. James, who claims to have on occasion helped run Garvey out of the park.[109] James nevertheless claims to have been influenced by Garvey during the events of 1919, when he regularly read the *Negro World*. Garvey's African theories, he alleges, "had no sense" but Garvey was preaching resistance, and that was positive.[110] James says that George Padmore, also still in Trinidad in 1919, was similarly influenced by Garvey,[111] which may explain Padmore's 1928 protest at Howard University, among other things.

In the United States, in the last decade of Garvey's life, at least one alleged Trinidadian was among those who tried to continue Garvey's work by founding new organizations based on his teachings. This particular Garvey disciple was one Antonio L. Paez who headed the International Negro Improvement Association of the World operating out of Chicago.[112]

Despite his experiences with the likes of de Bourg and Cyril Crichlow, Garvey maintained throughout his career his affection for Trinidadians and an interest in the island's affairs. In 1930 his *Blackman* newspaper (not to be confused with the *Black Man* magazine), commenting on Trinidad's *East Indian Weekly*, praised the progressive nature of Trinidad's Indians and wished them well.[113] In 1933 his *New Jamaican* considered Trinidadians to be leaders in politics, business sense, sports and "general pluck."[114] And in 1939, while objecting to a British scheme to resettle Jews in British Guiana on the grounds of the racial strife that would ensue, he cited the case of Trinidad where, he said, their introduction had caused trouble and their merchants were humbugging local small businessmen.[115]

After Garvey's death in 1940 his followers in Trinidad maintained contact with Garveyites elsewhere, especially in the United States, for many years. This contact was facilitated by *The African*, a Garveyite journal which had subscribers in Trinidad and whose correspondence columns contained many letters from Trinidadians. A central figure in this continuance of Garveyite ideas three decades after they had first entered the island was David R. Modeste. In 1946 Modeste was holding Yoruba classes in Claxton Bay with the help of alphabet sheets and a primer donated by New York Garveyites. By 1947 he was reported as having 62 students in a Yoruba school in California, South Trinidad, where he was helped by a Mr. G. Springer.[116] Modeste's contributions to African nationalism in Trinidad were manifold. He also taught Amharic and belonged to the Ethiopian Orthodox Church.[117] In 1947, too, the link between the UNIA and organized labour so evident in 1919 was still very much alive. For C.P. Alexander, then President of the Seamen and Waterfront Workers' Trade Union, was in touch with Garveyites during a visit to the United States and contributed an article on labour conditions in Trinidad to *The African*.[118]

Alexander's links with the movement thus illustrate again two linkages which reappear throughout this paper, namely the link between Garveyism and organized labour in Trinidad on the one hand, and that between African nationalism in Trinidad and in the United States (and elsewhere). This calls to mind the words of a secret British government document of 1919 which complained to the

American authorities about the spread of Black militancy throughout the world. "It is certain," this document lamented, "that the various negro organizations in the United States will not leave the British colonies alone."[119]

Officers of the Trinidad UNIA about 1927

The names of several officers of the association have already been mentioned in the text and footnotes. The following list comprises those names mentioned in the membership cards for UNIA branches contained in the Central Division (New York) UNIA files housed in the Schomburg Collection at the Harlem branch of the New York Public Library. They are published here both as a tribute to these early toilers in the struggle for African liberation and self-determination and as a possible help to other researchers interested in this topic. The first name in each case is that of the president of the branch. The second is that of the secretary. Addresses are given where they appear on the cards.

Balandra Bay	Francis Lynch; George L. Martineau.
Carapichaima	Richard R. Cuffy, Orange Field Rd., Carapichaima; Augustus Roberts, Colonial Village, Carapichaima.
Caroni	Donald Cuffy; Clarence Harris.
Cedros	F. Greaves; C.N. Sullivan, Bonas Village.
Chaguanas	Joseph Frederick; John Sealy, Endeavour Village.
Couva	John Asson; Ashby K. Robinson, Dow Village.
D'Abadie	Richard Brathwaite; J.R. Wilson.
Enterprise	David Cyras; L. Sampson.
Gasparillo	Robert Gilkes; Julian Baptiste.
Guaico	Isaiah Phillip; Edward C.A. Phillip.
Iere Village	W.R. McIntosh; Charles Hall.
La Brea	Charles Alfred; Lionel Goncher, Cabeaux Town (sic).
Lily of the Nile	(28 Prince St., Port-of-Spain) E.J. Louis, 28 Prince St.; Miss Catherine S. Richards, 2 Marine Square.
Los Bajos	James S. Henson; Morgan Joseph.
Mucurapo	William Beckles, 2 Clarence St., St.
(St. James)	James; H.O. Carrington.
Marabella	no names given.
Matura	Herbert Absolam (sic); Stephen Honow.

Morne Diablo	Isaac Martin, Penal Rock Junction; Jame James E. Cooper, Penal Rock Junction.
Palmira	James Herbert; Livingston Small.
Penal	J.A. Sergeant, Rock Junction, Penal; Thomas Jeffers, Rock Junction.
Port-of-Spain	Joseph Charles; E.M. Joseph, 72 George and 63 Duke Streets.
Princes Town	C. Bowman; Mr. Carr.
Rio Claro	Lewis Charles; Isaac Jackson.
St. Mary (Moruga)	J.M. Jones; L.J. Leotaud.
Ste. Madeleine	Henry Stewart; Vincent Arthur.
San Fernando	James Bobb; E.J. Sotere, 21 High St.
Siparia	no names given.
Tableland	D. Alleyne; V. Lewis.
Victoria Village	no names given.
Williamsville	no names given.

Notes

1. For a full list of UNIA branches worldwide, see Tony Martin *Race First: The Ideological and Organizational Struggles of Marcus Garvey and the Universal Negro Improvement Association* (Westport, Conn., Greenwood Press, 1976), pp. 361-373.
2. Notes taken by author at a lecture by the late Basil Brentnol Blackman, Secretary-Treasurer, Caribbean Congress of Labour, at the St. Ann's Community Workshop, Trinidad, in 1969; see also Martin, *Race First, passim,* for more on the Garveyite connections of West Indian labour leaders.
3. Denizens of Belmont will doubtless be familiar with Zampty Lane, named after Mr. Zampty's family. Material relating to Mr. Zampty comes mainly from a conversation between Mr. Zampty and the author recorded in Highland Park, Michigan, on April 17, 1973.
4. C.L.R. James, *The Life of Captain Cipriani* (Nelson, Lancs., Coulton and Co. 1932), p. 40.
5. E.g., *Negro World,* August 23, 1924; November 29, 1924.
6. *Blackman,* February 15,1930.
7. Governor J.R. Chancellor to Viscount Milner, Secretary of State for the Colonies, November 30, 1920, Public Record Office, London, Colonial Office records, C.O. 318/356.
8. W.M. Gordon, Acting Governor of Trinidad, to Govemor of British Guiana, June 10, 1919, Gordon to Milner, June 18, 1919, C.O. 295/521.
9. *Ibid.,* minute by "G.G."
10. Henry D. Baker to Secretary of State, December 8,1919, National Archives of the United States, General Records of the Department of

State, Record Group (R.G.) 59, 844g. 5045/2.

11. Baker to Secretary of State, October 5, 1919, National Archives of the United States, Records of the Post Office Department, R.G. 28, Box 56, Unarranged no. 500. There were three wrappers, addressed to Herbert Thompson, St. Joseph; George Thomas, c/o Smith Bros. and Co., Chacon St., Port-of-Spain; and Charles Mariners, 65 Nelson St., Port-of-Spain; see also *ibid.*, Otto Praeger, Acting Postmaster General to Secretary of State, October 30, 1919. (Herbert Thompson appears elsewhere as Herman Thompson).

12. C.L.R. James says he bought them every Saturday in St. Vincent Street, Port-of-Spain, in 1919, despite the ban "Document: C.L.R. James on the Origins," *Radical America,* II 4, July-August 1968, p. 24.

13. *Messenger,* July 1919, p. 22.

14. Brinsley Samaroo, "The Trinidad Workingmen's Association and the Origins of Popular Protest in a Crown Colony," *Social and Economic Studies, XXI,* 2, June 1972, p. 219. Samaroo states that some TWA members wore red shirts in solidarity with the Russian revolutionaries of 1917.

15. On Garvey and communism see Martin, *Race First,* pp. 221-272.

16. Acting Governor, Trinidad to Milner, July 29, 1919, Secret, C.O. 295/521; *The Caribbee,* III, 3, March 1935, p. 12.

17. For three occasionally overlapping accounts of the 1919 riots and general upheaval, see Tony Martin, "Revolutionary Upheaval in Trinidad, 1919: Views from British and American Sources," *Journal of Negro History,* LVIII, 3, July 1973, pp. 313-326; Samaroo, op. cit.; and W.F. Elkins, "Black Power in the British West Indies: The Trinidad Longshoremen's Strike of 1919," *Science and Society,* XXXIII, 1, Winter 1969, pp. 71-75.

18. R.G. 59, 844g. 5045/2, op. cit.

19. Augustus Duncan to Governor of British Guiana, January 9,1920, C.O. 111/630; Amy Jacques Garvey, ed. *Philosophy and Opinions of Marcus Garvey* (London, Cass, 1967, first pub. 1923 and 1925), Vol. II, pp. 359-362.

20. Chancellor to Baker, February 6, 1920, Baker to Secretary of State, February 7,1920, R.G. 59, 811.108/929.

21. *Negro World,* September 17, 1921.

22. *Emancipator* (New York), March 13,1920.

23. Rev. E. Urban Lewis to H.M. Consul, New York, September 24, 1924, Public Record Office, London, Foreign Office records, F.O. 37119633. On the African Orthodox Church see Martin, *Race First,* pp. 71-73.

24. John Sydney de Bourg, "Relative to the Charges Against Master and Chief Engineer S.S. Kanawha— Black Star Line, Inc.," sworn before American Consul Charles Latham, Kingston, Jamaica, June 14, 1921, National Archives of the United States, Records of the Bureau of Navigation, R.G. 41,122539.

25. Samaroo, *op. cit.,* pp. 208, 210.

26. Baker to Secretary of State, April 2, 1919, A.A. Adee, State

Department, to Baker, May 1, 1919, R.G. 59, 844g. 111/-; Baker to Secretary of State, December 8,1919, R.G. 59, 844g. 5045/2.

27. Garvey, *Philosophy and Opinions*, II, pp. 142,143, 279.
28. C.O. 318/356, minute of December 9, 1920. Garvey, *Philosophy and Opinions*, II, p. 143, contains among the signatories an I. Braithwaite. The Colonial Office official may have taken this for James Braithwaite. It was in fact more probably I. Newton Braithwaite, coprincipal with Trinidad born Cyril Crichlow of a business school in Harlem. Crichlow is also among the signatories. Similarly a Prince Alfred McConney appears among the signatories. Samaroo (*op. cit.*) mentions a Bruce McConney of the Workingmen's Association deported to Barbados.
29. *Negro World*, February 12 ,19 21; October 29, 1921; July 2, 1921; July 29, 1922.
30. *Negro World*, June 10, 1922; July 1, 1922. Many of the UNIA members here, as in Cuba, were British West Indian workers.
31. *African World*, June 23, 1923, clipping in C.O. 525/104; *Negro World*, March 5, 1921.
32. *New York Amsterdam News*, October 17,1923.
33. *Negro World*, August 23, 1924.
34. Garvey, *Philosophy and Opinions*, II, p. 278.
35. Chancellor to Milner, November 30,1920, C.O. 318/358.
36. *The Argos*, Friday, February 13, 1920, clipping in National Archives of the United States, Records of the American Consulate, Port-of-Spain, 1920 correspondence; Baker to Inspector Costello, February 16, 1920, R.G. 84, 840.1/2052; Costello to Baker, February 18, 1920, enclosing report by Sgt. Sylvester, R.G. 84, 840.1/2053; Sylvester to Detective Inspector, February 18,1920, R.G. 84, 840.1/2054.
37. *Negro World*, August 14,1920.
38. C. O. 295/621, minute of September 5,1919.
39. *Emancipator*, April 17, 1920.
40. Chancellor to Milner, November 30,1920, C.O. 318/356.
41. "Trinidad News Letter," *Crusader*, III, 5, January 1921, p. 23. This report mentions detectives seizing a copy of the *Promoter* from a house in Chaguanas; *Beacon*, August 1931, p. 3.
42. Baker to Secretary of State, March 5, 1920, R.G. 59, 844g. 04417; Baker to Secretary of State, March 5, 1920, R.G. 28, Box 53, Unarranged No. 398.
43. Quoted in *Negro World*, May 8,1920.
44. *Report of the Twentieth Annual Conference of the Labour Party, Scarborough, 1920* (London, the Labour Party, 1920?), p. 146.
45. "Calypso Lore and Legend, An Afternoon with Patrick Jones: Stories and Chants from the Lips of the Greatest Oldtime Calypsonian," Cook (1956?), Long Playing record.
46. *Negro World*, May 8, 1920.
47. W.F. Ellkins "Hercules and the Society of Peoples of African Origin," *Caribbean Studies*, XI, 4, January 1972, pp. 47-59.

48. *Emancipator,* March 20,1920.
49. *Negro World,* March 12,1921.
50. Quoted in James R. Hooker, *Black Revolutionary: George Padmore's Path from Communism to Pan-Africanism* (London, Pall Mall, 1967), p. 8.
51. Col. Hubert F. Julian, *Black Eagle* (London, Jarrolds, 1964), p. 41.
52. *Negro World,* June 4,1921. It never did get to Africa.
53. Statement by Parris to U.S. Vice-Consul, Kingston, Jamaica, June 17,1921, R.G. 41,122539.
54. *Negro World,* May 8, 1920; February 19, 1921; February 4, 1922; *Philosophy and Opinions,* II, p. 365.
55. *Negro World,* May 19, 1925.
56. *Port-of-Spain Gazette,* June 5,1921, reprinted in the *Negro World,* July 2, 1921.
57. "The Universal Negro Improvement Association ...," March 7, 1924, C.O. 554/64.
58. *Negro World,* July 2,1921.
59. On the South African UNIA see Martin, *Race First,* pp. 117-121.
60. *Gold Coast Leader,* August 10,1922.
61. Gov./18053, destroyed file of March 26, 1923 in the Colonial Office records, Public Record Office. As in the case of many destroyed files, a brief synopsis of its contents survived; "UNIA," March 7,1924, C.O. 554/64.
62. *Negro World,* July 28,1923.
63. Governor Wilfred Collet to Rt. Hon. Winston Churchill, July 6, 1922.
64. Churchill to officer administering the government, August 22, 1922, C.O. 318/371; Gov./51931, secret destroyed file, September 22, 1922; Governor Wilson of Trinidad to Churchill, January 20, 1923, F.O. 371/8450.
65. See Tony Martin, "Revolutionary Upheaval in Trinidad," *op. cit.*
66. *Negro World,* August 26,1922.
67. Ibid., August 15,1923.
68. Martin, *Race First,* pp. 370, 371. Professor Francis Mark of the State University of New York has suggested to the author that some UNIA branches may possibly have coincided with branches of the Workingmen's Association. Dr. Maureen Warner Lewis of the University of the West Indies (Jamaica) has informed the author that many of the areas named are pockets of relatively strong remembrances of, and identification with Africa.
69. Melville and Frances Herskovits, *Trinidad Village* (New York, Octagon, 1964), p. 263.
70. *Negro World,* December 30, 1922; one report speaks of Black Cross Nurses in the village (presumably) of Choorcoo—*ibid,* September 30, 1922.
71. *Ibid.,* March 7,1931.
72. *Ibid.,* September 30,1922; May 13,1922.
73. E.g., on April 7, 1927 a Rev. Benjamin of the A.M.E. Church dedicated the new Liberty Hall at Rio Claro—*Blackman,* May 20 1929; again, in

1924 we have A.M.E. clergyman Rev. Taylor officiating at a UNIA meeting in Penal—*Negro World*, October 4, 1924.

74. *Negro World*, June 14, 1924, February 2, 1924; December 30, 1922.
75. *Ibid.*, December 30, 1922.
76. *Ibid.*, September 20, 1924. There is no indication whether these were U.S. or British West Indian dollars.
77. *Ibid.*, August 19,1922, September 30, 1922.
78. *E.g., ibid.*, August 30, 1924.
79. *Blackman*, August 12,1929; *Negro World*, August 2,1930.
80. *Negro World*, September 17,1921.
81. *Ibid.*, October 21,1922.
82. *Ibid.*, December 15, 1923; September 6, 1930; May 9, 1931; November 15, 1930.
83. *Ibid.*, May 13,1922.
84. Martin, *Race First*, pp. 235, 267 n. 48.
85. *Negro World*, May 13,1922.
86. For the meeting see *ibid.*, August 23, 1924. *The New Jamaican*, September 1, 1932, contains a reference to Cipriani presiding over the monthly meeting of the Trinidad Workingmen's Association at Liberty Hall.
87. After elections in 1931, the Lily of the Nile executive comprised the following—President, E.J. Louis; lady president, Miss Edith Devonshire; vice-president, James Gallop; general secretary, Miss Mable Clarke; treasurer, Thomas Murdurch; chaplain, James Reid; Board of Trustees, H.J.J. Chortes [sic.], Samuel Lord, P. Thompson, James Gollop, E.P. Dair, James Reid, Thomas Murdurch, Edith Devonshire, Mabel Clarke, Josephine Baptiste, Floretha Louis, Laura Fox and W. Phipps. See *Negro World*, March 7,1931.
88. *Negro World*, February 24, 1923. Some reports spell his name "Burrowes," but most omit the "e."
89. *Negro World*, November 18,1922.
90. Garvey and P.L. Burrows, Secretary-General to J.H. Thomas, H.M. Colonial Secretary, January 25,1924, C.O. 554/60; *Negro World*, August 16, 1923.
91. *Negro World*, March 28,1925.
92. *Ibid.*, December 7, 1929.
93. *Black Revolutionary, op. cit.*, p. 7; *Negro World*, December 22, 1928; interview with Dr. Cyril Ollivierre, Harlem, New York, 1974; Martin, *Race First*, pp. 261-265.
94. Governor of Trinidad to Lt. Col. L.S. Amery, Secretary of State Colonial Office, December 20,1927, C.O. 318/391.
95. Alfredo L. Demorest, Vice Consul in Charge, Trinidad, to Secretary of State, strictly confidential, April 10, 1928, R.G. 59, 844g. 044/3.
96. *Negro World*, October 27,1928.
97. *Ibid.*, March 3, 1928.
98. George Padmore, *Negro Workers and the Imperialist War—Intervention in the Soviet Union* (Hamburg, I.T.U.C.N.W., n.d.), p. 16.

99. *Liberator* (New York), May 10, 1930, p. 1; the *Liberator*, organ of the Communist-backed A.N.L.C., also attacked Cipriani on December 7,1929, p. 2. It regularly attacked Garvey.
100. Minutes of July 15 and July 16,1937, C.O. 323/1518.
101. *Ibid.*, Murchison Fletcher to Sir Mark Young, Governor of Barbados, August 3, 1937.
102. *Ibid.*, two minutes of July 21,1937; W. Ormsby-Gore, draft letter to governors in the West Indies, July 26, 1937.
103. Martin, *Race First, passim.*
104. This news agency was run by Garvey's long time Communist foe, Cyril Briggs. Mitchell's statement was quoted from *The People*, a weekly workers' paper.
105. *The Caribbee* (Trinidad), Xmas Number, 1936, p. 8. Cipriani himself served on the City Council for close on two decades up to 1941 and was mayor eight times.
106. Governor Fletcher to W.G.A. Ormsby-Gore, November 10,1937, C.O. 323/1518.
107. *Daily Gleaner* (Jamaica), October 20,1937.
108. *Black Man*, II, 3, September-October 1936, p. 13; III, 10, July 1938, p. 19.
109. Adolph Edwards, *Marcus Garvey* (London, New Beacon, 1967), p. 33. Edwards says James told him this; also, lecture by James at the University of Michigan, April 2, 1972, notes taken by author. Apart from ideological differences, James was at this time running an organization in support of Ethiopia, and Garvey, though as hostile as anybody else to the Italian invasion of Ethiopia, was highly critical of Haile Selassie.
110. Michigan lecture, *op. cit.*
111. C.L.R. James, "Document: C.L.R. On the Origins," *Radical America*, II, 4, July-August 1968, p. 24.
112. Confidential memorandum, "To London," February 12, 1931, R.C. 59,800.00 B—International Negro Improvement Association of the World/7. This organization was said to have been founded in 1929. Some officials investigating Paez identified Garvey as a Trinidadian, so the possibility of a similar error in placing Paez' nationality cannot be discounted.
113. *Blackman*, August 23,1930.
114. *New Jamaican*, January 18,1933.
115. *Black Man*, IV, 1, June 1939, pp. 5,15.
116. *The African*, IV, 5, September 1946, p. 10; V, 6, June-July 1947, p. 5; V, 8, September 1947, p. 9.
117. Told to the author by Professor Maureen Warner-Lewis of the University of the West Indies.
118. *The African*, V, 9-10, October-November 1947, p. 16.
119. Secret document "Unrest Among the Negroes," Special Report No. 10, Directorate of Intelligence (Home Office), October 7, 1919, R.G. 59, 811.4016/27.

THE QUESTION OF IMPERIALISM AND ASPECTS OF GARVEY'S POLITICAL ACTIVITIES IN JAMAICA 1929-30

Rupert Lewis

Before examining the political role of the Garvey movement in the British colony of Jamaica during the years 1929-35, I intend to do two things. Firstly, to place the Garvey movement in the context of the worldwide struggle against imperialism in the early 20th century, and secondly, to look at some of the main aspects of imperialist enslavement in the colony from 1865-1930. This period of imperialist enslavement had at its core the land question because the main area of imperialist penetration was agriculture. It is in this context that I will examine Garveyism in Jamaica during the early 1930s, the focus being on the 1929-30 period and the program of the People's Political Party.

The Russian Revolution and Imperialism

The October socialist revolution of 1917 in Russia cracked open the foundations of imperialism and pointed the way forward to the millions of oppressed and exploited colonial peoples around the world. This socialist revolution led by V. Lenin and the Russian working class was also an anti-colonial revolution. Before the October Revolution over 35 million people of non-Russian nationalities, living mostly in Central Asia, were in colonial bondage. This revolution brought about the national liberation of all peoples who had previously been subjected not only to Tsarist colonial and national oppression but also to French and German capital invested in Russia.

This new development dealt a severe blow to colonialism and sparked off a crisis in the colonial system. Amy Jacques Garvey notes in *Garvey and Garveyism* that "on the death of Lenin in 1924, Garvey sent a cable to Moscow, on behalf of the Negroes of the world expressing sorrow at his passing."[1] This was done at a time when it was dangerous to sympathize with the Russian revolutionaries in any way and when the major imperialist states were working to undermine the revolution and restore capitalism and imperialist control in Russia.

A *Negro World* editorial referred to Lenin as "Probably the world's greatest man between 1917 and 1924"[2] and Garvey argued that what Lenin did for Russia should be emulated by Black men in the struggle for African emancipation.[3] This, of course, does not mean that Garvey was a marxist. One is making it clear that the leading democrats of the period were responding to a new international situation in the post-World War 1 period whose main feature was the emergence of the world's first socialist state.

What was the reaction of the imperialists to this stand of solidarity with the first socialist and colonial revolution and their determination to strive for national liberation? As early as October 1919, J. Edgar Hoover, who had initiated the campaign for Garvey's deportation, filed a memorandum on his activities to the Department of Justice, in which he wrote:

> In his paper the *"Negro World"* the Soviet Russian Rule is upheld and there is open advocation of Bolshevism.[4]

In the British colony of Jamaica the landowners and the *Daily Gleaner* which represented the interests of the merchants and planters were also of a similar opinion. They associated Garveyism and Bolshevism and saw the clear anti-imperialist content of the UNIA.

Prior to the October Revolution, imperialism and colonial domination held full sway. One of the main features of imperialism consisted in the whole world being divided into a large number of oppressed nations and an insignificant number of oppressor nations, the latter possessing great wealth and powerful armed forces.[5] The vast majority of the world's population was therefore in a state of direct colonial dependence.

Lenin points out in his classic study of imperialism that:

> For Great Britain, the period of the enormous expansion of colonial conquests is that between 1860 and 1880, and it was also very considerable in the last twenty years of the nineteenth century.[6]

By the start of the 20th century Britain controlled over 9.3 million square miles of territory obtained through plunder. Between 1884-1900 Britain acquired some 3.7 million square miles of colonial territory. The United Kingdom was in comparison only 121,000 square miles. The population of this empire was 431 million while that of the U.K. plus the white dominions such as Canada and Australia only amounted to 60 million. On the eve of World War II Britain's Empire included one $1/4$ of the world's population and $1/4$ of the world's area. The rate of British foreign investment at the turn of the century was:

1901-1905 under £50 million per year

1907-1913 £150 million per year

1911-1913 £200 million per year[7]

Forty-seven percent of Britain's foreign investment was in the Empire in places like Canada, New Zealand, India, Burma, Malaya, Ceylon, Africa and Latin America. British capitalists reaped huge profits from making loans at high rates of interests. It was through her finance capitalists that she met her frequent balance of payments problems. S. Pollard comments:

> Britain, it must be remembered, showed a substantial unfavorable balance on merchandise trade of the order of £150 million annually. This negative balance, to which must be added (net) bullion imports and tourist expenditure abroad of about £20 million, was almost exactly counterbalanced by large and rising credit items for net invisible exports: banking, insurance and shipping earnings. *The surplus was provided by dividends and interest rising from about £100 million to £200 million between 1900 and 1913, and it was these which allowed Britain to increase her foreign investments at an equally rapid rate.*
> Since foreign railways, docks or naval yards, if financed by British investors, would naturally favour British suppliers, a boom in capital exports was bound to be paralleled by a boom in the exports of merchandise.[8]

The indebtedness of colonial Jamaica and the high taxes imposed on the peasantry must be seen in the context of these economic relations.

The public debt in Jamaica grew from $1/4$ million pounds in 1875 to 1.5 million pounds in 1885 to 3.5 million pounds by 1905. Much of this was due to loans for railway construction. In 1884, for example, £130,000 of a £183,000 loan was raised in London at interest rates 3 to 4 times higher than that paid on the balance which was raised in Jamaica. This, of course, had to be paid for by tax increases on imports which affected the peasantry most of all.

This period of colonial territorial expansion and economic growth for British capital was at the same time one of intense competition with U.S. imperialism in Latin America and German capital in the Middle East. Chamberlain's (1895–1903) protectionist policy and his colonial policies cannot be understood outside of this context. The attacks against British colonialism by the early nationalist, Robert Love, at the turn of the 20th century centered on Chamberlain's land and fiscal policies and his statements concerning the withdrawal of the paltry political liberties granted to property owners in Jamaica in 1884 and 1895.

Inter-imperialist conflicts rooted in the late 19th century development of monopoly capitalism set the stage for World War I, the main issue of which was the re-division of the world and the struggle for markets. As a consequence of this, there was greater national oppression and the democratic rights promised the colonial peoples for their participation in that imperialist conflict were denied. It was in this new international situation that the Garvey movement developed into a powerful anti-colonial force representing millions of Africans who, along with other colonial and semi-colonial peoples in China, India and Latin America, were challenging imperialist domination.

Conditions in Post-War Jamaica

The post-World War I years found the colony of Jamaica in crisis. During June-July 1918 there were strikes in the parishes of Kingston, St. Catherine, Portland, St. Thomas, Clarendon, and Manchester, primarily among dockworkers, railway employees, and laborers on sugar and banana estates, who were protesting working conditions and calling for more wages. On the Amity Hall sugar estate in Clarendon, the reading of the Riot Act preceded the shooting to death of three workers.[9] The workers, generally, had resorted not only to strike action but also to the cutting of telephone wires and the burning of cane fields. Organizationally, the upsurge among the workers was reflected in the formation by Alexander Bain Alves of the Longshoremen's Union No. 1 of the Jamaica Federation of Labour on the 10th of January 1918.[10] The majority of workers, however, had no union organization and no political organization; their spontaneous anti-colonial movement shortly subsided.

The years following World War I witnessed the great expansion of the Garvey movement in the United States, the Caribbean and parts of Africa, the basis of which was to be found in the severe conditions of exploitation and oppression to which the African people were subjected.

Imperialist war and economic crises in the capitalist countries had disastrous consequences for the colonial peoples. This was the position during 1929-33 when an acute international capitalist crisis occurred. This was the longest, most destructive and profound economic crisis that capitalism had ever known. Industrial output in the capitalist world during the early 1930s shrank by 38%. Agricultural output dropped by over one-third. Thousands of banks crashed and currency depreciated in 56 countries. Unemployment in the capitalist world rose to 35 million. This included 16 million in America, 5.5 million in Germany, 3 million in Britain and 2.8 million in Japan,[11] for the colonies it meant that the prices received for agricultural raw materials and food dropped considerably in value on the world market. The imperialists increased their plunder in the colonies as the land of millions of peasants was seized by money-lenders and landowners and thus literally millions were on the verge of death by starvation.

In the West Indies these consequences were also experienced, in addition to the fact that thousands of migrants were returning from the United States, Cuba and the Central American republics. Between 1930-34 over 28,000 migrants returned to Jamaica to live in further misery.

This economic crisis expressed itself in the growth of the working-class struggle in the capitalist countries. There were 19,000 strikes involving 8.5 million employees during 1929-32 in 15 of the world's largest countries. There was also growing disaffection in the colonies which expressed itself in the widening of the anti-imperialist struggle throughout the world.

The high point of struggle in the British Empire at the time was in India where over 60,000 patriots were arrested in 1930 along with Gandhi and other leaders of the Indian National Congress. The only public figure (in Jamaica) who supported the Indian nationalists was Marcus Garvey. In militant articles and editorials he attacked *The Gleaner* whose editor, H.G. DeLisser, attempted to discredit and denigrate the anti-imperialist movement which was growing throughout the dying British Empire.

Garvey, in an editorial entitled "In Praise of Gandhi," wrote:

Today the whole civilized world is attracted to the movement of that wonderful man of India—Mahatma Gandhi—who has for several weeks been on the march through India toward a given point, arousing his countrymen to the consciousness of national independence. The Indians are an oppressed race—oppressed by some of their own as well as by external forces. Like the Negro they must struggle upward to justify their national existence, and so Gandhi is leading and pointing the way. [12]

Garvey, who was then living in Jamaica, was intensely involved in the political life of the country. His writings on the anti-colonial movement in China, India, Ireland, and Egypt are today the precious heritage of the anti-imperialist movement in Jamaica for they explicitly denounce the reactionary, narrow and pro-imperialist nationalism which forms the ideological basis of neo-colonial rule in Jamaica.

This, then, was the international situation during the early 1930s when Marcus Garvey confronted British imperialism in Jamaica. It was a period characterized by sharp conflicts between imperialism on one hand and on the other, anti-imperialist and socialist forces throughout the world.

Aspects of Imperialist Enslavement of Jamaica — 1866-1930

The 1865 rebellion clinched the victory for the plantation sector (then dominated by British capital) over small commodity peasant production. This led, politically, to the imposition of direct crown colony rule and economic underdevelopment which naturally benefited the absentee plantation owners in England and the United States. There was the growth of a local merchant-planter class which had exploitative relations with the small proprietor strata that formed the basis of the middle class in the 20th century and the further pushing into the ground of the mass of peasants, many of whom were forced back on the plantation either in Jamaica or in Latin America. The general decomposition of the peasantry was consequently speeded up. The major legal instrument through which London merchants secured Jamaican land which had either been abandoned or farmed by the peasants was the Encumbered Estates Act of 1854. Although British capitalist control of the land was predominant, most of the colony's exports in the 1870-90 period went to the United States where the cane producers did not have to face the stiff competition of the European beet sugar industry until the 1890s, after which time competition from Cuba, Hawaii and the

Philippines made the American sugar market a difficult one. This period marked the investment of the U.S. monopoly firm, United Fruit Company, in the banana trade. The colony was therefore tied to British and American capital, with the former maintaining the dominant position.

One of Governor J.P. Grant's assignments after the 1865 Morant Bay rebellion was to dispossess the peasantry of the land "by prohibiting squatting and inhibiting the development of isolated peasant communities where possible." Through the establishment of the Lands Department, the Crown foreclosed on thousands of acres farmed by peasants for which they had no legal titles. Between 1871-75 a total of 90,000 acres were reclaimed by the Crown.

At the same time that British and American capitalist penetration into agriculture grew, the conditions of the poor peasants deteriorated and many were forced into wage labour. However, the picture of the class composition of the society would be incomplete if one did not point to the growth of a middle stratum within the peasantry whose development had been determined by the objective economic relations in agriculture at the time and encouraged by British imperialism for its own interest. This is demonstrated in the fact that at the turn of the 20th century at least $1/3$ of the 7500 members of the Jamaica Agricultural Society were employed as rural constables. The majority of these were small property holders who employed a few wage-laborers. The growth of this middle stratum is seen in the fact that the number of holdings under 10 acres increased from 52,000 owners in a total population of 580,000 in 1882 to 81,900 owners out of a population of 650,000 in 1896. These middle peasants, to use Lenin's definition, were those small farmers who, either as owners or tenants, hold small plots of land which in good time may produce a surplus which may be converted into capital and therefore they quite frequently resort to employment of hired labor. One should distinguish between this stratum and the agricultural workers on the estates, and again between the latter and the poor peasants who worked occasionally on the plantation and on their own small plots of land.

The middle peasants were engaged primarily in minor export crops—such as coffee, pimento and bananas. Claude McKay's novel *Banana Bottom*, several of his short stories in *Gingertown*, and his unfinished autobiography—*My Green Hills of Jamaica*, reveal the lives of this upper and middle stratum of the peasantry and provide an insight into the contradictory and ambivalent nature of their relations with the other classes in the society.[13] As far as the period 1929-35 is concerned, the vacillation of the leading representatives of this stratum whom Garvey expected to play an important role in the anti-colonial struggle served more the interests of British imperialism, especially when they found that Garvey's program ran counter to the class interests of the big landowners on whom they depended.

Organizationally, the small and medium-sized farmers were to be found in the Jamaica Agricultural Society and the Jamaica Union of Teachers. However, in Dr. Robert Love,[14] whose influence on Garvey was significant as the latter himself later admitted, the left wing of the middle-stratum and the mass of poor peasants found their most consistent protagonist. Love's struggle against the system of land tenure and inequitable taxation brought about by British finance capital against the poor peasantry, his work in establishing a PanAfrican Association along with H. Sylvester-Williams,[15] his struggle against Chamberlain's reactionary colonial policy and his forceful democratic journalistic writings in the *Jamaica Advocate* made him an outstanding anti-colonial spokesman in the Caribbean.

The fiscal policies of the Crown in the post-1865 period clearly demonstrate the big planter interests of the colonial state. One of the main tasks of the Constabulary Force set up by the "liberal" Governor Grant, was the immediate imprisonment of all persons charged with non-payment of taxes which also meant the stamping out of any protests against tax collectors. Goods used by the peasants were heavily taxed, while the imports of the rich were exempt.[16] Land taxes were regressive, so that one paid proportionally less the larger the holdings were. In the 1880's taxes ranged from 1 shilling per acre for holdings under 100 acres to 1 shilling 1.5 pence for every acre over 500 acres, while on ruinate land belonging to the latter payment was a farthing per acre. Tax on peasant dwellings, draught animals, carts, and trade licenses was also high. The peasant practice of transporting produce to market by head instead of using carts or drays had to do with the unbearable taxation which made it impossible for them to afford draught animals. At the same time carriages, carts and wagons for plantation use were duty-free. It is no wonder then that so many people migrated to the Americas at the turn of the century.

In 1920 when Garvey traveled through Costa Rica, Bocas-del-toro, Panama, Nicaragua, Honduras and other areas of South America, he felt compelled to throw in his lot with West Indian workers on the mines and plantations and vigorously protested the disgraceful working conditions and poor wages. Black nationalist protest in the early 20th century was therefore inextricably bound up with the land question and the decomposition of the peasantry as a result of imperialist penetration of agriculture.

Garveyism in Jamaica

This section does not cover the entire period but focuses in particular on the People's Political Party, its program and battles during the years 1929-30. This is the most crucial and important period for Garvey.

Marcus Garvey returned to the colony in December 1927 after spending two years and nine months in the Atlanta Federal Prison as a political captive of American imperialism.

When he landed in Kingston the *Gleaner* reported that "Mr. Garvey's arrival was perhaps the most historic event that has taken place in the metropolis of the island" and "no denser crowd has ever been witnessed in Kingston."[17]

Black people in Jamaica saw Garvey as their spokesman but the planters and merchants necessarily saw him as an enemy. Anticipating his deportation two years before, in 1925, the *Gleaner* wrote:

> Whether Mr. Garvey comes here shortly or five years hence there can be no doubt that he will prove a dangerous element in Jamaica unless it is made unmistakably clear at the very beginning that the authorities are not prepared to tolerate any nonsense on his part....[18]

After Garvey returned, repression was not long in coming from the British Colonial government. His wife and himself were denied visa entries to visit British Guiana or any of the British West Indian islands. In Trinidad there was an anti-Garvey lobby among some school teachers who in their journal were opposed to Garvey's visit.[19] In Cuba, the government banned the *Negro World* in 1928 and declared the UNIA an illegal organization in 1929. Garveyites were charged with stirring up racialism under the Morua law, named ironically after an Afro-Cuban politician.[20] This law had been the basis for the brutal suppression and murder by the Cuban authorities and American marines of 3,000 Afro-Cuban peasant rebels in the Oriente province in 1912.[21] It was effectively used against the UNIA at the end of the 1920s. It was no wonder then that one of the leading figures of the constitutional reform movement in the West Indies at the time, T.A. Marryshow, could write in 1928:

> We will not be surprised to find that Jamaica is meant to be his St. Helena on authority of a powerful international combination whose interest some observers say is to keep Garvey down.[22]

It was therefore very clear that the prime tactic of the colonial authorities was to isolate Garvey from the main divisions of his movement in the Caribbean after his deportation from the U.S. through a denial of civil and political liberties. In April 1928 Marcus Garvey and his wife traveled to England. While in London Garvey concentrated on establishing contacts with African students and seamen. He assisted the West African Students Union out of which several nationalists emerged. His wife noted "... for the entire period of our stay he did splendid work in organizing and financing the underground movement to all parts of Africa..."[23] On the public level, he spoke in Hyde Park, sent circulars to members of Parliament, some churches, and to other liberals explaining his organization's program.

At a public meeting at the Royal Albert Hall on June 6, 1928 Garvey asserted the right to self-determination for all colonial peoples. This was repeated at meetings in Paris and other West European capitals where he spoke. In Geneva he presented a petition to the League of Nations on behalf of the Negro Peoples of the World. This petition includes important documentation of the worldwide economic exploitation and oppression of African people.

Garvey's activities in Europe were reported in the Jamaican press and pamphlets of his major speeches published and distributed through the UNIA on his return.[24] This showed that Garvey was battling against the limitations placed on him and was determined to conduct an international campaign against colonialism. This was repeated, on a lesser scale, during his 1931 visit to England.

Garvey's re-entry into colonial politics at the end of 1928 showed that he was neither cowed nor intimidated by the many threats and obstacles put before his path by the British colonial rulers and that for him there was no contradiction between the struggle for Africa and the fight for democratic, economic and political rights in the colonies outside Africa where African people lived. After launching the People's Political Party in Jamaica in December 1928 he promised to organize similar parties in the French and British territories of the Caribbean. Because of the priority which was given to organizing the Sixth UNIA Conference and establishing the headquarters in Kingston, the People's Political Party did not receive Garvey's full attention until September, 1929, when some 5,000 people were reported to have attended a party convention at Edelweiss Park in Kingston.

At the end of March 1929, Garvey's daily *Black Man* newspaper started publication. This newspaper served not only as the organ of the local UNIA, so complementing the American *Negro World*, but was a forum for the PPP's agitation.

The small and committed staff of the newspaper was supervised by Alexander Aikman, the literary editor, who at 50 years old had combined school teaching with journalism. He was assisted by Leo Rankin, the news editor, and A. Wesley Atherton, a talented journalist, was the chief reporter. J. Coleman Beecher who had compiled and published a history of cricket in Jamaica contributed articles on sports and was the business manager. Garvey, the editor-in-chief, wrote a daily column called "The World As It Is" and a weekend article which was sometimes published in the New York based *Negro World*. Stennett Kerr-Coombs, who along with H. Buchanan (ex-Garveyite and probably Jamaica's first Marxist)[25] published the *Jamaica Labour Weekly* newspaper in 1938, was at the time a printer's apprentice at the *Black Man's* office.

The *Black Man* newspaper achieved a very creditable circulation figure of 15,000 copies. However, it did so under pressure from the police who harassed the vendors and intimidated some post-mistresses into delaying the immediate delivery of the newspaper through the Post Office. During 1929 the P.P.P. registered three electoral victories to the Municipal (City) Council and the Legislative Council by-elections. J. Coleman Beecher was elected to the Municipal Council in early 1928 and in April Dr. Veitch won the legislative seat for the parish of Hanover. In another by-election Garvey set the precedent of being elected to the Municipal Council while serving three months in the St. Catherine District Prison for contempt of Court after being fined £100. This charge arose from the elaboration he had given on the tenth plank of his electoral manifesto which called for a "law to impeach and imprison judges who with disregard for British justice and constitutional rights dealt unfairly," at a public meeting in Cross Roads.[26] The plank had to be removed from the manifesto and could no longer be a part of his platform.

Garvey's historic 1929 manifesto was the first practical and realistic anti-imperialist political program in this country. It summed up briefly and clearly some of the major economic, political, legal, and educational demands of the working people as a whole. It was on that basis that Garvey fought the election campaign.

Before looking at the actual program, let us note Garvey's approach to the political struggle and the forces in the country whom, he argued, should unite in the anti-colonial struggle. In 1921 while on a visit to Jamaica, Garvey wrote a lengthy open letter to the *Gleaner* in which he outlined the economic and political conditions facing the African people. He suggested:

I recommend that the poorer classes of Jamaica—the working classes —get together and form themselves into unions and organizations, and elect their members for the Legislative Council. With few exceptions, the men in the Council are representing themselves and their class. The workers of Jamaica should elect their own representatives, and if the Government here will not pay the Legislators, as is done in England, and America, then the Unions and Organizations should pay these men so that they can talk out without caring whom they offend.[27]

This was his approach. (As regards the forces in the country that should unite), Garvey advocated a united front strategy which would involve the growing working class in the towns, the agricultural laborers, poor peasants and the small proprietors. Who constituted this latter category? These were the small farmers, produce-dealers, parsons, constables and teachers who also owned land. As a class, this petite-bourgeoisie was caught between the big landowners and the mass of poor peasants and agricultural laborers. Depending on the alignment of class forces and their objective economic conditions the petite-bourgeoisie was tugged between these two major forces. Moreover the absence of a Workers Party considerably weakened this strategy. Marcus Garvey appealed to this class largely in terms of the interests of the African race, and nationality. However, they did not respond favorably to this call but were in fact hostile at times and ambivalent towards the struggle against the colonial order because of their class position. Some of the representatives of this class tried to ignore or argue away the basic contradiction of colonial society between the foreign oppressors and the predominantly African population.

The British had, since the late 19th century through land grants, credit and limited educational concessions, made efforts to win the ideological support of the petite-bourgeoisie. This was one of the reasons why the Jamaica Agricultural Society was encouraged. The big farmers also did much to win their support through other commodity associations such as the Jamaica Banana Producers Association. These small proprietors constituted a social force of significance and functioned as an important buffer between the ruling class and the masses. The British and the big landowners dominated them through their control of the economy and distribution patronage. The latter was used to assure the support of the petite-bourgeoisie.

Garvey did not fully comprehend the economic basis of the wavering of this class of Black men and underestimated the danger they posed as opponents in the 1920s. He tried to win them to a democratic program from which they stood to benefit directly. Only a minority supported him.

Garvey's Program

Let us look at the 1929 program. The economic demands were:
1.   Protection of native labor.
2.   A minimum wage for the labouring and working classes of the island.
3.   A law to protect the working and labouring classes of the country by insurance against accident, sickness, and death occurring during employment.
4.   An eight hour working day throughout Jamaica.
5.   Land reform.
6.   A law to encourage the promotion of native industries.
7.   A law to compel the employment of not less than 60% of native labor in all industrial, agricultural and commercial activities engaged in, in this island.
8.   The establishment by the Government of an electrical system to supply cheap electricity to such growing and prospering centres as are necessary.
9.   The compulsory improvement of urban areas from which large profits are made by trusts, corporations, combines and companies.
10.   A law to prevent criminal profiteering in the sale of lands in urban and suburban areas to the detriment of the expansion of healthy home life of citizens of moderate means, profiteering such as has occurred in lower St. Andrew by heartless land sharks.
11.   A law to empower the Parochial boards of each parish to undertake, under the direction of the Central Government, the building of model sanitary homes for the peasantry by a system of easy payments over a period of from ten to twenty years.
12.   A law to empower the Government to secure a loan of three million (or more) pounds from the Imperial Government, or otherwise, to be used by the Government, under the management of a department of the Director of Agriculture in developing the Crown lands of the island, agriculturally and otherwise, with the object of supplying employment for our surplus unemployed population and to find employment for stranded Jamaicans abroad; and that the Government purchase such ships as are necessary from time to time, to facilitate the mar-

keting of the produce gathered from these Crown lands, and at the same time offering an opportunity to other producers to ship and market their produce.

This last plank cannot, of course, be separated from the demand for land reform. These then are the economic demands of Garvey's manifesto. They reflect the intensity of the class struggle not only in the colony but in particular in Britain and the United States, the imperialist countries to which the economy was subordinate. Most of these planks are self-explanatory. I would, nevertheless, like to comment on Plank 11. This demand for reform in rural housing is based on the view that local government reform is necessary and that the working people must have their representatives in the Parish Councils to oppose the planter policies. The Parochial Boards were direct instruments of the landowners and were utilized as a means of systematic exploitation of the peasants primarily through trade or hawkers' licenses, market fees, and water rates. For example, in St. Ann, the parish of Garvey's birth, in 1903-4 over 20% of the revenue came from market fees. The rural populace hardly benefited from the parochial taxes they paid. During the electoral campaign Garvey lashed out against inequitous taxes in the rural areas.

On the question of political self-determination the manifesto simply called for:

13.   "Representation in the Imperial Parliament for a larger modicum of self-government." Garvey argued that greater political and civil liberties would provide the pre-conditions for the advance of the working people in their struggle against colonialism.

On the question of legal and penal reform the planks read:

14.   A law to impeach and imprison judges who, with disregard for British justice and constitutional rights, dealt unfairly.

15.   The appointment of official court stenographers to take the official notes of all court proceedings in the Supreme Court, Resident Magistrates Courts and Petty Sessions Courts of the island.

16.   The creation of a Legal Aid Department to render advice and protection of such persons who may not be able to have themselves properly represented and protected in courts of Law.

17.   Prison reform.

For plank 14, as we noted, Garvey was tried for contempt of court, sentenced to three months imprisonment and fined £100. He served the sentence in the Spanish Town District prison and paid the fine. The British saw this demand as an attack against the entire legal basis of their rule which had been established in the post-1865 period. Justice Clark, who disagreed with the harshness of the sentence imposed by the Chief Justice, nevertheless made it clear in his opinion that:

> The Courts are the King's Courts administering the King's justice, and an insult to the Courts is an insult to the Crown itself...[28]

The courts were the main instrument of peasant dispossession in land cases and were used to destroy the democratic-nationalist movement in the colony. Garvey's manifesto speaks directly to this situation.

Plank 15 is crucial because judges took their own notes and hence discrimination and abuse of the peasants and radicals who filled the courts were inevitable. But the impoverishment, which forced people into crime and the innocent into the courts, had its roots in British and American private capital, which dominated the economy and created hardship for the working people.

The remaining nine planks deal largely with the country's social and cultural development.

18.   A Jamaican University and Polytechnic.
19.   The establishing of a Government High School in the capital town of each parish for the supply of free secondary education. Attached to the said High School to be a night continuation school to facilitate those desiring to study at night in order to advance their education.
20.   A public library in the capital town of each parish.
21.   A National Opera House with an Academy of Music and Art.
22.   The expansion and improvement of city, town or urban areas without the encumbrance or restraint of private proprietorship.
23.   A law for the imprisonment of any person who by duress or undue influence would force another person to vote in any public election against his will, because of obligation or employment or otherwise.
24.   The granting to the townships of Montego Bay and Port Antonio the corporate rights of cities.
25.   The beautifying and creating of the Kingston Race Course into a National Park similar to Hyde Park in London.
26.   A law to establish clinical centers from which trained nurses are to be sent out to visit homes in rural districts and to teach and demonstrate sanitary and better health methods in the care of home and family.

Plank 23 exposes public immorality in politics, attacking the patronage system of the large landowners who sought to prevent the emergence of radical anti-colonial spokesmen in the island's legislature. Plank 26 embodies very modern ideas with regard to para-medical services.

The program embodies a broad statement of demands around which the nationalist forces could have been consolidated. This was Garvey's aim. In his campaigning he explained with concrete examples what he was calling for and pointed out that he was "against the class system here which keeps the poor man down; and the poor are mostly Black people. It is only natural, therefore, that their interest should be nearest, and dearest to my heart..."[29]

It was on this basis that Garvey was prepared to forge an alliance with R. Ehrenstein, a white Jewish planter who supported his program and ran for the election in the parish of St. Thomas.[30] However, the petite-bourgeoisie, on the whole, could not be budged in large numbers to support this program. One of its leading ideologues, D.T. Wint, a teacher and small proprietor who supported the big planters, argued:

> Garvey said the laboring men should get 4/- per day, with an eight hour day. Could the smaller people who had to employ labor send such an impossible man to the Council? ... If Garvey wants to go to Africa, let him go, but it is an insult to every Jamaican to tell him he should go back to African savagery—to darkest Africa—Garvey's Mecca.[31]

This shows the anti-democratic and ridiculous British colonial view of Africa that this Black man used not simply as a demagogic attack on Garvey but to whip up support among the small proprietor class by suggesting that insofar as they employed wage laborers Garvey's program would damage their interests. By implication they had more in common with foreign and big local capital than with the mass of working people. The frustration of Garvey's program came from this class, as the small proprietors, in a system where political liberties were based on property ownership, constituted the largest section of the electorate. They took the side of the imperialists and the large landowners. The defeat of Garvey himself and most of his candidates in the January 1930 election to the Legislative Council was due, firstly, to the fact that the masses had no vote. Secondly, the big landowners, merchants, and the colonial officials had won the support of the small proprietor class—i.e. farmers, produce dealers, inspectors, parsons, teachers, policemen, and shopkeepers—in the urban and rural areas. Thirdly, the People's Political

Party was not a strong political organization. It went out of existence after the election. However, in the 1930 electoral combat the
first two factors were decisive.

This election was a political victory for the Jamaica Producers
Association which gained 12 out of the 14 seats[32] in the Legislative
Council. The political representatives of the United Fruit Company
were also defeated. A.B. Lowe, a director of the Jamaica Banana
Producers Association who had been defeated, succinctly summed
up the situation when he wrote:

> It seems to me that the issue which has been decided is, that no
> agent of any foreign company will be allowed to represent any
> parish in the Legislative Council.[33]

Lowe is referring to the United Fruit Company. But this did not mean
a triumph for national interests for it was British capital that was in
conflict with American in the colony and this election marked a vic-
torious battle for the former in which the colonial petite-bourgeoisie
was on the front line. The largest section supported Britain, the
remainder supported the United Fruit Company or the PPP.

I have focused on Garvey's practical political program because
it is a turning point in the history of the struggle of our people against
imperialism. There are of course other areas—such as his trade union-
type activities in the Jamaica Workers and Labourers Association,
his cultural work at Edelweiss Park, his activities in the Kingston and
St. Andrew Corporation and the international conferences of the
UNIA which were held in Kingston in 1929 and 1934, in addition to
his political visits to Europe.

One should bear in mind Garvey's own statement:

> To fight for African redemption does not mean that we must give
> up our domestic fights for political justice and industrial rights.[34]

To deny the one and assert the other—a position current among repa-
triationists, who stress Garvey's ideas for African redemption and
ignore whatever else he may have done—is to misrepresent the man's
work and ideas. However, more than this, it is to capitulate and sur-
render to the exploitation and continued oppression of African people by imperialism and to a fatalism which denies the importance of
our struggle outside of the continent.

One should pay close attention to the actual political struggle
of Garvey in this period because they provide the only way of understanding the man and the period in which he lived.

Notes

1. Amy J. Garvey, *Garvey and Garveyism,* Collier Macmillan, New York, 1970, p. 96.
2. Edmund D. Cronon, *Black Moses—The Story of Marcus Garvey and the Universal Negro Improvement Association,* Univ. of Wisconsin Press, 1968, p. 197.
3. Amy J. Garvey, ed., *The Philosophy and Opinions of Marcus Garvey,* Vol. I, Atheneum, New York, 1969, p. 96.
4. Edgar Hoover, Memorandum for Mr. Ridgely, October 11, 1919, National Archives, R.G. 60,198940. I—Items 2-4 and 291-293 in this file (198940/1-293) of the Dept. of Justice on Marcus Garvey. At present items 6-290 are closed. Quoted from W.F. Ellkins, *Origins of the Deportation of Marcus Garvey* (ms.), p. 15.
5. V. Lenin, *Selected Works in One Volume,* International Publishers, New York, p. 602.
6. *Ibid.,* p. 224.
7. Sidney Pollard, *The Development of the British Economy, 1914–1967,* Edwin Arnold, London 1969, 2nd rev. ed., p. 19.
8. *Idem.*
9. Rupert Lewis, "A Political Study of Garveyism in Jamaica and London, 1914-1940," M.Sc. thesis, University of the West Indies, p. 74.
10. Central Bureau of Statistics, *Trade Unionism in Jamaica, 1918–1946,* Kingston c. 1946, p. 9.
11. Institute of Marxism-Leninism and Central Committee of the C.P.S.U., *Outline History of the Communist International,* Progress Publishers, 1971, pp. 296-298.
12. *Black Man,* April 12,1930.
13. See Rupert and Maureen Lewis, "Claude McKay's Jamaica," *Caribbean Quarterly* 23: 2 & 3, June/September 1977, pp. 38-53.
14. See Rupert Lewis, "Robert Love: a democrat in colonial Jamaica," *Jamaica Journal* 11: 1 & 2, August 1977, pp. 59-63; Joy Lumsden, "The political career of J. Robert Love: the earliest years," History Department Seminar, University of the West Indies, Jamaica, November 1978.
15. See J.R. Hooker, *Henry Sylvester Williams: Imperial PanAfricanist,* Rex Collings, London, 1975; Owen Mathurin, *Henry Sylvester Williams and the Origins of the Pan-African Movement, 1969–1971,* Greenwood Press, Connecticut, 1976.
16. In 1870 property taxes yielded £68,500, customs receipts £221,300, while in 1890 property taxes had declined (due to economic depression) to £17 ,300, but customs receipts had increased to £344,ooo. Customs receipts were the most important source of revenue judging by the items taxed (smoked fish, flour, salted or cured beef, soap and salt), and those exempted (books, carriages, carts and wagons, dogs, diamonds, fresh fish and meat, manure, pipes, ploughs, barbed wire, apples, grapes, peaches, strawberries and bacon, etc.) Land taxes also

hit the peasants hardest. See Graham Knox, "Political Change in Jamaica (1866-1906) and the Local Reaction to the Policies of the Crown Colony Government" in *The Caribbean in Transition,* F.M. Andic & T.G. Matthews, eds., Institute of Caribbean Studies, 1965, pp. 150-151.

17. *Daily Gleaner,* December 12, 1927.

18. *Ibid,.* February 11,1925.

19. Cf. *The Herald,* February 25,1928.

20. Morua was a Black politician from Matanzas province who rose to the Senate after the establishment of the first Republic in 1902. He held moderate views, having previously sided with those calling for Cuban autonomy within the Spanish empire rather than independence. He laid emphasis on the cultural emancipation of Cuban Blacks and on their educational advancement along lines suggested by Booker T. Washington. He was opposed to Black separatism and was responsible for introducing a law proscribing organizations based on racial principles. It had the negative effect of outlawing Black—rather than white-based organizations, but its immediate aim was to destroy the Independent Party of Colour. In later years, the UNIA and the British West Indian Association were among groups affected by this proscription. In addition, oral evidence suggests that the UNIA incriminated itself by its military-type practice sessions—though sticks and stones were used— which were geared towards the projected war to liberate Africa from white domination. The Cuban authorities may have suspected that these aggressive postures would have found outlet in local grievances. (Interview by the author with Charles Mitchell, Marianao, Cuba, March 1978.)

21. One aspect of the strong United States lobby in the early regimes of independent Cuba was their vigorous suppression of Blacks and the enforcement of racial segregation. Cf. Esteban Montejo, *The Autobiography of a Runaway Slave,* Bodley Head, London, 1968, p. 215 ff. This particular uprising was sponsored by the Independent Party of Colour. In the early days of the Republic however, there were many ill-armed uprisings all over Cuba. These were not necessarily racial in character.

22. *The Herald,* February 11,1928.

23. Amy Jacques Garvey, *Garvey and Garveyism,* p. 191.

24. See, for example, speech delivered by Marcus Garvey at Royal Albert Hall, London, June 6, 1928 in setting forth "The Case of the Negro for International Racial Adjustment," *More Philosophy and Opinions of Marcus Garvey,* Vol. III, E.U. Essien-Udom and Amy Jacques Garvey, eds., Cass, 1977, pp. 44-58.

25. See Rupert Lewis, "Hugh Clifford Buchanan: Jamaica's first Marxist," *Socialism!* 1:6, December 1974, pp. 19-28.

26. Amy Jacques Garvey, *ibid.,* pp. 208-209.

27. *Ibid.,* p. 65.

28. *Ibid.,* p. 209.

29. *Ibid.,* p. 212.
30. Although contradictory, the alliance with Ehrenstein was politically pragmatic. The Black peasantry and petite-bourgeoisie looked up to and respected the mulatto/white planter and merchant classes. Individuals from these classes who won popular support were called 'people's men'. (Evidence from interview with Iris Patterson by Maureen Lewis, Kingston, July 1978. Cf. also Rupert & Maureen Lewis, *op. cit.* These social attitudes account in part for the powerful popular appeal of Bustamante and N.W. Manley who rose to prominence in the late 1930s.
31. Amy Jacques Garvey, *Garvey and Garveyism,* pp. 212-213.
32. J.A. Carnegie, *Some Aspects of Jamaica's Politics, 1918-1938,* Institute of Jamaica, 1973, p. 106.
33. Rupert Lewis, "A Political Study of Garveyism...," p. 140.
34. Amy Jacques Garvey, ed., *Philosophy and Opinions of Marcus Garvey,* Vol. II, Atheneum, New York, p. 36.

AFRICA AND THE GARVEY MOVEMENT IN THE INTERWAR YEARS[1]

Arnold Hughes

While it is no easy task to assess the overall influence of Marcus Garvey on the evolution of African political consciousness, there is sufficient evidence available to suggest that during the years immediately following World War I, the UNIA (Universal Negro Improvement Association and African Communities League) aroused widespread interest and enjoyed a strong measure of support in Black Africa and, even after the swift decline in Garvey's political fortunes in the late twenties, many Africans remained true to his ideals.

It was the holding of the First Convention of the Negro Peoples of the world in New York City in August 1920 which first brought Garvey to the attention of the African public and European colonial officials. The plenary sessions in Madison Square Garden and the large and colorful street processions in Harlem were designed to attract the attention of the world; Garvey's bellicose warnings to the colonial powers to pull out of Africa and the disclosures of grandiose plans to bring the scattered sections of the Black race together under the aegis of the UNIA and its economic subsidiaries generated an unusual degree of enthusiasm among Africans as well as those of

African descent across the Atlantic. Some measure of this impact on Black Africa is provided by contemporary accounts: writing home in 1920, a British missionary on the Gold Coast (now Ghana) stated

> The Africa for Africa Movement ("Marcus Garvey") has gripped the coast and many of the towns are seething with it.[2]

Support for this view was afforded by editorial comments in African-owned newspapers: the *Times of Nigeria* considered the idea of a shipping line owned entirely by Blacks ... "a sublime concept for which everybody of African origins will bless the name of Marcus Garvey."[3] In similar vein the *Sierra Leone Weekly News* thrilled to the thought of a "West African Negro republic" which it considered to reveal... "the workings of the mind of a man who is the child of visions."[4] On the other side of the continent, in Uganda, E.B. Kalibala recalled the arrival of the Garveyite newspaper, the *Negro World*, as a "sensational development"[5] and similar reactions were recorded in South Africa where the white-owned *Cape Argus* was obliged to admit that

> One of the many absurd stories that are being circulated among the natives is that the notorious Marcus Garvey ... will soon arrive in South Africa with a large force of Black soldiers to drive the white man out of the country.[6]

This presumably was a reference to the activities of Wellington Butelezi, a semi-literate "prophet" who achieved a short-lived but widespread following in the Eastern Cape by preaching a garbled version of Garveyism according to which all Europeans would be driven into the sea by American Blacks and their goods taken over.[7] Similar phenomena were recorded in Central Africa,[8] causing consternation among European administrators already facing a range of problems associated with a new sense of racial awakening among colonial Africans. From the coastal and urban intelligentsia to untutored rural masses the appeal of Garvey's message of racial emancipation could be discerned.

Race Consciousness

By the early twenties a significant level of racial consciousness and cooperation could be detected among Black people. Even before World War I numerous contacts between Africans and transatlantic Blacks had been established —missionary and educational ties being the most common but there had also been more overtly political links such as the Pan-African Conference in London in 1900. The war had aroused Black hopes on both sides of the Atlantic and their frustration generated a shared sense of aggrievement. Added to this failure to reward Black sacrifice on behalf of the Allies was the disregard of Black opinion in the matter of the disposal of the German colonies. Belief in the imminent rise of the colored races, precipitated by the rise of Japan as a world-class power and the assertion of Indian and Arab nationalism, was also discernible in these years and Garvey was to make frequent reference to this "rising tide of colour." Viewed in the light of this race consciousness and the rapid political changes which had occurred over the last few years, Garvey's proposals did not appear too impossible to many thinking Africans.

It is quite likely that Garvey's first connections with Africa were established during his two-year sojourn in London in 1912-14. Working on the anti-colonial newspaper, the *African Times and Oriental Review*, which was owned by a consortium of West Africans and edited by an Egyptian with Sudanese-African ancestry, Garvey is likely to have come into contact with African nationalists and to have imbibed a romantic notion of African history.[9] Much later, in 1920, he was to seek the aid of his former employer, Duse Mohammed Ali, in promoting his World Convention. He also used the services of John E. Bruce, a leading Black American nationalist and scholar-journalist, to spread his name among Africans and seemed to have corresponded independently with a number of politically prominent or aspiring Africans as well. Several Africans attended the 1920 Convention and two of these, Gabriel Johnson of Liberia and George Marke of Sierra Leone, were appointed to two of the highest offices in the UNIA—"Supreme Potentate" and "Deputy Potentate." African visitors to the United States were to turn up at later Conventions and at local Divisional meetings of the UNIA as well, and some of these returning travelers were to carry Garveyism back to Africa.[10]

By the time Garvey had established himself in New York Africa had come to occupy a central place in his thoughts. From the *Philosophy and Opinions* and Garvey's editorials in the *Negro World* a general, if not always coherent or detailed, picture of Africa's position in his thinking emerges.[11] "Negro Redemption," Garvey's life mission, could only be achieved through the liberation of Africa from European rule and the creation in that continent of an economically advanced, politically powerful and militarily impregnable national homeland for all Black peoples. Such a country would not only enable Africans to enjoy their "right divine" to self-government, a right at that time being extended to many minor European and Middle Eastern peoples, but would also enable them to offer protection and refuge to the threatened Blacks of the Diaspora. Garvey was fearful of the future of the Black race, at home and abroad, because of the head-start enjoyed by other races over the Negro, and because of the danger posed by racial and cultural assimilation of Blacks overseas.[12] Racial survival, as well as racial dignity, lay behind the desire for a "big, Black republic," for only a free and powerful Africa, with its uncontaminated and teeming populace, could ensure the continuity of the race.

From this concern for the future of his race were born two slogans indelibly linked with Garvey's name, though in fact neither was original to him —"Africa for the Africans" and "Back to Africa." Neither rallying calls were precise in their meaning and argument continues to this day over exactly what Garvey had in mind. "Africa for the Africans," put simply, meant a free continent in the utilization of whose resources all people of African descent could share. However, difficulties arose in defining who was a "real" African and in determining the political relationship between indigenous and repatriate African. Garvey was noticeably vague in deciding who was African; although principally a Pan-Melanist, he attributed Negro origins to North Africans, some Indians and even Southern Europeans.[13] His notions of government were equally elusive; at times he envisaged the UNIA as an ally of African nationalist movements working for their own liberation, but on other occasions he indicated a hegemonic role for the UNIA. Certainly, the formal structure of the Garvey Movement suggested a parallel government of Blacks based on global representation through the local Divisions and Chapters of the organization. Similar ambiguities surrounded the notion of repatriation. Garvey does not seem to have decided in his own mind whether he wanted selective return of skilled Afro-Americans or a wholesale abandonment of the Americas in return for Africa.[14] The uncertainties surrounding these two key slogans were a source of confusion and mistrust in Africa, for it was not only white administrators who balked at the idea of millions of ungovernable immigrants pouring into the continent; leading Africans were also anxious to know how many of their racial compatriots intended returning and under what political conditions.

Garveyism penetrated Africa in several ways in the early twenties; principally at the level of ideas but also at a practical and institutional one. Apart from the publicity surrounding the World Conventions and the numerous public statements and telegrams to world leaders, we have observed that word-of-mouth communication was very important in spreading Garveyism in Africa. With high levels of illiteracy and a well established system of oral transmission of information, news of Garvey's doings, inevitably garbled, spread rapidly. Literate Africans corresponded directly with transatlantic Blacks but the main source of information for the reading public was the UNIA's weekly journal, the *Negro World*. Despite censorship in many parts of Africa, the newspaper got through to provide its readers (who in turn retold its contents to those who could not read) with the latest news concerning Garvey and the UNIA; all presented in an uncompromisingly anti-colonial and Pan-Melanist style. The *Negro World* gave wide coverage to African issues, frequently denounced colonial injustices and made full use of African source material. Its African correspondents were numerous and extensive use was made of editorials and news stories from Pan-Africanist newspapers such as the *Gold Coast Leader* and the *Abantu Batho* (of South Africa). Without the *Negro World*, it is unlikely that Garvey's fame would have spread so quickly and widely in Africa; after all, radio and television were not available and much of the North American press of the day, both Black and white, was hostile to the UNIA.

The UNIA and Africa

Regarding itself as a world government and parliament of Black people, the UNIA sought to establish itself in Africa as well as invite African representation at its annual gatherings in America. Information concerning the penetration of Africa by the UNIA is not easily come by, but the records of the Movement itself,[15] police files, and African newspapers, indicate that Divisions of the organizations were set up in several parts of West and South Africa. Colonial repression prevented open organization in the French and Belgian territories, though we know that a branch of the UNIA existed briefly in Senegal and that Garveyite agitation occurred in Dahomey and Cameroon.[16] The Belgians showed considerable concern lest English-speaking Blacks from America and West Africa and Francophone Africans from Senegal introduce Garveyite and other Pan-Melanist ideas into the Congo.[17] The frequent outbursts of millenarianism, *Ngunzism,* were recognized to have anti-white features and believed to be fomented by alien Blacks. A UNIA agent, a Gold Coaster named Wilson, was expelled in late 1920 for allegedly seditious activities. Both the Belgians and the French were prepared to accept the most fanciful links between the UNIA and Bolshevism, Pan-Islamism or even Indian and Japanese agitation. The wilder allegations were usually made by journalists on the right of the political spectrum, such as Coty and Daye, and there was also a predilection for racial conspiracy theory in the British press which was picked up on the

European continent.[18] Some of these charges were picked up by colonial officials and not always without substance. The attempts of the Communist movement to infiltrate the UNIA are well documented,[19] and Asian nationalists played some part in organizing resistance to colonialism among Africans in East Africa.[20] It should also be remembered that in Paris Indo-Chinese, Arab, African and West Indian opponents of French imperialism worked closely together on numerous occasions.

It was in English-speaking Africa that the UNIA made greatest headway. The settler colonies of East and Central Africa, mindful of earlier disturbances involving American-educated Africans, notably John Chilembwe's abortive revolt in Nyasaland (now Malawi) in 1915, prevented the establishment of UNIA branches in their midst and sought to restrict contact between their African charges and America. That they could not keep out Garveyism or the *Negro World* is shown by the correspondence between proto-nationalists in several of these territories and Garvey and the illicit distribution of the UNIA journal. Harry Thuku, founder of the East African Association in 1921, sought the advice of Garvey and soon after the *Negro World* began to appear in Kenya.[21] According to King, "it would be difficult to exaggerate the sort of effect it began to have from 1921 onwards."[22] Nyasalanders also seem to have been aware of Garvey. Rothberg[23] states that at least one of the Nyasa founder members of the first African political body in Northern Rhodesia (now Zambia) had been in correspondence with Garvey and that another Nyasalander, Isa Macdonald Lawrence, had been arrested in 1926 for handling seditious journals, which included the *Negro World.* When Dr. J.E.K. Aggrey visited Nyasaland in 1920 as a member of the Phelps-Stokes Education Commission to Africa many indigenes thought that he had come to liberate them by force,[24] an ironic confusion, seeing that a major part of Aggrey's work was to seek to counter radical Pan-Melanism.

In English-speaking West Africa, branches of the UNIA were established in all territories save The Gambia. We know most about the Lagos Division, formed in late 1920 and which recruited some 300 members at one stage.[25] Concentrating exclusively on racial and economic uplift, its plans aroused considerable local interest and, initially, the Garvey Movement was tolerated by the Nigerian government, though two years later the *Negro World* was banned. It appears there was another branch at Kano and additional interest in Garveyism is known to have existed in Minna and Ibadan.[26] In the latter town, J.A. Obisesan led a Garveyite discussion group in the early twenties, indicating that even where there was no open UNIA presence Africans were eagerly discussing Garvey's ideas. No member of the political elite wished to be associated with the UNIA, although Herbert Macaulay, the leading nationalist leader of the period, had corresponded with Garvey and offered him commercial advice.[27] Instead, the Lagos UNIA drew significant support from independent churchmen such as Abiodun and Euba, and West Indians, such as Amblestone, Shackleford and Hawkins. Even when Garveyism had formally retreated from Nigeria, Joyce Carey,[28] then administrative officer in the north, reported coming across garbled accounts of Garvey as a Black liberator, similar to those in circulation in South and Central Africa.

Unlike Nigeria, some leading nationalists on the Gold Coast were drawn to Garveyism. Kobina Sekyi, a conservative African nationalist, but very race-conscious for that, had a guarded admiration for Garvey's work;[29] while Joseph Caseley Hayford, the dominant political figure of the twenties, editor of the *Gold Coast Leader* and founder of the National Congress of British West Africa, appeared very close to the UNIA.[30] Hill[31] has suggested, with some conviction, that the young Garvey was intellectually indebted to Hayford and certainly he was held in high regard by the UNIA. The *Gold Coast Leader* was quoted more frequently in the *Negro World* than any other African newspaper, and Hayford was "knighted" by the UNIA in 1920. There were two divisions of the UNIA on the Gold Coast but no members' names are available. Wilkie mentioned Accra, together with Lagos and Calabar, as a center of Garveyism at this time.

Freetown, in Sierra Leone, also had two divisions of the UNIA despite the ancient loyalty to the British Crown. Creoles were active in seeking to establish divisions in Senegal[32] in these years and the more radical members of this peripatetic community had an old reputation for preaching "Africa for the Africans." The mysterious George Marke, mentioned above, was believed to be from Sierra Leone, although he must have spent most of his adult life away from that colony in Liberia and North America. Liberia's links with the UNIA were more extensive and are considered separately.

Garveyism made a great impact on South Africa[33] where the circumstances of the Black population, a considerable degree of social and economic advancement, well-established ties with Black America, and mounting racial discrimination in the twenties, favored the spread of Garveyite ideas. Garvey's influence was felt in three ways: at a syncretistic level as in the case of the "Wellingtonians" in the Eastern Cape; through the participation of Garveyite sympathizers in the activities of the two leading African political organizations,

the African National Congress and the International Commercial
Workers Union; and in the establishment of some seven divisions of
the UNIA, mainly in the Cape Town area. Additionally, as elsewhere
in Africa, Garvey's ideas were discussed and upheld even where no
formal organization existed. Certainly the numerous letters to the
Negro World from South African correspondents suggest a widespread admiration for the UNIA. In Cape Town, as in Lagos, West
Indians were prominent in the Garvey Movement, the most active
being Arthur McKinley and J.G. Gumbs.[34] The latter was also
President of the International Commercial Workers Union for a number of years. Perhaps the leading Garveyite at the Cape at this time
was "Professor" James Thaele,[35] who had imbibed Garveyism during his stay in the United States and established a "race-conscious'
newspaper, the *African World* (not to be confused with the London
newspaper of the same name). Thaele was also President of the
Western Cape Division of the African National Congress. Other leading Congress members with UNIA affinities were Mweli Skota, W.B.
Makasube and Josiah Gumede. It was Skota who, as General
Secretary of the ANC in 1925, proposed a UNIA type governmental
structure for the ANC and a continental convention to which all leading nationalist groups in Africa would be invited. He also favored the
adoption of the UNIA colors, red, green and Black, for the ANC. His
Pan-Melanist views were regarded as too advanced by his colleagues
and he was replaced. Makasube also harbored advanced racial views,
so much so that he left the ANC to set up his own short-lived Africa
Party. Gumede was torn between Garveyism and Marxism but his
newspaper, *Abantu Batho* (The People) was frequently cited in the
Negro World. Walshe[36] notes that Garvey's influence on Black nationalism in South Africa developed later than in West Africa, was subject to local interpretation, but was never a major factor in the
essentially interracial ideology of the period.

Realizing the limitations placed on its expansion by the colonial
powers, the UNIA naturally sought to establish footholds in the two
remaining independent African states. Although individual
Garveyites made the long and difficult journey to Abyssinia,[37] lack
of support from the government of that country, transportation problems, and unsettled conditions, led Garvey to concentrate instead on
Liberia. After all, the "Black Republic" had been founded by an earlier generation of Black American repatriates, had an open-door policy on immigration, and was about the nearest part of Black Africa
to North America and the Caribbean where potential emigrants were
located. The details of the Liberian Colonisation Scheme promul-
gated by the UNIA between 1920 and 1924 have been told else-

where;[38] in the main it was a sad story of great hopes dashed by treachery, mismanagement, and tactlessness.

The Black Republic

With his customary ebullience Garvey planned to raise millions of dollars for investment in Liberia and "guaranteed" President King 20,000-30,000 suitably qualified settlers in 1924-25 to aid in the development of the country.[39] Although privately opposed to the UNIA scheme as early as 1921, King permitted the organization to establish two divisions in his country and to go ahead with its preparations for the creation of five "colonies" each of 500 settlers. The UNIA, with great difficulty, raised enough money to establish a second shipping line, the Black Cross Navigation and Trading Co., which acquired one ship (the S.S. "General Goethals," re-named the "Booker T. Washington") for trade and colonization in West Africa. Bolstered by the support of his colonial neighbors, who were very much opposed to Garvey's demand for the incorporation of Sierra Leone and the Ivory Coast into an enlarged Liberia[40] (to be obtained on behalf of American Blacks by the United States government in return for the cancellation of British and French war debts), and by an upturn in the Liberian economy in 1923;[41] and alarmed by the presence of his political opponents in the local divisions of the UNIA and by the opportune disclosure of the contents of the "Garcia Report" by a hostile British newspaper[42] (the document hinted at the possibility for an alliance between tribal and Americo-Liberian opponents of the King administration and the UNIA), the Liberian President reneged on an earlier agreement and expelled the UNIA mission from Liberia in July 1924. A ban on further immigration by known Garveyites was also imposed and the Movement's assets seized.

The collapse of the Liberian venture was a major blow to the UNIA, both in Africa as well as in the United States. In West Africa it raised doubts about Garvey's political motivations and questioned the soundness of his economic plans. Apart from sharing with the UNIA its stress on race pride, West Africans also took enthusiastically to its commercial program. The idea of a Black-owned shipping fleet trading directly between Black producers in Africa and the West Indies and Black manufacturers in North America was very attractive at a time when European and Lebanese competition was felt to be ruining African traders and reducing the value of produce sold by African farmers. Great interest had been shown in 1920 for shares in the Black Star Line but no sales had taken place because of the indifference (or incompetence) of the parent body to the local incorporation of the company.[43] The local agent at Lagos, Akinbami Agbebi, had sound commercial ideas for the expansion of the Black Star Line in Nigeria but these were ignored in the pursuit of wider schemes. Wilson, the Dakar agent of the Black Star Line, was no more fortunate, for he was far too busy avoiding detection by the French and Belgian authorities to sell many shares. The collapse of the Black Cross Line and the Liberian settlement scheme of 1924 further eroded public confidence in the economic judgment of UNIA leaders and encouraged Africans to set up their own business enterprises. The Gold Coaster, Winfried Tete Ansah, emerged in the late twenties as the inheritor of the intra-racial trading schemes of the UNIA although he was no more successful.[44] After his failure a trend towards territorial business activity could be detected, together with a move to seek economic redress through political action at the local level rather than through Pan-Africanist trading combines.

Garveyism received additional support in Africa from the activities of independent Black churches and the missionary work of Black American churches. In East, Central and Southern Africa, where formal political opportunities were barred or restricted, independent churches provided a political as well as spiritual outlet for Black frustrations. Several of these local churches were natural vehicles for the propagation of Garvey's ideas and one, the Afro-Anglican Constructive Church of Kimberley, actually incorporated Garvey's name into its creed.[45] The African Orthodox Church, a Black American church close to the UNIA, had a mission in South Africa and its local leader, Archbishop Alexander, visited Uganda and Kenya in the early thirties to ordain priests.[46] One of these, Reuben Spartas, the Ugandan proto-nationalist, had learned of the African Orthodox Church from the *Negro World*. In Central Africa, Rothberg[47] states that Yesaya Zerenji Mwasi, who founded the "Blackman's Church of God which is in Tongaland" in 1933, had earlier corresponded with Garvey and it was commonly held, though not proven, that Black American missionaries and syncretistic churchgoers alike, were involved in disseminating Garveyism in the Belgian Congo.[48]

The Garvey Movement also reached Africa indirectly through Europe. Pan-Melanism flourished among West Indian and African exiles in Britain[49] and France[50] and there were several divisions of the UNIA in Britain in the early twenties, though not in France. "Ambassadors," Richard Tobbitt and Jean Adam, were appointed to these countries and, in the case of Paris, links established with local Pan-Melanist groups. The first of these was Kojo Tovalou Houenou's LUDRN *(Ligue Universelle pour la Défense de la Race Noire)* which had a short-lived newspaper, *Les Continents*, and which exchanged material with the *Negro World*. In 1924 Houenou enjoyed a brief but friendly relationship with the UNIA, being feted at its World Convention in New York and elected "Potentate" and "UNIA Representative" in France, in succession to Adam. Never an uncritical admirer of Garvey, Houenou, nevertheless, was responsible for broadcasting UNIA views among Blacks in Paris and his native Dahomey.

Following Houenou's return to Africa and political obscurity in 1925, other Pan-Melanist organizations appeared, led by such persons as Lamine Senghor (from Senegal), Tiemoho Garan-Kouyate (a French Soudanese from present-day Mali) and most importantly, according to Spiegler,[51] the *métis* Emile Faure. Their small organizations, first the CDRN (*Comité de la Défense de la Race Nègre*) and then the LDRN (*Ligue de la Défense de la Race Nègre*), both in their deliberations and their newspapers, *La Voix des Nègres* and *La Race Nègre*, displayed intense race-consciousness as well as leftwing attitudes. Garvey seems to have been a nominal member of the CDRN[52] and may well have had dealings with Francophone Pan-Melanists during his visit to Paris in 1928. African visitors to the imperial capitals could well have learnt of Garvey from these sources and then carried them back to their homeland like the Ugandan, Daudi Bassude, mentioned by King.[53]

Virtually nothing is known of Garveyite contacts in the capital cities of other European colonial powers. Garvey did visit Brussels in 1928 and spoke cryptically of having made contact with kindred spirits.[54] There was a Union Congolaise in the Belgian capital, whose secretary in 1921, was accused of harboring Garveyite sentiments.[55] There is no trace in the bulky files on the UNIA in the Belgian Archives[56] of any reference to local Garveyite activities and it was probably Du Bois' Pan African Congress, which met in Brussels in 1921, which aroused the greater interest. In the case of Portugal, the *Liga Africana*, an organization of *assimilados* based at Lisbon, sought good relations both with the UNIA and the Pan African Congress, and the Poston Mission to Liberia in 1924 briefly made contact with the Liga when their ship stopped at Lisbon *en route* for West Africa.[57] There is also a French confidential report of "Garveyite" activities in the Portuguese colony of Guinea in these years.[58]

With the collapse of the Liberian Colonisation Scheme, on which Garvey had pinned so much hope for gaining a foothold in Africa—even intending moving the UNIA headquarters to Monrovia and holding the 1924 World Convention there[59] —UNIA support in Africa ebbed. Pockets of organized Garveyism survived, notably in

South Africa, and admiration for Garvey's vision and sacrifice never disappeared; but any prospect of establishing a significant and concrete foothold in Africa vanished with the Liberian venture. From then on Garvey was in no position to give much time to Africa although it always remained in the forefront of his thoughts. Legal persecution, the break up of the American UNIA, imprisonment, and finally deportation to Jamaica in December 1927, forcibly removed Garvey from the helm of the movement and its center of power in New York. From 1928 there was a gradual attempt at rebuilding support among the loyal divisions of the UNIA and, at subsequent World Conventions at Kingston and Toronto, new and even more ambitious plans were revealed for the redemption of Africa. The paucity of news coverage in the African press from this time on (and, equally significantly, a loss of interest in Garvey in police files) indicates that much of the old magic had gone.

The UNIA Declines

After a period of moving between London and Jamaica, Garvey rightly calculated that he would have to re-form his Movement in the imperial capital and, in 1935, he settled down there until his death in June 1940. Not a great deal is known about these last years and Cronon[60] and Lewis,[61] who appear to disagree on the extent of Garvey's decline, tell us little about his political activities. As far as Africa is concerned, there is little to suggest that Garvey was able to create a new following to replace the one he had lost, or was in the process of losing through the attrition of death. It has been suggested[62] that he was active among West African students and radical exiles in the West African Students Union and the International African Service Bureau, but the former was too conservative and the other too left-wing to suggest a close tie with Garvey.[63] Garvey's last newspaper, the *Black Man,* has little to say about his activities in London and the general impression gained is one of increasing isolation, both ideologically and organizationally. Apart from his newspaper activity, itself a pale reflection of the *Negro World* days, Garvey spent time on arranging UNIA Conventions in Canada and in promoting Black studies. He held summer schools in "African Philosophy" in Canada and set up a correspondence school for Negroes only in London on similar subjects. His intention was to create a new UNIA leadership drawn from the graduates of his educational institutions, some of whom were African.[64] The one great opportunity offered in these last years was the Italian invasion of Abyssinia. Black reaction was intense and global and, while some of

Garvey's old spirit returned,[65] he never featured prominently in the pro-Abyssinia protest movement in London. On the contrary, he had harsh words for the exiled emperor, attacking him for cowardice, dislike of Negroes and failing to modernize his country.[66] More personally, Garvey still rankled over Haile Selassie's failure to reply to a letter sent him many years before.[67]

There is some evidence[68] from his writings in this period that Garvey was less intransigent in his opposition to the colonial powers, while still believing in the eventual destiny of the Black man. He found time to praise British policy in West Africa and, perhaps aware of the growing menace of Fascism to Black and Briton alike, stressed the loyalty of the Negro to the Empire. As early as 1925 Garvey had admitted the shortcomings of the belligerent posture of the earlier period, arguing that it had been a tactical necessity to shake a complacent world out of its indifference to the plight of the Black man.[69] Perhaps again, the milder reproach of the colonial powers reflected the new strategy, reinforced, possibly, by the advice of West Africans in London. Regardless of any change in approach, Garvey's political message no longer evoked the eager response of fifteen years earlier and even his death in June 1940 produced little more than a ripple of interest, occurring as it did at a time when the very British Empire itself seemed faced with imminent extinction. It would be a number of years before the spirit of Garveyism, if not Garvey himself, would play its part in the decolonization of Africa.

Why did this Movement, which seemed poised on the edge of success in Africa in the early twenties, fail to obtain a political breakthrough? There is no single explanation for this failure and the answer must be sought on both sides of the Atlantic. Garveyites were undoubtedly correct in pointing out the difficulties posed by the colonial powers, either in the form of outright repression or in less severe but equally effective forms, such as harassment and ostracism. This last technique should not be overlooked, given the desire for social as well as political recognition on the part of the nationalist elite. Yet the severity of sanctions varied from outright persecution in the Belgian and French colonies, through a combination of harassment and bare tolerance in the British dependencies, to a paradoxical guarded legal recognition in the Union of South Africa, where the Smuts government tended to play down its importance.[70] Clearly, additional reasons must be sought for the Garvey Movement's inability to establish itself.

A second important reason for its failure in Africa was the collapse of the parent body and its economic auxiliaries in the United

States. As early as 1921 major difficulties were hindering the UNIA in its international activities:[71] policy differences between the "regionalists" and the "internationalists"; tension between American and West Indian components; personality clashes; treachery; official harassment; incompetence; mismanagement; fraud; and a yawning gap between the soaring aspirations and popularity of Garvey on the one hand, and the ability of the organization to keep up with them. The legal persecution of Garvey succeeded more than anything else in disabling the Movement, for even before he was jailed and later deported, Garvey was obliged to spend a great deal of time in his legal defense, which diverted his energies and the financial resources of his organization away from its international task. The disintegration of the American organization deprived Garvey of funds and reduced the credibility of his Movement in Africa. The anti-Garvey press, both Black and white, had a field day publicizing the problems and shortcomings of the parent body and this slanted coverage duly found its way to Africa.

The bankruptcy of the two shipping lines and the ignominious withdrawal from Liberia were particularly felt in West Africa. Much was expected of "industrial Garveyism" while the revelations of the "Garcia Report" raised doubts about Garvey's political intentions on African soil. Attacking the Liberian government following its expulsion was as tactically unwise as allying with President King's opponents. West African nationalist leaders were quite familiar with the shortcomings of the Liberian regime but were reluctant to condemn it lest it strengthen the arguments of those who claimed Blacks to be incapable of self-government. By adding his voice to racist opponents of Liberia, Garvey was seen to endanger the independence of the lone "Black republic." It should also be noted that there were strong ties of culture between the Liberian ruling elite and leading families in Freetown and other parts of British West Africa and, indeed, some measure of intermarriage. The prospect of being incorporated into an enlarged Liberia is likely to have further reduced the appeal of the UNIA to the African elite of Sierra Leone.

The Liberian episode also brought to a head the issue of who would control the Pan-Melanist movement. It was only in South Africa that a political struggle between local Garveyites, West Indian at that, and indigenous Africans, came to a head.[72] Yet Kadalie's determination to prevent Gumbs and other UNIA leaders taking over the ICU was echoed in the leadership struggle of the ANC and most nationalist leaders would have endorsed Sekyi's interpretation of "Africa for the Africans" to mean emancipation under the control and direction of "African Africa and thoroughly African Africans."[73]

In this respect it is significant how few leading nationalists joined the UNIA. After years of struggle themselves they were not prepared to share power with alien Blacks, however strong the race bond.

The "American-ness" and "West Indian-ness" of the UNIA was also a cause of complaint. "Patriarch" Campbell of Lagos objected to American civilization "with all its brag and big talks,"[74] and Sekyi felt that "the Americanization of the American Negro" militated against his success in Africa.[75] Perhaps the unbridled enthusiasm of West Indian exiles in Africa led some Africans to regard the local UNIA Divisions as social clubs for Antilleans. The absence of first-hand knowledge of Africa, or its disregard, led to errors of judgment of the kind that took place in Liberia. A typically insensitive action was the conferment of bogus aristocratic African titles—Duke of the Nile, Viscount of the Niger—on worthy American and West Indian members of the UNIA at the 1920 World Convention, and Garvey's own assumption of the Provisional Presidency of Africa. Not only did they expose the Movement to ridicule but they also led to doubts about the political aspirations of these newly-ennobled dignitaries. Although Africans were generally in support of unimpeded immigration by Black Americans and felt they had much to learn from them, the UNIA's use of such terms as "colonizing" and "civilizing" Africa did not always go down well among professional Africans.

Garvey's desire to create a "big, Black republic" both attracted and repelled. The dominant view in British West Africa was that it was impracticable and ran counter to the objective of territorial or regional self-government.[76] Further, it was seditious, and the thought of disloyalty to the Crown weighed heavily on the minds of a generation of constitutional nationalists, many of whom were barristers and lawyers. Besides, the British made several small concessions in the mid-twenties aimed at providing the local political elite with some minor say in the government of three of their four West African colonies.[77] The creation of a small electorate and of a number of highly coveted seats in the local Legislative Councils had its effect; it convinced local nationalists of the value of reformist politics and distracted them from PanMelanism. It was not only the UNIA which suffered eclipse in the late twenties, the NCBWA was also in a state of collapse by then. The "indigenization" of politics continued in the thirties with the tendency to recruit inwards into the colonial interiors rather than outwards among the various colonies. In French West Africa the myth of eventual assimilation was maintained by Blaise Diagne,[78] the Black deputy for Senegal, and even Kojo Tovalou Houenou advocated independence only as a substitute for full equality within the French Empire.[79]

Black radicals in Europe and Africa were divided between Pan-Melanism and revolutionary socialism, as is revealed by the tensions within the CDRN and LDRN in Paris, or the ANC in South Africa. With the consolidation of revolutionary power in the Soviet Union, Moscow's version of socialist internationalism appeared very attractive to anti-colonialists in Africa and elsewhere. The Soviet Union made a determined attempt to recruit Blacks through such front organizations as the League against Imperialism or through the Africa section of the Profintern (Red International of Labour Unions), set up initially by the Trinidadian radical, George Padmore. Padmore bitterly denounced Garveyism[80] as an empty deception and sought to win away its adherents whom he conceded were regrettably numerous. Failing to penetrate the UNIA, the Communist International emulated its policy of Black separatism in the late twenties in the hope of winning over Pan-Melanists in South Africa and elsewhere. In the thirties the policy was abandoned for that of the "Popular Front" alliance against Fascism, mobilizing Black support on such issues as the Italian occupation of Abyssinia.

Garveyism had to contend not only with revolutionary internationalism as an alternative to Christian-liberal reformism; moderate socialism was also being taken up by younger Africans. The reforms of the Popular Front government in France enabled the French Socialist Party (SFIO) to establish branches in Senegal while the British Labour Party, particularly through the Fabian Colonial Bureau, forged links with colonial Africans. The International African Service Bureau was closely associated with the Independent Labour Party. Even within the Pan-Melanist field the UNIA had to face continued opposition from an increasingly radical Du Bois, whose Pan-African Congress movement had always enjoyed a measure of support among Africans.

In the twenties Garveyism, in its political aims, had appeared too revolutionary and seditious for a generation of constitutional nationalists; but by the thirties it was being attacked as too reactionary, a petit-bourgeoise Black capitalism, by a more stridently anti-colonial generation of Africans. In the short run it was the reformist territorialists who succeeded in dominating African nationalism but the price of accommodation still leaves a yearning for Garvey's vision of an independent and unified Africa.

Notes

1.   This paper is a summary of a longer study on *Marcus Garvey and Black
      Africa,* in preparation by the writer. Reference to the activities of the
      Garvey Movement in Africa in the secondary literature are all too
      often brief, scattered, inaccurate or politically biased. Undoubtedly the
      fullest and best account is to be found in Chapter 7 of T. Martin, *Race
      First* (Greenwood Press, Westport/London, 1976). Other useful
      accounts are those by J.A. Langley, "Garveyism and African
      Nationalism," *Race* XI, 2, 1969; I. Geiss, *The Pan-African Movement*
      (Translated by Ann Keep, Methuen, London, 1974), Chapter 12; R.G.
      Weisbord, "Marcus Garvey, Pan-Negroist: the View from Whitehall,"
      Race Xl, 4, 1970, and T.G. Vincent, *Black Power and the Garvey Movement*
      (Ramparts Press, San Francisco, 1971), pp. 176-185.
      E. Cronon's standard biography of Garvey, *Black Moses* (University of
      Wisconsin Press, 1955), provides *very* little information on the UNIA
      in Africa. The "official" Garveyite sources, *Philosophy and Opinions of
      Marcus Garvey,* III Vols. (Compiled and edited by A.J. Garvey and E.U.
      Essien-Udom. Frank Cass, London, 1967 and 1977), and A.J. *Garvey
      and Garveyism* (Collier Books, New York, 1970), are more useful in
      defining Africa's place in the ideology of the UNIA than in providing
      details of its involvement there. The one important exception is
      Liberia, which is discussed in a highly partisan manner in Vol. II, pp.
      352-412.
2.   A.W. Wilkie to J.H. Oldham, Gold Coast, 8. 12. 20. Conference of
      Missionary Societies in Great Britain and Ireland. Box 265. Gold Coast.
      File C. Correspondence with Rev. A.W. Wilkie, 1917-31.
3.   24 May 1920.
4.   18 September 1920.
5.   K. King, *Pan-Africanism and Education.* (Clarendon Press, Oxford, 1971)
      p. 71, citing interview with Kalibala.
6.   29 January 1923.
7.   M. Hunter, *Reaction to Conquest* (Oxford University Press, for
      International Institute of African Languages and Culture, London,
      1936), p.p. 570-573.
8.   G. Shepperson, "Nyasaland and the Millenium," in S. Thrupp (ed.),
      Millenial Dreams in Action (Mouton, The Hague, 1962), pp. 145-159.
9.   R.A. Hill, "The First England Years and After, 1912-1916," in J.H.
      Clarke (ed.), *Marcus Garvey and the Vision of Africa* (Vintage Books,
      New York, 1974), pp. 38-70.
10.   E.g. James Thaele of Cape Town.
11.   There is no systematic discussion of Africa but numerous editorials,
      essays, reflections, etc. dwell on African themes. Perhaps the most
      coherent statements are the two petitions presented to the League of
      Nations in 1922 and 1929 and reprinted in *Philosophy and Opinions,* Vol.
      III, *op. cit.,* pp. 195-224; and "The Declaration of Rights of the Negro
      Peoples of the World," reprinted as Appendix I in Vincent, *op. cit.*

12. E.g. *Philosophy and Opinions,* I-II, pp. 46-49. "Shall the Negro be Exterminated?"
13. *Ibid.,* pp. 18-19, 82.
14. *Ibid.,* for instance, contrast the two statements which appear on pp. 53 and 107.
15. List of Divisions, 1925-27, held in the Central Division Records of the UNIA. Reel 1, Papers (Microfilm). Schomburg Center for Research in Black Culture, New York Public Library. These papers provide very little information on the UNIA's activities in Africa but some additional material is to be found among the J.E. Bruce Papers, also on microfilm at the Schomburg Center.
16. For a general account of Garveyism in French Colonial Africa see A. Hughes, "French and Belgian Reactions to the "Menace' of PanNegroism in the Twenties." Unpublished paper; SLOTFOM III, 84, 2. "Garveyisme." Archives Nationales, Section D'Outre-Mer, Paris; CO 96/625. "The Black Star Line." Secret, 10 June 1921. Inclosure from Governor-General, French West Africa, to Governor, Gold Coast. Dakar, 25 March 1921. Public Record Office, London. For *Senegal* see "Garveyisme" file above; and 3/59 Confidential: Universal Negro Improvement Association: Activities of Representatives of 21 June 1922. Gambia Public Record Office, Banjul. For *Dahomey* see Langley, *op. cit.,*p. 169; and *West African Aspects of the Pan-African Movement* (Clarendon Press, Oxford 197 3), pp. 293-294; M. Crowder, *West Africa Under Colonial Rule* (Hutchinson, London, 1968), pp. 447-448. For Cameroun see Commissioner of the French Republic in the Cameroun Territories to Minister of Colonies. Yaounde, 9 July 1923. SLOTFOM III, 84, 2, op. cit.; R.L. Buell, *The Native Problem in Africa* (Macmillan, New York, 1928), II, p. 304.
17. Hughes, *op. cit.;* AE/II No. 1375 (3240) "Affaire Black Star Line." Archives de l'ex Ministere des Affaires Africaines, Brussels; AF 1-1 (2ieme Serie, 1920-21) and AF 1-17 (Congo/USA 1884-1925) Ministry of Foreign Affais Archives, Brussels; C. Du Bus de Warnaffe "Le mouvement pan-negre aux Etats-Unis et ailleurs," *Congo,* May 1922; "Le Garveyism en action dans notre Colonie." Congo, June-December 1 1921; P. Daye, "Le Mouvement pan-negre." *Le Flambeau* 4, 2, 1921. Shepperson, *op. cit.,* pp. 153-154; Buell, *op. cit.,* II, pp. 601-609; E. Andersson, *Messianic Popular Movements in the Lower Congo* (Translated by D. Burton et al., Kegan Paul, London, 1958), pp. 71, 250-254; Martin, *op. cit.,* p. 116; Langley, "Garveyism...," op. cit, p. 169.
18. E.g., the sensationalist article on an alleged anti-white conspiracy in Africa which appeared in the *African World* (London) as a Supplement to its issue of 30 November 1921, was translated by the Belgian authorities and filed as part of the dossier on the Black Star Line, cited above.
19. E.T. Wilson, *Russia and Black Africa before World War II* (Holmes and Meier, New York/London, 1974), pp. 117-119;146-148; 167-168; 204, ft 258; and Martin, *op. cit.,* Chapter 10.

20. King, *op. cit.*, p. 73.
21. CO 533/277. Northey to Churchill, 4 May 1922.
22. King, *op. cit.*, p. 77.
23. R.I. Rotberg, *The Rise of Nationalism in Central Africa* (Oxford University Press, 1966), p. 125.
24. Shepperson, *op. cit.*, 145.
25. CO 583/109. "Report on U.N.I.A. Activities in Nigeria." 27 February 1922, Public Record Office, London; *Lagos Weekly Record,* 29. 20; 9. 10. 20; 27. 11. 20; 6. 12. 20; Langley, "Garveyism...," *op. cit.*, pp. 159-161; Martin, *op. cit.*, pp. 116-117.
26. Martin, *op. cit.*, p. 143, ft 50. For Obisesan's activities at Ibadan see Geiss, *op. cit.*, pp. 275-278.
27. Macaulay Papers III, 27. Ibadan University Library. It is not clear whether the letter of advice was sent. Macaulay strongly supported the Black Star Line but a confidential report by the Deputy Inspector General of Police in Lagos, dated 28 March 1921, claimed to have seen a letter from Macaulay to his followers advising them to avoid Garveyism because of its treasonable connotations. CO 583/109, *op.cit.*
28. Quoted by Geiss, *op. cit.*, p. 488, ft 65.
29. Langley, "Garveyism...," *op. cit.*, pp. 164-168.
30. Martin, *op. cit.*, p. 116.
31. Hill, *op. cit.*, pp. 51-54-
32. 3/59 UNIA Report, Gambian Archives, *op. cit.*
33. Martin, *op. cit,* 117-121; A.P. Walshe, "The African National Congress of South Africa" (Oxford, Unpublished D. Phil. 1967), 2 Vols. pp. 165-167; 297-305.
34. Martin, *op. cit.*, pp. 118-120.
35. Walshe, *op. cit.*, pp. 302-305; M. Benson, *The African Patriots* (Faber and Faber, London, 1963), pp. 70-72.
36. Walshe, *op. cit.*, pp. 165, 304-305.
37. Martin, *op. cit.*, pp. 137-138.
38. The fullest accounts are those of Martin, *op. cit.*, pp. 122-137; and M.B. Akpan "Liberia and the UNIA: the Background to the Abortion of Garvey's Scheme for African Colonisation," *Journal of African History,* 14, 1973, pp. 105-127. Garvey's own account is to be found in *Philosophy and Opinions* I-II, pp. 352-412.
39. Garvey to King, 5 December 1923. Reproduced in *Philosophy and Opinions,* I-II, p. 368. This was at a time when there were only some 10,000-12,000 Americo-Liberians in a total population of 600,000-700,000. Buell II, op. cit., p. 709.
40. *Philosophy and Opinions* I-II, p. 40.
41. *Akpan, op. cit.*, p. 121.
42. *The African World.* See Martin, *op. cit.*, p. 126.
43. Bruce Papers, *op. cit.* A. Agbebi to J.E. Bruce, 15,18 May;and 25 June 1920. 100,000 shares at 30/- each were offered to Nigerian subscribers as late as June 1921. *Lagos Weekly Record,* 18-25 June 1921, and subsequent issues.

44. For an account of Tete Ansah's career and the implications of his failure see A.G. Hopkins, "Economic Aspects of Political Movements in Nigeria and in the Gold Coast, 1918-1939," *Journal of African History*, 7, 1966, pp. 133-152.

45. B.G.M. Sundkler, *Bantu Prophets in South Africa* (Oxford University Press, 1961), p. 58.

46. R.L. Wishlade, *Sectarianism in Southern Nyasaland* (Oxford University Press, 1965), pp. 141-142.

47. *Op. cit.*, p. 150.

48. Shepperson, *op. cit.*, pp. 153-154.

49. There are numerous reports from UNIA Divisions in Britain to be found in the *Negro World* in the early twenties. The London branch was particularly active while the Manchester Division was presided over by a Sierra Leonian.

50. The most extensive account of Pan-Melanist organizations in France in the interwar period is by J.S. Spiegler, "Aspects of Nationalist Thought among French-Speaking West Africans, 1921-1939" (Oxford. Unpublished D. Phil. 1968). See also Langley, *WestAfrican...*, *op. cit.*, Chapter VII.

51. Spiegler, *op. cit.*, p. 219, ft. 3, "We want a single Negro State, encompassing all of Black Africa, and the West Indies... ," *La Race Negre*, July 1935.

52. According to Vincent, *op. cit.*, p. 283, a CDRN membership card in Garvey's name exists among Mrs. A.J. Garvey's papers. Spiegler mentions that Garvey also subscribed to *La Race Negre* while at Atlanta Prison in 1927. Aspects of Nationalist Thought..., p. 160, ft 6. He adds that during his visit to Paris in 1928 "He may have been received by the LDRN, but evidence conflicts on this point." However, neither Garvey nor *La Race Negre* made any mention of this and there is nothing in French police reports about such a contact.

53. Pan-Africanism..., op. cit., p. 78. Bassude published his favorable impressions of Garvey in an interview in the Swahili newspaper, *Sekanyolya*, January 1922.

54. *Negro World*, 18 August 1928. He claimed to have established a "sub-European head-quarters" in France with a "wing" in Belgium.

55. Le Mouvement pan-negre, *op. cit.*, pp. 371-372.

56. Neither is there any mention of Garvey's visit to Belgium although a visa was normally required to enter the country.

57. Geiss, *op. cit.*, p. 241; Martin, *op. cit.*, p. 127.

58. SLOTFOM III, 84, 2, "Garveyisme." French Consul, Bisso, [sic] to Minister of Colonies, 10 Mars 1921.

59. *Negro World*, 16 June 1923.

60. Cronon, *Black Moses*, Chapter 6, "Days of Decline."

61. R. Lewis, "The Last London Years, 1935-1940," in Clarke, *op. cit.*, pp. 330-341.

62. Lewis, *op. cit.*, pp. 334-335.

63. Ras Makonnen, *Pan-Africanism from Within* (Oxford University Press,

1973), pp. 127-128 states that Garvey's generosity to WASU—a house in Camden—caused some difficulty to this rather middle-aged and conservative association which had links with the Colonial Office. Martin, *op. cit*, p. 143, ft 53, cited an official Colonial Office report of July 1937 stating that after giving the IASB 10/-6 and some advice, Garvey would have nothing further to do with it. This seems quite likely given that George Padmore, a virulent Marxist critic of Garvey, and Amy Ashwood Garvey, Garvey's former wife, were prominent in this organization.

64. *The Black Man,* IV, 1, February 1939.
65. *The Black Man,* Issues 8-10, 1935.
66. *The Black Man,* II, 2, July-August 1937; II, 5, January 1937; II, 6, March-April 1937.
67. *The Black Man,* II, 2, July-August 1937. This was an invitation to the UNIA World Convention of 1920.
68. *The Black Man,* No. 12, March 1936; II, 1, May-June 1936; II, 3, September-October 1936. E.U. Essien-Udom in his introductory comments to Part VII of *Philosophy and Opinions, III,* also detects changes in Garvey's attitude towards the colonial powers; noting his strong aversion to Japan and the European Fascist powers, on the one hand, and the USSR, on the other. He supported a tactical alliance with the USSR to defeat Fascism, the immediate danger to a Western civilization of which he felt part.
69. *Negro World,* 1 August 1925. In an editorial Garvey characterized the period 1914-22 as a radical period "when we spoke out..." but the new policy was to be one of "silent penetration."
70. FO 371/8513. J.C. Smuts to British High Commissioner in South Africa, 28 February 1923. Public Record Office, London.
71. For the international disintegration of the UNIA and its ancillary organizations see Martin, *op. cit.,* pp. 151-214; Cronon, *op. cit.,* Chapters 4-6; Vincent, *op. cit,* Chapter 8.
72. C. Kadalie, My *Life and the ICU* (Edited with an introduction by S. Trapido. Frank Cass, London, 1970), pp. 220-221.
73. Cited in Langley "Garveyism...," *op. cit.,* p. 165.
74. *Times of Nigeria,* 8 November 1920.
75. Cited in Langley, "Garveyism...," *op. cit.,* p. 166.
76. J.G. Campbell, himself an enthusiastic Pan-Africanist, summed up this feeling in an editorial in *The Times of Nigeria,* 24 May 1924, when he stated—"the idea of independence entertained by Africans, at least by British West Africans, certainly does not chime in with that propounded by the Hon. Marcus Garvey... each distinct African nation, while having the most cordial relations with every other sister nation, will infinitely prefer remaining as a separate political entity to being drawn into one huge melting pot of a Universal Negro Empire."
77. Crowder, *op. cit.,* p. 455.
78. His frequently cited letter in the *Revue Indigene,* 1922, p. 275, sums up the attitude of the more conservative section of the French African elite.

79. Spiegler, *op. cit*, Chapter 3, offers several illustrations of Tovalou's assimilationism. This tenacity for French values and attitudes even on the part of race-conscious radicals was noted by Garvey during his French trip in 1928. He wrote of the educated French African: "Because of the privileges allowed him, he has not developed a race consciousness in France as racially helpful as that we have developed in America and other parts...." *Negro World*, 11 August 1928.

80. Principally in the columns of *The Negro Worker*. He also wrote a book, *Life and Struggles of Negro Toilers*, published by the Profintern in 1931, praising the achievements of the African proletariat and dismissing Garvey as a Black bourgeois utopian. For the various shifts and approaches to Soviet policy towards Blacks in these years see Wilson, *loc. cit.*

GARVEY
AND NIGERIA

G. O. Olusanya

One of the external factors which stimulated the development of political consciousness in Nigeria in the post World War I period was the race-conscious organization, the Universal Negro Improvement Association (UNIA), formed and led by Marcus Garvey. To appreciate this fully, it is pertinent to give a short biography[1] of Marcus Garvey himself. Garvey was born in Jamaica, West Indies on August 17,1887. After leaving school he was apprenticed to a printing establishment in Kingston where, as a result of his ability and intelligence, he rose to be a foreman within a short time. While with this establishment Garvey displayed a keen sense of social justice which continued to shape his life until his death. He also displayed an organizing ability which proved very useful to the cause to which he later dedicated himself. In 1907 he was involved in the Printer's Union Strike in which he played a prominent role. Garvey did not need to participate in the strike but his sense of social justice and sympathy for his fellowmen took him into the thick of it. As a foreman at Benjamin's Printery, he was promised an increase in pay if he kept out of the strike. This, however, did not deter him from joining his fellow workers. The strike was not successful and this cost him his job. After this incident he worked for a short time in the

Government Printing Office. He resigned from there to set up a newspaper, *The Watchman*, but the paper collapsed because of financial handicaps. Thereafter, Garvey decided to seek his fortunes in Latin America. This decision took him to Costa Rica, Panama, Ecuador, Nicaragua and other South American countries. Everywhere he went he was dismayed by the conditions of the colored peoples and was angered by the fact that they were heartlessly exploited by the whites and had no means of redress whatsoever. He decided to return to Jamaica in 1911 and awaken Jamaicans at home to the true conditions on the Spanish mainland,[2] but success did not crown his efforts because of lack of cooperation amongst the Negroes themselves and the hostility of white Jamaicans.

Garvey emigrated to England in 1912 in search of better opportunity. Little was he aware that his stay in England would exert the greatest influence on his life and make him a determined champion of the Black race. In London he came into close contact with Africans from different parts of the continent and became keenly aware of the evils of colonialism and the conditions of the African subject race. He was a sensitive and attentive listener to tales of economic exploitation, of racial discrimination, and of white arrogance which were not dissimilar to his experience in the West Indies. His job with Duse Mohammed Ali, the famous Egyptian traveler and journalist, also gave him an opportunity to acquire a fair amount of knowledge of African history, geography and culture. He was also at this period exchanging correspondence with Booker T. Washington and came to realize the suffering and indignities under which Black Americans lived. He came to realize that all Black people needed emancipation and he therefore decided that his life mission was to accomplish this. He returned to Jamaica and established the UNIA and the African Communities Imperial League with the main objective of working for the general uplift of the Black peoples of the world, and of conserving their rights while respecting the rights of all mankind. As in the past Garvey received little or no support in his island home. Meanwhile, he had been invited by Booker T. Washington to the United States on a speaking tour. In 1916 he set out for that country, notwithstanding the fact that Washington himself was by this time dead. Within a short time of his arrival in the United States, he was able to gather the support of a large number of followers from the Black American community because of his sincerity, his passionate belief in the cause which he had chosen and his uncompromising Black nationalism.

By 1920 he had been so successful that he began to receive serious attention from the American Press. In that year he decided to hold a Negro Convention in New York to which were invited Black people from different parts of the world. It was at this Conference that he worked out his scheme of establishing a Black African Government and designated himself "His Excellency the Provisional President of Africa." This Convention brought him to the attention of the whole world, and the journal of his organization, the *Negro World*, was read avidly by Black people throughout the world. So fearful were the colonial powers of the influence of this journal in their colonial territories, that it was banned, and in French West Africa in particular, the possession of the journal was made a capital offense punishable by death. This, however, did not stop its circulation. It only drove it underground.

Garveyism in Nigeria

Garvey's movement caught the imagination of Africans. This was because the socio-politico-psychological climate in Africa favored it. By 1920 the whole of the African continent, except Ethiopia and Liberia, had been parceled out among European colonial powers and Africans had been brought to the reality of colonization with its racial intolerance, economic exploitation and social injustice. They were therefore receptive to any movement which sought to emancipate them from European subjugation. It is therefore not surprising that a branch of the UNIA was organized in Nigeria in 1920. The credit for this goes to Rev. S.M. Abiodun and Rev. W.B. Euba.[3]

The organizers of the Nigerian branch of the movement were however more realistic than Garvey. They were fully aware of the realities of their colonial situation and were conscious of the fact that for the organization to be allowed to exist at all, they had to operate within the framework of the colonial administration and ensure that the movement did not possess an anti-white bias: "We are not against cooperation with the white man; we say that cooperation amongst the Negroes is the first necessity without which it will be futile to try to cooperate with other people." The leaders of the Nigerian Branch emphasized time and time again their abiding loyalty to the British Crown "while at the same time pursuing their course of race advancement with grim determination."[4] They also were aware that Garvey's dream of a Black State in Africa was not destined to find fulfillment. They therefore limited themselves to the objective in which economic freedom could be achieved. This fact was well advertised by the founders: Rev. W.B. Euba emphasized that the Negro should ensure his own advancement in the order of things by his own independent effort, that he had been too dependent on others in the past, and that one of the basic objectives of the new organization was to help the Negro to help himself.[5]

Reactions of the Nigerian Press

At its formation, the Nigerian Press gave the new organization strong support. For instance, the *Nigerian Pioneer,* a pro-government paper, commenting on the limited objectives of the organization, stated:

> Those who formed the UNIA in Nigeria have been attracted by the underlying structure of the movement and not by the details of the methods as worked out by Marcus Garvey himself. Any scheme for better education of the Negroes for business possibilities, for enlargement of scope and outlook of our people is bound to appeal to every right-minded Negro.[6]

But though attracted by the limited aim (self-help) of the Nigerian branch, the newspapers were very critical of the political program of the parent body which they rightly regarded as impracticable, and they seized the opportunity to comment on this at length. The *Times of Nigeria* was enthusiastic about the Nigerian branch and supported its objectives, but criticized at length the political program of the parent body, particularly the idea of a Negro Republic that would absorb all Negroes of the world. It observed that such a program was absurd and would not in any way help the image of the organization. It pointed out that it was certainly the desire of Nigerians that their American brothers should aim at political autonomy since liberty was man's highest right and Africans themselves looked eagerly forward to the day when they would be masters in their own home. It asserted that the request for political freedom was even more urgent in the case of Black Americans who were subjected to all types of hardship and disadvantages, and that it was therefore desirable for them to have a portion of their ancestral land where they would, in freedom, shape their own destiny and spread their own culture among their less enlightened brethren—"de ole folks at home."

It asserted that the idea of independence held by Africans, particularly British West Africans, differed radically from that of Garvey. It concluded:

> If at all that day should come and it must in the process of evolution—when Africa shall be controlled by Africans, each distinct African nation while having the most cordial relations with every other sister nation, will infinitely prefer remaining as a separate political entity to being drawn into one huge melting pot of a universal Negro Empire.[7]

The *Nigerian Pioneer* in its own comment observed that Garvey's
dream of a Pan-Negro Republic was impracticable for the very simple reason that thousands of ethnic groups in any section of Africa
did not at any time regard themselves as one nation—that differences in language, customs and institutions created mental and social
barriers, and as a result, Garvey's dream of the unification of Africa
on the basis of one nationality was incapable of realization. It
observed that Africa might be united as Europe was on the basis of
nationality limited to certain territorial spheres and "not as the whole
continent the sphere and Africa the nation." It pointed out that
Garvey's warlike speech in which he advocated driving out European
powers from Africa would increase racial hostility. It however sym-
pathized with Garvey's attitude, particularly when viewed against
his background— Garvey was a direct descendant of those who had
borne and suffered the horror of slavery in that continent. It observed
however, that when this allowance had been made, Garvey ought to
realize that all Africans were not the same even in the West Indian
Islands and in America, or in any two West Indian Islands, and since
Garvey's scheme ignored this important fact, it could not but fail. It
advocated the adoption of the strategy of the National Association for
the Advancement of Coloured Peoples led by W.E.B. Dubois and
Booker T. Washington's program for Negro emancipation because of
its belief that these methods were already achieving gradually the
very objectives of Garvey. It observed that instead of Garvey working with these men and their groups, he had only succeeded in alien-
ating them. It claimed that the Negro Convention of August 20, 1920
was not representative of the Negro world since no Nigerian
attended and only one Sierra Leonean was there, and even then he
was there as an observer. It then warned Nigerians to beware lest
they be found in bad company while pursuing a patriotic and worthy end. It concluded on a note of loyalty to the British Government,
saying that Nigeria's destiny was closely interwoven with that of the
British Government and that there were mutual objectives between
the British Empire and its African subject race, that Nigerians still
believed that the British system represented a civilizing mission
among them, and their response to this mission would determine in
future their political independence. It further observed that Nigerians
were well aware that the British did not always uphold their best
traditions in the country, but that Nigeria's main consolation was
that whenever any departure occurred, an appeal could be made to
British public opinion which would always be found to be solidly in
their support, and that it was this that ensured for the British
Government the love and loyalty of Nigerians.[8]

These hostilities and reservations expressed by the newspapers regarding the parent body notwithstanding, the Movement began actively to organize itself and was able to acquire some following throughout the country.

Membership

The Movement attracted quite a reasonable following at the onset. Amongst its early members was Ernest Sesei Ikoli who had earlier resigned from his job as Assistant Master at King's College, Lagos, the premier secondary school in Nigeria at that time, because of the treatment meted out to him by the Acting Principal of the School, a Briton. This incident is worth relating to demonstrate our viewpoint that the time was favorable for the reception of Garvey's ideas. Before the start of a football match between King's College ex-students and a European club, Ikoli, an old boy himself and one of the organizers of the match, went to the Principal's Office to collect a ball to be used for the match. The Acting Principal of the School reprimanded him openly in the presence of the students and guests. He took him to task for not obtaining his permission before taking the ball from the Principal's Office. Ikoli felt humiliated and the following day resigned his appointment. He later forcefully stated his case in a letter to the Director of Education, Southern Province, when he wrote:

> This was most aggravating to me as a personal insult and disgrace for which my pride and honor compelled me to seek redress. By addressing me as he did in the presence of the boys, I feel my authority undermined and my influence with the boys minimized.[9]

It is instructive that on leaving King's College, he took up the post of Assistant Editor, *Lagos Weekly Record*, which was at that time the greatest champion of the African cause.

Rev. Euba who was one of the founders of the movement had been attracted to Garvey's scheme of self-help mainly because of his experience with the Methodist Mission. For instance, although he acted as the Principal of the Wesleyan (now Methodist) Boys' High School for a number of years and established a creditable record in that post, nevertheless, the mission refused to confirm him as principal because of his race.[10] To him therefore the only way by which Africans and other Black people could achieve self-respect and dignity was by self-reliance enshrined in Garvey's self-help scheme. As proof of his determination, he founded in 1913 the Eko Boys' High

School, Lagos, which became very successful and is today one of Nigeria's leading secondary grammar schools.

As would normally be expected, it was in Lagos that the movement acquired the largest following. Here was to be found the largest concentration of Western-educated people who were involved in the administrative and commercial activities brought about by the British presence, and who were therefore in direct contact and conflict with the British and with private commercial organizations, very often at a personal level. Being more closely in touch with Europeans on the spot, they were also more exposed to racial arrogance and intolerance on the part of Europeans and therefore more sensitive to a movement of this nature. There was no organized membership of the body outside Lagos, but there were individuals throughout the length and breadth of the country who became either members or sympathizers of the organization, although such membership was limited to West Indians, educated Southern Nigerians and other Africans of this class resident in the North.

The Reaction of the Colonial Government and Colonial Administration

When the news of the formation of the Lagos Branch of the UNIA reached London, the Colonial Office took the matter seriously. This was due to a number of reasons. Firstly, Garvey, the founder of the parent body, had already attracted the attention of the British Government to himself in 1920 when, during the Negro Convention in New York, he declared the support of his organization for the Irish Revolutionary leader, De Valera, and for the Irish Movement for Independence. This had won him the hostility of the British Government. Secondly, Garvey's pronouncement that the objective of his movement was "Africa for the Africans" and that the movement would, if necessary, employ force to drive out the white man from Africa did not, of course, endear him and his movement to the colonial powers, not because they feared that he was capable of carrying out his boast but because his movement might gain ground and provide some difficult moments for them in their colonial territories. This of course made the British Government hostile. The hostility and fear were clearly demonstrated by the reaction of the British Government to Garvey's demand for a passport to visit West Africa on a speaking tour so as to correct misrepresentations of the aims of his organization. His application was rejected by the Colonial Office on the ground that his visit would lead to more unrest in the territory. They observed that although Garvey had more following in the

United States and in Britain than in West Africa, it was (nevertheless) in Africa that he hoped to establish his Negro State. Consequently, his aim would be to stir up trouble and to incite sedition. It was further stated, without any justification whatsoever, that all Garvey wanted in the West Indies was money, and that this might probably be his chief objective in Africa too, and that for him to achieve this, it would be necessary to create an atmosphere of unrest not conducive to peaceful colonial rule.[11]

The Nigerian administration, taking its cue from the attitude of the Colonial Government, was equally hostile to Garvey's demand for permission to visit West Africa. The administration, like the Colonial Office, stated without any basis that Garvey would utilize such a visit to collect further sums of money on false pretenses from the semi-educated Africans of the West Coast. A ban was placed on the importation of the *Negro World* which was described as "coming within the category of seditious, defamatory, scandalous, or demor- alizing literature."[12] Thirdly, the activities of the various branches in other parts of Africa convinced the British Government that all branches of the UNIA were subversive. For instance, an attempt had been made by the parent body to settle some Black Americans in Liberia. This attempt failed because of the justifiable opposition of the Movement to the Firestone Rubber Company, an American business organization operating in Liberia and a symbol of white economic exploitation of Africans and therefore totally opposed to Garvey's aims and objectives. To make matters worse, Garvey spared no pains in attacking in the most virulent language the Liberian Government which he rightly described as the puppet of American imperialists. All this led the Liberian President to change his attitude, and the result was that the scheme did not materialise.[13] Moreover, the branch of the UNIA which was established at Rufisque in Senegal as a result of the initiative of Sierra Leoneans such as Francis Webster, Farmer Dougherty, H.W. Wilson and John Kamara, became so active in disseminating the ideas of the parent body that the French colonial authorities became very worried, so much so that the members of the organization were kept under constant surveillance and the branch was in the end suppressed.[14]

All these factors led the British Government to take the Garveyite movement seriously. Thus when news of the formation of the Nigerian branch of the Movement was received in London, a secret despatch was sent to Sir Hugh Clifford inquiring about its activities.[15] On receiving the despatch, the Governor and his Executive became anxious and took immediate decision to investi- gate the Movement. Clifford requested the Lieutenant-Governors and the Deputy Inspector-General of Police to report on the activities of the organization.

The Lieutenant-Governor of the Southern Provinces, H.C. Morehouse, in his own report claimed that though an American Negro by the name Cockburn, formerly of the Marine Department, had been appointed the commercial agent in Nigeria of Garvey's Black Star Shipping Line, the Association had not made much progress and that if it became discredited in the United States, as it probably would, the Nigerian branch of the Movement would gradually peter out. This was indeed prophetic. The Lieutenant-Governor of the Northern province, W.F. Gowers, stated that copies of the *Negro World* were circulated amongst Africans and West Indians to a limited extent in some provinces in the North, mainly Kano, Minna, Ilorin, but that the possibility of the movement gaining ground amongst the indigenous Northerners was very remote.[16] This was not surprising for the Northern Nigerian at that time was still greatly sheltered from the inroads of Western forces, and thereby to some extent free from the frustrations of a subject people in a colonial situation.

The Deputy Inspector-General of Police in his own report stated that a number of Nigerians had purchased shares in the Black Star Shipping Line and that a branch of the UNIA had been formed in Nigeria, with its Headquarters at 72, Tinubu Square, Lagos; that its president was Wynter Shackleford, a West Indian employed by S. Thomas & Company, and its first Secretary, Ernest Ikoli, editor and manager of the *African Messenger.* He claimed that Ikoli was succeeded as Secretary in 1922 by Rev. Ajayi of the Church Missionary Society. He also claimed that the Movement membership was 300, although financial members as a result of heavy subscription fees and levies, were only 28; that the Movement owned a brass band for the purposes of playing the UNIA Anthem—"Ethiopia Land of my Father," and that the Nigerian agent of the industrial arm of the organization was Mr. Agbebi. He further claimed that Nigerians were opposed to the Movement and substantiated this by stating that he was in possession of a private letter written from London by Herbert Macaulay, the founder of the Nigerian National Democratic Party (NNDP) and the leading nationalist of the period, to a friend in Lagos advising him not to have anything to do with the Movement as it was "perilously near the borderline of treason and sedition." Finally, he stated that Ernest Ikoli had resigned from the organization on the grounds that he was opposed to the political aims of the movement, though he strongly believed in the industrial scheme.[17]

The Deputy Inspector-General of Police therefore came to the conclusion that the movement did not constitute a threat to peace and stability in the country and that, as its leaders expected, most of its members were apathetic and the general public indifferent because, as he put it, they were aware that they were much better off under British rule and had no desire whatsoever to change this for American Negro rule.[18]

On the basis of information provided by the three officials, Governor Clifford reported back to the Colonial Office that the Nigerian branch of the Movement was ineffective and consequently harmless.[19]

Obstacles to Success

The Nigerian branch of the UNIA was not able to achieve concrete results for a number of reasons. First was the hostility of the British Government and the local administration to the Movement as demonstrated above—hostility which did not disappear until it was found that the organization was harmless. Second was that some organizations and institutions in Nigeria were opposed to the organization and did their best to frustrate its efforts, the most important being the Nigerian Branch of the National Congress of British West Africa (NCBWA) and the *Nigeria Pioneer*—a pro-government paper. This was partly due to the fact that many members of the NCBWA tended to base their judgment of the local branch on the objectives of the parent body rather than on the group's own limited objectives, and partly because they saw in the organization a rival to their own movement. They were of the opinion that all efforts should be concentrated on the NCBWA, which they regarded as the best institution for achieving Nigeria's political objectives. They therefore believed that the existence of the UNIA in Nigeria when the NCBWA was still struggling to find its feet was undesirable. Also, the Accra Conference which led to the formation of the NCBWA had endorsed Garvey's economic program, which was the main objective of the Nigerian Branch, therefore the Nigeria Branch of the UNIA should disband itself and its members be absorbed into the NCBWA. The refusal of the UNIA to commit suicide led to their hostility against it, and it became common amongst NCBWA members to claim that it was not right for any loyal British subject to take part in the political program and aspirations of the American Negroes.[20]

Moreover, some members of the NCBWA were convinced that the existence of a branch of the UNIA in Nigeria might deter the colonial administration from granting political concessions being demanded by the NCBWA. This belief was based on the hostile attitude of the Government to the UNIA, an attitude well advertised by the *Nigerian Pioneer* which had by this time become intensely hostile to the organization and had begun a campaign of hatred and destruction. In an editorial of December 17, 1920, the *Pioneer* carried a bitter attack on Marcus Garvey himself. It stated that the Jamaican, Garvey, who had no success in his own country, had migrated to the United States to reap where he had not sown, because he possessed a silver tongue and was therefore able to rally round him a number of American Negroes who, like himself, wanted to make hay while the sun shone. The paper ridiculed Garvey's assumption of the title "His Excellency the Provisional President of Africa" and his creation of an African nobility and an African Orthodox Church, all of which were considered inconsistent with republican ideals. It concluded: "If only Gilbert and Sullivan were still collaborating, what a splendid theme for a musical opera Garvey's pipe dream would be."[21] The *Pioneer* was also very much concerned with the circulation and influence of the *Negro World*, the journal of the UNIA. It was of the opinion that its circulation might incite Nigerians to political insurrection, and it therefore called on the colonial administration to ban it. It asserted:

> In order to further his (Garvey's) scheme, and incidentally to get in the *shekels*, the paper called the *Negro World* is sent to all places where Africans most do congregate.... We must still warn the Government that these copies may do incalculable harm amongst those who, whilst able to read, will not understand aright. The paper may also be read to the illiterates and in the hands of a frothy-mouthed agitator, generally a man of no substance, such a sheet could be used to the detriment of good government and perhaps eventually prove the direct cause of disorders, when the real culprits would, if possible, flee the country, whilst their dupes would bear the brunt of the clearing-up process.[22]

The paper claimed, without authority, that Nigerians were not yet ripe for substantial political progress because, according to it, Lagos and a few other towns might be described as civilized; but, it asked: "What of the teeming millions along the coastland and hinterland?" It asserted that the British Government had demonstrated (though it never stated by what means) that it would be prepared to grant political concession to Nigerians if demanded by a fully representative body (which did not exist). It condemned Garvey's slogan "Africa for Africans" as "bunkum and foolish twaddle." It cited the political conditions of Haiti and Santo Domingo which were described as lands of unrest, groping in darkness, corruption and fetishism, and contrasted this with Jamaica where it claimed representative

Government existed. This comparison was made in order to demonstrate that the white man's influence was necessary if Africans were to attain political maturity. It then concluded: "The truth is that Garveyism is both fatuous and futile, and whilst beyond the dream of practical politics is not beyond the dream of avarice. We desire and must have for many years yet government as it is now."[23] It is obvious that this was a government-sponsored paper claiming to speak for a people it did not represent.

Provoked by the *Pioneer's* unwarranted and virulent attacks on Garvey and his movement, and irritated by its self-assumed championship of the interests of Nigerians, the *Lagos Weekly Record* came out to defend the cause of the UNIA. It praised the aims of the Lagos branch of the Movement and poured scorn on those who were hostile to it.

> These certainly are not the aims any man can find fault with. To us they are neither traitor nor revolutionary, neither fantastic nor visionary, and it is iniquitous to label a class of men who profess such aims as traitors and foolishness to think them insane.[24]

However, true to its objectivity, the paper (at the same time) called into question the political program of the parent body:

> While we Nigerians will hesitate to endorse the political program of Marcus Garvey with its aggressive militaristic tendencies, we entertain no doubts whatever in the soundness of the doctrine of world-wide cooperation among Negroes for their economic and industrial uplift. There is far more in this than we can see at present under the leadership such as the local organization can boast of at present. We have no doubt of the good that will ultimately come from it.[25]

Caught in such cross fire, it is not surprising that the Nigerian branch of the Movement was short-lived. It became discredited because of the imprisonment of Marcus Garvey for an alleged mail fraud in connection with the sale of stocks in his Black Star Shipping Line in 1925. This virtually destroyed the faith of people in the Movement. After 1925 the Movement quickly disappeared from the Nigerian political scene.

An Assessment of its Influence

It is obvious from what has been said above that the Movement existed for a very short period, barely five years, and that in terms of concrete achievement there is nothing to record in its favor. But it would be wrong to believe that it exerted no influence on the political development in Nigeria. Achievement can be viewed from two angles: practical and inspirational, and it is to the second that we must turn if we are to grasp the significance of the UNIA in the history of Nigerian politics. There is no doubt that it contributed its own quota to the race consciousness which was already rapidly developing in Nigeria as a result of the racial intolerance of the British Raj, and that it inspired some very key Nigerians such as Ernest Ikoli and Dr. Azikiwe who played very significant roles in the nationalist struggle for freedom from the thirties. Dr. Azikiwe himself admits this:

> The motto of Garveyism appealed to me: "One God, One Aim, One Destiny"—and I resolved to formulate my philosophy of life, as far as practicable, towards the evangelization of the universal Fatherhood, universal Brotherhood and universal Happiness.[26]

Dr. Azikiwe summed up the influence of the Movement upon him, on another occasion, when he asserted: "Marcus Garvey's epigram (sic) made me ambitious to serve Africa." His influence on Nigerian politics was given full expression at his death in 1940 when Dr. Azikiwe's *West African Pilot* editorialized:

> Marcus Garvey has lived and died leaving an indelible impression of his footprints on the sands of time which neither the forces of space nor those of time can obliterate for ever... He revolted against the idea that the African was destined to take the back seat for ever. He refused to admit the alleged inferiority of the African. He poo-poohed all ideas which identified Black people as inferior beings. And throughout his short life (he died at the age of fifty) he inspired Africans to regard their Black complexions with pride and to develop race-consciousness so as to look forward to a place under the sun. Marcus Garvey was the fountain from which sprung (sic) other more scientific, constructive and effective ideas of Pan-Africanism. His memory should be revered by all those who believe in the future of Africa.[27]

Notes

1.   This is based on Amy Jacques Garvey, *Garvey and Garveyism*, Collier Books, New York, 1970.
2.   Amy Jacques Garvey, *op. cit.*, p. 7.
3.   *Lagos Weekly Record*, 29 November 1920, cited in G.O. Olusanya, "Notes on the Lagos Branch of the Universal Negro Improvement Association" *The Journal of Business and Social Studies*, 1: 2, March 1969, p. 136.

4. *Ibid.*
5. *Lagos Weekly Record,* 27 November, 1920, also Olusanya, *op. cit.*
6. *Nigerian Pioneer,* 19 October 1920. Cited in Olusanya, *op. cit.*
7. *Times of Nigeria,* 24 May 1920. Cited in Olusanya, *op. cit.*
8. *Nigerian Pioneer,* 22 October 1920. Cited in Olusanya, *op. cit.*
9. Cited in F.I.A. Omu, *Pioneer Heroes of the Nigerian Press* (Unpublished), p. 33.
10. See Olusanya, *op. cit.,* p. 134.
11. C.O. 583/118/34197/ of 9/7/1923 (Nigerian Confidential).
12. *Ibid.*
13. *African World,* 1923, pp. 124-5.
14. R.C. Maugham, British Consulate General, Dakar to His Excellency the Governor of Gambia. 15/6/1922/Confidential No. 348/255/ 22, Gambia 3/59 Confidential M.P. No. 727. I am indebted to Dr. J.A. Langley for this reference.
15. C.O. 583/109/281/28194 of 22 February 1922.
16. *Ibid.*
17. *Ibid.*
18. *Ibid.*
19. *Ibid.*
20. Olusanya, *op. cit.,* pp. 138-139.
21. *Nigerian Pioneer,* 17 December 1920. Also Olusanya *op. cit.,* p. 139.
22. *Ibid.*
23. *Ibid.*
24. *Lagos Weekly Record,* 27 November 1920, see also Olusanya op. cit., p. 140.
25. *Ibid.*
26. Cited in K.A.B. Jones-Quartey, *A Life of Azikiwe,* Penguin, 1965, p. 29.
27. *West African Pilot,* 23 May 1940. See also Olusanya, op. cit., pp. 141-142.

MARCUS GARVEY
AND THE LEAGUE OF NATIONS,
1921-1931
AN EPISODE IN THE
INTERNATIONAL
RELATIONS OF THE U.N.I.A.

George Huggins

Between 1921 and 1931 Marcus Garvey, on behalf of the UNIA, approached the League of Nations several times on questions relating to the four hundred million Africans the world over that the UNIA claimed to represent. The Association sent two delegations to the League Assembly, in 1922 and 1928, presented two Petitions in those years, and generally sought diverse means to bring African problems and aspirations before the world assembly of nations. This excursion of Garvey into international diplomacy is one of the lesser known and researched aspects of the vast and complex history of the UNIA. Yet these efforts are worth examination; not only because they illustrate another dimension to this history, but particularly because they shed light on the hostile international structures which the

UNIA had to challenge in its campaign for Africa and Africans. Mrs. Garvey herself made few references to the relations with the League, the most extensive being a mere page in *Garvey and Garveyism*.[1] A scrutiny of the Garvey and the UNIA files at the Archives of the League in Geneva, Switzerland, reveals however a somewhat lengthy correspondence between Garvey and Sir Eric Drummond, Secretary General of the League, and Mr. Rappard, Director of the Mandate Section, as well as notes and minutes of the international civil servants of the League. Together they give a good picture of the hostility, indifference or misunderstanding Garvey had to face.

Garvey's First Approach

Garvey's first approach to the League dates from 1 August 1921. It was a cable to the Secretary General of the League carrying the text of a resolution voted by the Second Convention of the Negroes of the World, intended for "universal circulation in Europe, America and Africa."[2] It was a long text of over 750 words aimed primarily against the intended Pan African Congress by W.E.B. Du Bois. Garvey and Du Bois were bitter enemies. The latter's strategy, based on leadership of Negroes by the "talented tenth"—the intellectual and social elite of Black America—estranged him from the masses. It was partly this strategy, so opposed to Garvey's own, as well as personal jealousy, which created the enmity between the two. The Congress to be held in London, Paris and Brussels in August and September had been greatly publicized by Du Bois. In July he had written the Secretary General of the League, through the Bureau International pour la Défense des Indigènes in Geneva, asking him to present the resolutions of the Congress to the General Assembly of the League due to be held in September. Du Bois intended to visit the League himself as part of a Commission which would be created at the Congress in Paris.[3] Garvey got word of these plans and sought to forestall them—hence the strongly, yet soberly, worded cable. It is perhaps ironical that this first contact with the League should have been prompted by his enemy, to forestall an action Garvey would himself undertake later.

A second cable followed a month after, in September, protesting "the distribution of lands of Africa by the Supreme Council and the League of Nations among white nations of the world."[4] Africa, Garvey asserted, was for Africans, just as Asia was for Asians and Europe for Europeans. He included a veiled threat of wars to come since Africans demanded their rightful place in the sun. He claimed the right of four hundred million Africans to a nation of their own, in the homeland of Africa. It was the first statement to the League of an idea he would repeat often. On the sixth of that month Du Bois made a visit, as head of a delegation, to the League, and this provoked another incensed telegram from Garvey.[5] He asked the Secretary General to "repudiate any requests made of the League by representatives of a so-called Pan African Congress who are self-appointed and self-seeking," and confirmed his two former telegrams. None of these cables brought any positive action beyond acknowledgment. The League received the delegation of the Pan African Congress, and Du Bois held talks with Rappard, Albert Thomas, then Head of the International Labour Office, and Dantes Bellegarde, Haitian Delegate to the League Assembly.[6] Two sets of resolutions voted at the Pan African Congress were published as an official communique and distributed to the Council and Secretariat. The contents were not debated at the Assembly and consequently no action was taken on their proposals. These were threefold:1. that a section be set up at the I.L.O. to deal particularly with the needs of Negro labor; 2. that a man of Negro descent be appointed to the Mandates Commission; 3. that an "International Institute for the study of the Negro Problem and for the Evolution and Protection of the Negro Race" be created by the Colonial Powers at the instigation of the League.[7] Garvey and Du Bois were never more apart.

In May 1922, Garvey informed the Secretary General of the forthcoming Third Annual Convention and the plans to elect a deputation of representative Negroes to attend the Assembly and to present the case of Africans to the Member States.[8] This approach was different from the impersonal ones that preceded. The Secretariat was at a loss as to how to treat the letter. A request for information on the UNIA was made to the Library. It turned up little: a note on the Conference in New York in 1921 (Garvey's second Convention) and one in London (Du Bois' Pan African Congress), but could not distinguish clearly between them. Of Garvey the note said: "Mr. Garvey's organization seems to be of a much more radical and even violent character... and is not supported by the best Negro element in the States."[9] On the basis of this adverse comment the original draft reply to Garvey's letter was amended. The original said in part:

> Should you decide to send representatives to Geneva during the month of September, I shall endeavour to find time to see them myself, and would, in any case, put them in touch with officials of the Secretariat.[10]

This was changed to:

> The Agenda of the Assembly consists of questions put before it by
> States Members of the League. There is, however, nothing to pre-
> vent your Association from communicating to the Delegates of the
> States represented at the Assembly a memorial stating forth any
> facts to which the Association might wish to give publicity. [11]

This terminology was seen as a compromise, which avoided "the
danger of the Secretariat usurping powers it did not have"[12] while
giving the addressees some slight satisfaction. One of the criticisms
against the original was precisely that "it may arouse hopes or results
which *will not, in fact,* be achieved, [my emphasis] and the delegation
may, therefore, go away with a feeling of disappointment and bitterness."[13] Even the slight satisfaction the amendment was supposed
to bring was to be denied the UNIA, as the final copy accepted held
out no offer of a meeting or of distribution of a memorial. Its relevant
paragraph ran thus:

> As regards your wish that a delegation of your Association should
> be heard by the Assembly, I have to inform you that the agenda of
> the Assembly consists of questions submitted by the States
> Members of the League and that the rules of procedure do not pro-
> vide for the hearing of delegations other than those officially rep-
> resenting such States Members.[14]

We have chosen to deal at some length with this matter of reply by
the League Secretariat because it indicates the trend of thinking which
marked the Secretariat in its relations with Garvey and the UNIA. The
international civil servants were particularly cautious, above all with
questions that involved internal disputes of Member States. The
major reason which seemed to prompt the alterations is expressed in
this minute:

> It is likely that the complaints voiced may come under the category
> of the interior affairs of States Members. Further, as the presence
> of a Negro delegation will be a novelty, it will be referred to by the
> Press—especially the American Press—and it might antagonize
> many of our friends in America.[15]

Even though the U.S.A. was not a Member of the League its influence
was strong, in part because the very idea of a League had originated
there. Added to the professional caution of these men was their lack

of sympathy with the "Negro question," as they termed it. The majority of these people were recruited from their national civil services, and primarily from offices dealing with European or North Atlantic affairs. A man like William Rappard who headed the Mandates Section, a Swiss national, had had little contact with the colonial world. Yet, if the hands of the Secretariat were tied, as was claimed, a means to introduce a petition and arrange meetings could have been found, had the political will to do so existed.

Self-Determination for Africans

The Third Convention was duly held in New York in August of 1922 and a Petition in fourteen points was drawn up. It was intended that the delegation to the League Assembly referred to in Garvey's letter should present the Petition to States Members, were they allowed. The Petition called for a Government for Africans to be formed in the homeland of Africa. In more precise terms it said:

> Your Petitioners pray that you may grant to us for the purpose of racial development the Mandates now given to the Union of South Africa: namely German East Africa and German South West Africa [today Tanzania and Namibia]. We feel that if the League will pass over to our control as a race the development of these two later German colonies we shall be able, within 20 years, to prove to the world and to the League our ability to govern ourselves.[16]

It was not such a novel idea. Three years earlier Du Bois had also conceived of the idea of an Internationalized Africa, whereby the former German colonies at first, then parts of Belgian and Portuguese Africa, would come under the control of an international government, representing "not simply the white world but the civilized Negro world."[17] This was as far as Du Bois had then got in self-determination for Africans. Garvey's plan was bolder by far. In 1922, also, an American Senator proposed the idea that the U.S. could get rid of its "surplus colored population"[18] by exporting it to Africa. Where in Africa? Precisely in the former German colonies now ruled by Britain, France and Belgium, in exchange for which the United States would wipe off the Allied War Debts owed to her. Although it was a vicious white American way to keep America white and did not please the majority of Black Americans, Garvey accepted the proposal, since it fitted so neatly with his own plans. Garvey was undoubtedly influenced by such views in the drafting of his Petition. However, Senator French's views got little support, either from those whites who looked carefully at the cheap labor force Afro-Americans still were, or from the integrationist-minded Afro-Americans. At any rate, the Mandates were already established and it would have entailed a massive effort to change them.

The delegation of the UNIA was a high-powered one, headed by G.O. Marke, and comprising also Jean-Joseph Adam, secretary and interpreter, William Le Van Sherrill and James O'Meally. Marke had been elected Deputy Potentate of Africa, a position which ranked him second only to the Supreme Potentate, but placed him immediately above Garvey himself as President General of the UNIA and Provisional President of Africa. Today these posts would be roughly equivalent to Head of State, Deputy Head of State and Head of Government. Like other aspects of the UNIA, these posts were intended to lay the structures for government. The four delegates arrived in Geneva on the 11th September and the following day wrote to request a meeting with the Secretary General.[19] Each bore a letter of credentials from the UNIA with the seal of the Association, attesting their quality as diplomats of this body. In his reply the Secretary General chose to be evasive and "diplomatic." He regretted not being able to see them because of the "calls upon [his] time by the simultaneous meetings of the Council and of the Assembly, together with the work necessary for the preparation of those meetings and the execution of the decisions taken."[20] He asked Rappard, and Colban, Director of the Administrative Commission and Minorities Section, to see them.

In the meanwhile the delegates had begun lobbying among the various delegations to the League Assembly. One man who agreed to receive them was Dantes Bellegarde, the Haitian Envoy Extraordinary and Minister Plenipotentiary. He suggested they would have a better reception from Rappard, and on the 15th of September Marke wrote the latter, even before the reply came from the Secretary General making this very proposal.[21] This was to cause a minor confusion. Marke had entrusted his "purely private and informal letter to Rappard" to two members of the delegation, asking them to deliver it personally to its addressee. Rappard, with the contents of the Secretary General's reply in mind, received them and held a discussion which he interpreted to be the meeting referred to in the reply. Marke was incensed, and saw things quite differently. As far as he was concerned these talks could in no way be construed as the meeting requested in his own letter of 15th or Drummond's letter, equally of the 15th. The 16th was a Saturday, and the following week Marke wrote to Drummond to explain his views, asking him to "exercise [his] good offices in respect of the Petition ... so that it may without further delay be submitted to the Assembly."[22]

Marke had every right to be angry over the interview that Rappard held with Sherrill and Adam. It was certainly not the meeting he had asked for, and which, in fact, had been agreed to. As head of the delegation he had a right to courtesy from the League Secretariat, even if it was felt that the members of the Secretariat could comfortably depart from the rules of protocol, not having to deal with a delegation of a sovereign state. Drummond's letter sent off on Friday evening at earliest could not have been received before the 18th. It is difficult to ascertain whether Rappard sought this easy way out or was sincere in his mistake. His report to Drummond on the meeting sheds partial light. Rappard evidently took the matter lightly, and the mild irony running through his report tends to suggest he shrugged off the whole affair and tried to finish it easily with the meeting.[23] Colban "accepted to be present for part of the interview," showing it was far from the official meeting with these two men that had been promised. He was of the opinion that the two delegates "seemed preoccupied particularly to receive an official document from the League to show their mandators explaining the failure of their mission." He agreed to write to Marke. A copy of the letter, he said to Drummond, he was "pleased — and courageous enough! —to join to this report." The strange term: "courageous enough" is ample testimony to our mind of his lack of serious concern.

These efforts failed but Marke sought a new approach. On September 28th he wrote the Head of the Persian Delegation, asking him to present the text, on their behalf, to the League Assembly. His Highness Prince Arfa ed Dowlah wrote an ambiguous letter on the question to Secretary General Drummond.[24] He refrained from taking position on the terms of the Petition but felt "it would be in the interest of the League of Nations not to refuse a right to Petition to the numerous organizations which placed a sincere hope in our League." "That is why," the letter continued, "we ask Your Excellency to judge if it would be possible to submit a copy of this Petition to each of the Delegations present." The note contained in annex 70 copies of the Petition. Rappard, who received the letter, took the decision to agree to the request and so informed the Persian Ambassador. Drummond was hopping mad. In a stern internal note to Rappard, he correctly pointed out that the letter asked for an opinion and did not constitute a formal request.[25] He would have preferred Rappard to say that circulation was not possible unless formally requested by a member state, in which case he felt the Persian Delegate "would not have pressed the point... We must be very careful about circulating documents from non representative organizations," he concluded. Rappard countered by saying he read the note as a specific request but he was somewhat shaken by the incident.

Why did Marke approach the Persian Delegation? The only other sympathetic sovereign countries were Haiti, Liberia and Ethiopia. Of these, Liberia was a foundation member of the League, but ineffective, and Ethiopia became a member in September 1923 only. Haiti would certainly have been willing, but with its economy and foreign affairs controlled by the Americans since 1916, it could not dare such a step that would antagonize the Americans. But further, the UNIA had already made contacts with Persian diplomats. At the Third Convention a month earlier, the Persian Consul General in the United States, who represented Abyssinia there, read a personal message from the King and Queen of Abyssinia to the elated participants of the Convention. Marke reminded Prince Arfa ed Dowlah of the incident and certainly influenced him this way.

The net result of three weeks of lobbying and effort in Geneva was minimal. The League Secretariat distributed the Petition, and had a notice to this effect inserted in the official journal of the League. There is no reason to believe that the member states even considered it seriously, if their delegations read it at all. It is difficult to envisage what could have happened in fact. No colonial power would have offered an inch of their African territories, and would not have dared to recall the spoils of war given out to South Africa. In many respects Du Bois' requests were more immediately feasible, yet even these met with little positive response. Garvey had failed before he started, but could not easily admit or realize this. The logic of the UNIA's dynamism forced him to draw up and present such a Petition. An official of the Secretariat having to work out the seating arrangements for the four-man delegation sized up the dilemma of Garvey better than many others: "They have a real case which we cannot totally ignore and should not greatly encourage. Seats for the Assembly would seem to be the least, and the most, we can do."[26] It was little indeed.

The following year Jean-Joseph Adam was again elected as a delegate to the Assembly, but apparently did not attend. 1923 was a difficult year for the UNIA. The Federal Government had begun its lawsuit against Garvey. No Convention was held that year as Garvey was in prison during August, Convention month. The following year, 1924, all that came out of the 4th Convention was a reminder to the League of the 1922 Petition and a call for immediate action on its terms. By 1925 Garvey was committed to prison, and was deported two years later. The backbone of the UNIA was broken.

Final Attempts

In 1928 Garvey went to London to try to reactivate the international movement. The Head Office still remained in New York but a European Headquarters was established in London, with a sub-European Headquarters in Paris, while the Foreign Head Office was in Kingston. A new Petition was drafted that year, far more lengthy than the former.[27] It gave a long description of the subjection and exploitation Africans suffered and the failure of colonization to live up to the lofty ideals of the Berlin Decree of 1885. It included a detailed, accurate list of prohibitive and discriminatory laws against Africans in South Africa. The Union of South Africa was the main target of the UNIA attack, explained by the fact that Garvey again sought the transfer of the South African mandated territories to the UNIA. No new requests were included but those of the 1922 Petition, included integrally in the text, were reconfirmed.

At the same time Garvey undertook to write to each delegation to the Assembly, enclosing copies of the Petition and requesting the support of the delegation when the Petition was brought before the house. It was an excellent initiative, although few delegations did more than acknowledge receipt of the letter. South Africa's reply is well worth quoting in part:

> ... The South African Delegation supported by its Government will always resolutely uphold the ideals of the League, one of which is the speaking of Truth.
> On this account, therefore, the South African Delegation is precluded from rendering your Petition the assistance sought.[28]

One Government's token assistance, if indeed it were conceived as such, entailed sending Garvey's letter with a covering note to the League Secretariat. Garvey was not contented with this, but had also planned a campaign of direct support from individuals in the United States and the West Indies. Between the 19 October 1928 and the 22 October 1931 no fewer than 63 letters came from individuals and groups to the League Secretariat asking that the terms of the Petition be considered. Many of the letters bore hundreds of signatures, and several letters coming from the United States were identical, suggesting close coordination or concerted planning. A pathos and frustration runs through many of these. One from Cuba went thus:

...We respectfully beg to consider us the Four hundred Million Negroes who is [sic] without a Government of our own and we sincerely ask you pay attention to our President General ['s] Petition; who represent [sic] us, to witch [sic] we are perfectly satisfied. We your Petitioners lay at your feet our grievances and sorrows to plead before you for justice.[29]

An American from New York wrote:

... I feel that we should be given some part of Africa that we may form a government of our own. We believe down [in] our heart that Africa is ours [by] God-given right. We are prepared even to die for it if possible ....[30]

Neither these efforts nor the others brought any success to Garvey. The Petition was never discussed. In 1929 Garvey had visited Geneva and tried in vain to have meetings with League officials. Two years later, on a visit to Europe from Jamaica where he had established himself once more, he visited the League and succeeded in having talks with one of the League's Secretariat members. Garvey inquired of the action that would, or could, be taken on the 1928 Petition. In reply the official brought him up-to-date on the achievements of the Mandates Commission—a slim satisfaction in the way of an answer, and gave him a copy of a letter of 1928 confirming that the copies of the Petition had been distributed and a note to this effect inserted in the journal of the Ninth Assembly.

Ten years of discussions and battling with the League had resulted in slim accomplishments. Why? The reasons are to be found far less in any inherent faults of Garvey or the UNIA than in the structures in which they had to fight. The major weakness lay in the fact that Garvey represented no government—and the League was the sacred preserve of nation-states. The lack of a sovereign state denied him direct access to the League. It was a tragic illustration of the very principle Garvey held dear: that nationhood, including sovereignty and government, is the only means whereby the race can protect itself. Because he did not have this single all-important factor, Garvey was as impotent as a child despite the four hundred million backing he claimed. Within these limits, Garvey played the game well. The essence of a good diplomat may be seen as the capacity to prepare a good brief, a knowledge of the other party, and the ability to use all the means at one's disposal in presenting one's case. On all these counts Garvey acted creditably; it was lack of real power that failed him.

Today the successor body to the League, the United Nations Organization, is far more open to such bodies as the UNIA. Nationalist leaders have been invited to appear before the General Assembly to present their case, while the Committee of 24 on Decolonization sits permanently to accelerate the decolonization of the remaining dependent territories. Other organizations, such as the Organization of African Unity, have granted observer status, and at times full participant status, to nationalist and liberation groups in various conferences and in General Assembly. It is no exaggeration to say that there is an indirect co-relation between these later achievements and Garvey's efforts. Indeed it was primarily at the insistence of African governments that these attempts to hasten decolonization have been undertaken. In these efforts, one name, among many others, stands out: Kwame Nkrumah. The late Ghanaian President and unyielding Pan-Africanist has often borne testimony to the inspiration he drew from Garvey in the evolution of his own Pan-African thought. From Garvey to Nkrumah through men like George Padmore, C.L.R. James, and Isaac Wallace Johnson,[31] there is a virtually unbroken tradition of militancy, and of harassment of the structures imperialist nations have erected. One such was the League of Nations. Garvey put faith in it, tried to negotiate with it and harangued it, with little overall success. Still, the spirit of his effort lived on, and in time bore fruit among these other leaders. Africa and Africans have been well served by Marcus Garvey.

Notes

1. Amy Jacques Garvey, *Garvey and Garveyism,* New York, Collier Macmillan, 1974, pp. 105-6.
2. UNIA to League of Nations, 1 Aug. 1921, League of Nations Archives, 1/14410.
3. W.E.B. Du Bois, *The Autobiography of W.E.B. Du Bois,* New York, International Publishers, 1969, pp. 271-2.
4. UNIA to League, 2 Sept. 1921, League of Nations Archives, 1/15345.
5. *Ibid.,* 7 Sept. 1921, League of Nations Archives, 1/15499.
6. W.E.B. Du Bois, *The World and Africa,* 2nd ed., New York, International Publishers, 1965, p. 240.
7. *Ibid.*
8. UNIA to League, 23 May 1922, UN Archives 1/21159.
9. League of Nations Archives 1.21159.
10. Draft Reply of League of Nations, 8 June 1922, League of Nations Archives 21159.
11. Minute by E.H. Abraham, 15 June 1922, League of Nations Archives, 21159.

12. *Ibid.*
13. *Ibid.*
14. League to UNIA, 20 June 1922, League of Nations Archives 21159.
15. Minute to Abraham, loc. cit.
16. Petition of the UNIA and African Communities League to the League of Nations, Geneva, Switzerland, 26 July 1922.
17. W.E.B. Du Bois, *The World & Africa*, pp. 11-12.
18. *New York Times,* 17 April 1922. Quoted in Amy Jacques Garvey, *op. cit.,* p. 82.
19. G.O. Marke to Drummond, Sec. Gen. of League of Nations, 12 Sept. 1922, League of Nations Archives, 21159.
20. Drummond to Marke, 15 Sept. 1922, League of Nations Archives, 21159.
21. Marke to Rappard, League of Nations, 15 Sept. 1922, League of Nations Archives 21159.
22. *Ibid.,* 21 Sept. 1922, League of Nations Archives, 21159.
23. Record of Interview, 16 Sept. 1922, League of Nations Archives, 21159.
24. ed Dowlah to Drummond, 28 Sept. 1922, League of Nations Archives, 21159.
25. Memo, Drummond to Rappard, 3 Oct. 1922, League of Nations Archives, 21159.
26. Minute by Swenster, League of Nations, 12 Aug. 1922, League of Nations Archives, 21159.
27. Renewal of Petition of the UNIA and African Communities League to the League of Nations, Geneva and to the Separate and Distinct Nations of the World, and their Nationals and Peoples on behalf of the Hundreds of Millions of Black, Struggling and Oppressed People of the World, Sept. 1928.
28. South African delegation to UNLA, 13 Sept. 1928, League of Nations Archives, 6/A/7 158.
29. Bertha Hodge, Cuba to League of Nations, 30 Oct. 1928.
30. Robert Martin to League of Nations, 1 Nov. 1928.
31. Padmore and James —Trinidad-born Pan-Africanists; Wallace Johnson—Sierra Leone nationalist and Pan-Africanist.

THE EVOLUTION OF
THE SPLIT BETWEEN
THE GARVEY MOVEMENT
AND THE ORGANIZED LEFT
IN THE UNITED STATES
1917-1933

Theodore Vincent

T he arrival of Marcus Garvey on the international scene was contemporaneous with the rise of the New Negro movement. The New Negroes emerged during the First World War and by 1920 had become a major force in Black communities across the United States and in the Caribbean. By far the most successful of New Negroes was Marcus Garvey. His Universal Negro Improvement Association would grow to have over a million dues paying members, and recently uncovered evidence suggests there might have been twice that number.[1]

The New Negro was eager to establish international connections between Blacks in all parts of the world. He created a plethora of international Black trading companies, and innumerable regional and international organizations to link Blacks together; among the latter were the African League, Pan-African Congress, International

League of Darker Peoples, *Comité de Défense de la Race Nègre,* and the West African National Congress. The UNIA built by far the most extensive international network.

In part the New Negro phenomena represented the impatience of Black youth with the apparent failure of established Black leadership, its "abject crawling and pleading" to whites. However, the essential distinction between the New and Old Negro was not so much that the former was angry and the latter complacent as it was that the New Negroes sought to replace the institutional framework used by the Old Negroes with a new one. Garveyites took the lead in this struggle, especially in creating new economic institutions. The UNIA had its own steamship company and a cooperatively owned Negro Factories Corporation, and also helped promote numerous other cooperative ventures like the "Harlem Retailers Cooperative," "United Produce Dealers," "Colored Tenants Combine," "Knights Developing and Trading Company," and "Homes Progressive Association."[2]

With the coming of the New Negro, socialism found favor among a sizable number of Blacks. The New Negro was eager for action, and willing to risk the consequences in waging a struggle to better his standard of living. The socialists' reputation as fighters for better working conditions on the job won them converts. The Black nationalist Garveyites showed as much interest in this kind of struggle as did the political left, at least this was the case up through 1920. For instance, in the 13 February 1920 *Negro World,* the weekly organ of the UNIA, there were articles on labor strikes of Blacks in Costa Rica, on a sugar plantation in St. Lucia, on the waterfront in Boston, and among transportation workers in Cuba.

Reform in the relations of Blacks to electoral politics was sought by the New Negroes, and here again the activity of the Garveyites was commendable. In 1920 the UNIA's James Walker Hood Eason was presidential candidate for the first all-Black political party in the U.S., the Liberal Party.[3] During the 1920s, in cities across the northern U.S., Garveyites paved the way for the shift of Black voting patterns from Republican to the more liberal Democratic Party.[4]

New Negro Militancy

The militancy of the New Negro was severely tested during 1919 when white mobs, intent on putting the Black American back in his old position of subservience invaded Black neighborhoods in over two dozen cities. However, Blacks fought back. As the New Negro journal the *Veteran* noted of the race riot in Knoxville, the whites came in anticipating great fun seeing the Negroes "scurrying before them like so many rats driven by the flames." Instead, the whites "saw fire—deadly well directed fire, and volley after volley of it, belched forth from the mouths of rifles and revolvers held by the hands of Black men who now have "stiff backs, straight shoulders, and know how to shoot," having been taught how to handle a gun in the recently passed World War.[5] New Negroes roundly applauded and encouraged these acts of self defense; for, like the Garveyites, they waged a forceful verbal assault in their journals upon all forms of racial oppression. Blacks must "prepare to meet fire with hell-fire," declared Marcus Garvey in reaction to white mob violence in Omaha, Nebraska.[6]

The New Negro sought his political rights, but at the same time he looked with disdain upon the political system of the United States. The young editor of the Oklahoma City *Black Dispatch*, Roscoe Dungee, explained at a meeting chaired by the governor of that state. "You have had what was termed a NEW NEGRO described to you as an insolent, arrogant individual;" and if that is the case, said Dungee, it is because "this New Negro... finds himself in America and in this state, physically bound and shackled by LAWS AND CUSTOMS THAT WERE MADE FOR SLAVES ... I want to tell you, if you were to creep up to-night to a place where there are 10,000 Negroes gathered, you would find no division on this one point. I know that they all would say, 'WE HAVE NO CONFIDENCE IN WHITE POLICEMEN.' Let there be one hundred or one hundred thousand, they would with one accord all say, 'WE HAVE NO CONFIDENCE IN THE WHITE MAN'S COURT'."[7] Garveyites applied this position of Dungee in regard to a proposed federal anti-lynch law. The UNIA refused to fight for its passage in Congress (it never passed), on the grounds that it would not be enforced, and that the only defense against the lyncher was the self-defense of the intended victim.[8]

The position of W.E.B. DuBois in this period sheds light on the meaning of the New Negro movement. Despite his long record as a champion of racial equality, DuBois was ostracized by the New Negroes. The root of the differences was the insistence of DuBois on identifying the interests of the Black man with the United States. The distinction between the way the New Negro and DuBois related to the United States can be seen in a comparison of two articles on Black soldiers returning from the First World War. The first article is by DuBois, the second by self-proclaimed New Negro, William Bridges. The concluding part of the DuBois article reads:

This is the fatherland for which we fought! But it is *our* fatherland. It was right for us to fight. The faults of *our* country are *our* faults. Under similar circumstances, we would fight again. But by the God of Heaven, we are cowards and jackasses if now that war is over, we do not marshal every ounce of our brain and brawn to fight a sterner, longer, more unbending battle against the forces of hell in our own land.

We return

We return from fighting We return fighting

Make way for Democracy! We saved it in France, and by the Great Jehovah, we will save it in the United States of America, or know the reason why.[9]

The foregoing is from one of the most quoted articles in the *Crisis* ever penned by DuBois. Equally as militant, and all but forgotten, is Bridges' piece on the same subject. But then DuBois identified the Black cause with America, while Bridges all but repudiated such ties. Said Bridges, in an article in his *Challenge* monthly, titled "Six Demands":

We demand, first, that instead of being re-Americanized into accepting sterner patriotic obligations we be thoroughly informed why we should be loyal to any Government that does not protect our lives and property the same as it protects those of other people with less claim to protection... Second, that we be told why we should disclaim all previous respect for Germans and Germany, when, no matter how diminished the respect of white Americans for them may be, it still transcends that which white Americans have for us... Third, that the full responsibility for lynching be placed where it properly belongs on the American Government; not upon the feebleminded groups that practice it, not upon the governors that permit it, not upon the States where it is carried on. Each and all of these are component parts simply of the organism of the United States subject to its laws and not above them...[10]

Bridges goes on to question the legitimacy of sending Black Americans into the World War in the first place. The initial break between DuBois and the New Negroes had come in 1918 when in a *Crisis* article, "Close Ranks," DuBois had urged: "Let us, while this war lasts, forget our special grievances and close our ranks..." in support of the war effort.[11] Hubert H. Harrison replied to DuBois in an article in Harrison's *Voice*, one of the first New Negro monthlies.

"The essence of the present situation," wrote Harrison, "lies in the fact that the people whom our white masters have "recognized" as our leaders (without taking the trouble to consult us) and those who, by our own selection, had actually attained to leadership among us are being revaluated and, in most cases, rejected. The most striking instance from the latter class is Dr. W.E. DuBois ... DuBois's case is the more significant because his former services to his race have been undoubtedly of a high and courageous sort." Harrison declared that DuBois had "palpably sinned" in the "Close Ranks" editorial, that the Blacks in America could not "forget [their] special grievances" and "preserve either their lives, their manhood or their vote...."[12] Harrison was founder and head of the Afro-American Liberty League, an organization formed to express Black opposition to the World War and to champion armed self-defense against white lynchers and mobs.

DuBois of this period could still sound like a militant, as in his article on returning soldiers. However, the conditions under which one conducted militant struggle had changed from what they were when DuBois had fought against the policies of Booker T. Washington. At the turn of the century it had taken a good deal of courage and foresight on the part of DuBois to argue that Washington's policy of industrial education and political accommodation was a failure and that the predominantly rural Black American should seek the highest individual goals within the established system, and should fight for whatever political rights could be salvaged in a period of lynch terror. It had been a militant act in 1910, when DuBois and a few other Blacks joined with white socialists, social workers and philanthropists to create the National Association for the Advancement of Colored Peoples. To launch an interracial, though white-dominated, organization for civil rights was, in the context of that day, a progressive venture. The all Black Niagara movement having folded, the NAACP was a means of setting up at least some organizational basis for the needed fight against the on-going terror and intimidation of Black folk.

The Gathering Forces

Then came the great migrations of southern Blacks to northern cities, the influx of West Indian immigrants, and the eye-opening experience of a World War in which the Western European world degraded itself in a mean and bloody debauchery. It no longer made sense to try to work "within the system," and New Negroes sought to "seize the time" and create a comprehensive movement for Black liberation. Here entered the new forces, Black nationalists, communists and socialists, aligned under the New Negro label, (along with an assortment of apolitical angry young men and women). During the War years there was very little evidence of any significant difference between the future nationalist leader Marcus Garvey, the fledgling promoter of communism, Cyril V. Briggs, or the most prominent socialist, A. Philip Randolph. Garvey and Briggs had cooperated with socialist Hubert Harrison in the latter's antiwar Liberty League. For his antiwar views Randolph served a brief period in jail in Cleveland, Ohio. Garvey and Randolph had joined with other New Negroes in 1918 to create the short-lived International League of Darker Peoples, which was to draw up a list of demands upon the European powers concerning the treatment of colonized peoples.[13]

By the mid-1920s Black nationalists, communists, and socialists had become embroiled in a bitter feud, and in their official positions each group blamed the other for a virtual collapse of the New Negro Movement. From that time on, cooperation in the liberation struggle between the proponents of these various views was tenuous at best, and often, impossible. A few rough observations should be made before going into the specifics of the development of this split.

First, the splintering of the New Negro Movement was into three main factions, specifically, a break between (1) Garveyites, (2) the African Blood Brotherhood which was left-wing, and (3) the officially recognized Black spokesmen for the Socialist Party of the United States — A. Philip Randolph, Chandler Owen and their *Messenger* group.

Second: the confrontation developed in the New Negro Mecca of Harlem, New York. Belatedly and often grudgingly, other parts of the Black world were drawn into the battle. Scattered evidence from Trinidad, Guyana, the Union of South Africa, and California suggests some forms of cooperation between Garveyites and communists continued on into the 1930s.[14] Two years into the bitter battle between Harlem Garveyites and Socialists, Charlotta Bass of the Los Angeles *California Eagle* was still singing the praises of both Garvey and Chandler Owen.[15] It appears the division in Black militancy was even slow in reaching down from Harlem to Brooklyn, where Randolph's friend George Frazier Miller continued to attend UNIA meetings when Randolph was in open opposition.[16]

Third: in Harlem, the African Blood Brotherhood and its offspring, the Harlem Section of the Communist Party, had a much closer relationship to the Garveyites than had the *Messenger* group of the Socialist Party. The Brotherhood seemed far more interested in infiltrating the massive UNIA than did the *Messenger* group. After 1921, when the New Negro Movement was torn apart by political fac-

tionalism, Randolph and his associates went into permanent opposition to Garvey, whereas the African Blood Brotherhood and its
Black communist successors made repeated attempts to come to
terms with Garvey. Had the divisions in Black radicalism arisen primarily over differences in economic systems one could expect to find
the Communists rather than the Socialists the most alienated from the
"welfare state liberal," Marcus Garvey.

Perhaps a brief glance at the attitude with which Garvey, Briggs
and Randolph had come to view race would better explain their inter-
relationships in the later New Negro Movement.

Race or Class

According to Amy Jacques Garvey, her late husband had from
his youth been proud of his pure African heritage and his ancestral ties
with the once independent nation of Maroons in Jamaica. All students
of Marcus Garvey know of the education in nationalism he received
from the Egyptian Duse Mohammed Ali, and of the inspiration that
came to Garvey upon reading Booker T. Washington's autobiography,
a book which prompted Garvey to ask "Where is the Black man's
Government? Where is his King and his kingdom? Where is his
President, his country, and his ambassador, his army, his navy, his
men of big affairs?" Because Garvey could not find them, he declared
"I will help to make them." The objectives of Marcus Garvey are also
well known from the Manifesto of the UNIA set down in 1914.[17] What
is not so well known is the young Garvey's analysis of the "class or
race" question: is oppression more a problem of social and economic
class relationships, or of racial ones? It has been generally assumed
that Marcus Garvey was solidly on the racial side of this question.
After all, he had to be on one side or the other, or so it was thought.
And if Garvey declared for race, then on these ideological grounds one
would expect him to have a difficult time with communists and socialists, whose theories were based on a class analysis.

The position of the young Garvey is expressed in a revealing letter to Major R.R. Moton of Tuskegee Institute sent by Garvey from
Jamaica in 1916.[18] Moton was planning a visit to the island and
Garvey wished to inform the "prominent American Negro leader" of
the conditions existing "among our people," by which Garvey meant
the Black, as opposed to the "colored and white." At length Garvey
described the hardships of Blacks, their economic poverty, their
unsanitary living conditions, their inadequate education, and the
police brutality they experienced. Garvey explained to Moton that the
relationship in Jamaica between the Black, colored and white was

"unlike other parts" of the world; that in Jamaica it was much easier to understand exploitation in racial rather than class terms, even though "we have no open race prejudice here." The point was that in Jamaica "the Black people.... form the economic asset," the laborers; and the colored and white were the upper classes. Garvey would have Moton understand that on even a short visit one could quickly distinguish the exploited from the privileged, the dark skinned being the former, the light skinned the latter.

What Garvey seemed to be attempting in this letter to Moton was a complex analysis similar to the one presented by John Rex in an article on the economic system of the Union of South Africa.[19] There Rex found each separate racial and ethnic group "separated out by economic functions assigned to them, and the rights and privileges they enjoy." With acknowledged exceptions to the rule, Rex found certain races comprised the lower classes and the white race comprised the upper class. Rex wanted it understood that unlike the racist he was not arguing that the exploitation of the Blacks, colored and Indian minorities in South Africa was a result of normative factors like social prejudice; but neither was exploitation entirely the result of economic relationships and class structure; these factors had been made virtually identical to categories of race and ethnicity. The thing which kept the system going was "the capacity of the employers to command the use of coercive violence, during and after colonial conquest." The armed might which was first used to conquer was then used to strip the Africans of the "means to perpetuate their own economy, society, and culture, and (they) were therefore forced into *de facto* dependence on those who had placed them in this position." Garvey informed Moton that the Black Jamaican had gained little in the 78 years since emancipation from slavery and that the Black had adopted "his master's ideals, and up to today you will find the Jamaica Negro unable to think apart from the customs and ideals of his old time slave masters."

In discussions with Amy Jacques Garvey in 1969, this writer raised with her the question of how the young Garvey interpreted the problem of exploitation in Jamaica. She declared, "He always saw it in class terms." I then mentioned Garvey's statements that appeared to me to identify exploitation with race, and Mrs. Garvey retorted, "You see, he interpreted it as a class question!" At the time I did not see. It was only after reading the argument of John Rex that I realized that Marcus Garvey, a half-century earlier, had superimposed racial categories in the traditional class analysis of exploitation. Garvey informed Moton that the poverty ridden Blacks were driven to distraction, and "mad houses are overcrowded with our people much to the absence of the other classes." Garvey noted that the only avenue of social mobility open to the Black was in education, "and he dominates there because the wage is not encouraging enough for others."

According to Garvey, just as exploitation in Jamaica was best understood in racial rather than class terms, so too, in combating the problem it would be useful to interpolate the factor of race consciousness for class consciousness. Garvey tells Moton, "Racial ideals do no people harm, therefore, the Jamaica Negro has done himself a harm in not thinking on racial ideals with the scattered Negroes of other climes." (The word "climes" was an insert, written over the original typed word "classes," which was crossed out). Garvey continued, "The coloured and white population have been thinking and planning on exclusive racial ideals—race ideals which are unwritten and unspoken. The diplomacy of one race or class of people is the means by which others are outdone."

One has to question the applicability of the analysis of Garvey or Rex in a country like the United States where there were only two basic racial distinctions, and where there were large numbers of poverty stricken whites. In the U.S. Garvey would appear to have made some modification of his position. He did not distinguish between light and dark Blacks—he called for unity of everyone of African descent. "What Garvey did attack," says Maglangbayan, "was the assimilationist, integrationist Black —of whatever hue he may be ...."[20]

As for the poor whites in the U.S., they simply were not Garvey's problem. Blacks were. In Jamaica Garvey had found the Black "at the foot of the ladder" economically, socially and politically; in the U.S. he found the overwhelming majority of people of African descent, of whatever hue, at the foot of the same ladder. But, according to Garvey, whenever the African improved his social position he took an Aryan identity; a Marxist describing the same process calls it the adoption of a bourgeois ideology on the part of the socially mobile worker. For Garvey such a Black was a traitor to his race, to the Marxist he was a class traitor. In either case, the person in question was often the same, as in Garvey's condemnation of "the capitalist class of Negroes whose only concern is to rob and exploit the unfortunate of their own race...."[21] Thus, one can say that the young Garvey's analysis of the workings of Black society was hardly inimical to socialist class analysis. And one could expect some cooperation between Garvey and those socialists who had in addition to a class analysis of society, a strong identification with Blacks. The future leading Black Communist, Cyril V. Briggs, tried to be this kind of leftist.

The Black Communists

Cyril Briggs was a frail, extremely light-skinned native of the island of St. Kitts. He had come to New York at the age of 16, in 1905.[22] By the advent of the World War Briggs had cultivated friendships that no doubt helped him to feel a strong Black identity; people such as John E. Bruce and Arthur A. Schomburg of the Negro Society for Historical Research, and Richard B. Moore, agent for the *African Times and Orient Review,* the organ of Duse Mohammed Ali. Briggs was close to Hubert H. Harrison one of the earliest political radicals on the Harlem scene, and an organizer in the 1913 Paterson textile strike led by the anarcho-syndicalist Industrial Workers of the World.[23] In 1915 Briggs inaugurated a monthly *Colored American Review,* with Harrison's blessings. For Briggs, the press was an instrument through which he could proclaim his race consciousness. His *Review* did not last long, probably because he antagonized most of his potential advertisers by making the bold move of calling upon Blacks to "discriminate" against, and boycott, retail shops in Harlem which did not hire Black employees.[24] In 1917 Briggs was pressured to resign a post as editorial writer for the *Amsterdam News* after writing a piece titled, "Security of Life for Poles and Serbs Why Not for Colored Nations." It was a scathing indictment of Woodrow Wilson's peace proposals.[25]

In 1917 Briggs became acquainted with A. Philip Randolph, but Briggs would declare that he never became a part of the *Messenger* group: according to Briggs the Socialist Party had nothing special to offer the Negro. Politically, Briggs was inspired by the Russian Revolution. But as he noted years later, he was not interested in "Bolshevik socialism *per se.* My sympathies were derived from the enlightened attitude of the Russian Bolsheviks toward national minorities."[26] It was Lenin's proposal for creating autonomous states for national minorities of the Soviet Union that caught Briggs's eye. Like Garvey, the young Briggs had his attention turned toward Africa where he hoped to create a "great Pan-African army" that would descend from the hinterland upon the coastal plantations and drive out the European imperialists.[27] Briggs was quite sympathetic toward Garvey's Back to Africa idea, at least until 1920. In 1919, Briggs wrote in his *Crusader* monthly that "it should be a comparatively easy matter for the American Negro in particular... to pull up stakes from out of the hellish soil of American mobocracy."[28] In another article he declared, "it seems that the only sure and permanent solution of the race problem in America, the only honorable and mutually beneficial solution, is government of the Negro, by the Negro, and for the Negro in a Black man's country." Briggs would build this nation in the "ancestral land," and he surmised that "the United States Government could very well afford to give a bonus of several hundred dollars to, and pay the passage of, every Negro who would voluntarily leave this country."[29]

Throughout the New Negro period Briggs displayed little interest in the intricacies of Marxist theories of economic surplus value, or the materialist conception of history. Briggs' *Crusader* magazine, published from 1918 into 1922, carried virtually nothing of a Marxist theoretical nature, and very little on trade unionism, a favorite cause of the orthodox advocates of class struggle. The magazine ran a monthly horoscope column, which was hardly compatible with doctrinaire Marxism. The important thing to the young Briggs was the noble act, rather than the correct theory. One of Briggs's first connections in the New Negro Movement was with Harrison and Garvey in the Liberty League, an organization which promoted the use of armed self-defense against lynchers.[30] Early in 1919 Briggs formed his own para-military self-defense organization, the secret African Blood Brotherhood, which included special cadres to which were admitted "only the best and most courageous of the race." Initiation in the Brotherhood included a Blood Ceremony which Briggs modeled after "ancient African traditions."[31] Members also adhered to a Race Catechism which declared that duty to one's race was to

> love one's race above one's self and to further the common interests of all above the private interest of one. To cheerfully sacrifice wealth, ease, luxuries, necessities and, if need be, life itself to attain for the race that greatness in arms, in commerce, in art, the three combined without which there is neither respect, honor, nor security.[32]

The African Blood Brotherhood had been in existence for over half a year when in September of 1919 the first Communist Parties were formed in the United States. As an avowed revolutionary, Briggs was looking for ultra-radical groups with which he could align himself. The Communists represented connections with the one big successful revolution of that day, the one in the USSR. Briggs wrote in the October 1919 *Crusader*, "If to fight for one's rights is to be a Bolshevik, then we are Bolsheviks;... we would not for a moment hesitate to ally ourselves with *any* group, if by such an alliance we could compass the liberation of our race and the redemption of our Fatherland." Since Briggs equated liberation with a violent revolution, he was gradually driven to conclude that the Communists were the only allies and in

1925 he abandoned the ABB entirely for the Communist Party. The steps taken leading to this decision are not clear. It appears that there was some connection between the Brotherhood and the CP as early as 1920; and it is known that early in 1921 Briggs established a formal alliance between the Communist International and the ABB; from that time forward, his racial attitudes would diminish as ever more import was given to Party line.[33] But at the onset of the New Negro Movement Cyril Briggs held racial attitudes that would make him eager to work with Garvey and the UNIA. The nationalism of Briggs reflected a trend found among early white communists in the U.S. The Communist Party grew out of nationalistic organizations of immigrant ethnic groups, particularly among Finns and Lithuanians. These Communists expected to return to their homeland and wage the revolution, much as the immigrant Briggs looked toward ancestral Africa. Garvey was building a transportation system and making connections throughout Africa, and Briggs was at first quite favorably inclined to the Garvey movement. But the Party line would change; nationalism would be denounced, and the Party became "Americanized."

The Black Socialists

A. Philip Randolph, from the start of the New Negro period, appeared to have a markedly distinct position on race, when compared with Garvey and Briggs. The son of a self-educated Florida preacher, Randolph came to New York in 1911, originally intent on a career as a Shakespearean actor. His parents dissuaded him from that profession, and he began attending night school at the City College of New York and there met his first socialists. For him, reading Marx was "like finally running into an idea which gives you your outlook on life."[34] With Marx, exploitation could not be explained in racial terms; it was economic.

The socialist colleagues of Randolph at City College of New York and at the Rand School of Social Science where Randolph also studied were representatives of the intellectual side of the American Left. They prided themselves on their "scientific radicalism," a term Randolph used in describing the policy of his *Messenger* magazine. To be a scientific radical one had to do a great deal of studying, and this rigorous training had its beneficial results. The *Messenger* of Randolph and his co-editor Chandler Owen was an excellently edited and well-written monthly. An interesting description of Randolph's and Owen's first meeting is given by Randolph's biographer Jervis Anderson. "Randolph was at once impressed by the similarity of

Owen's political temperament to his own. Here, Randolph recognized with delight, was a 'natural-born iconoclast,' a man 'who did not believe in anything, including the church,' and who was 'just as discontented as I was about the racial problem.'"[35] Randolph seemed to collect iconoclast intellectuals, like Theophilus Lewis and the cynical George S. Schuyler.

As noted by Sterling Spero and Abram Harris in *Black Worker*, Randolph and his associates "attributed race prejudice to capitalism. They held that in an individualistic economic system, competition for jobs and the profitableness of race prejudice to the capitalist class were incentives to race conflict. Therefore the removal of the motive for creating racial strife was conditioned upon the socialization of industry and the nationalization of land, in short, upon the elimination of economic individualism and competition through social revolution."[36] There is little room here for interpolating race for class. In this orthodox class analysis, race is divorced from its human context and becomes only a tool used by the capitalist to beat down the workers of all colors. The Black has no alternative but to struggle for an alliance with white workers.

In a 1918 secret report, titled "Socialism Imperiled, or the Negro—A Potential Menace to American Radicalism," written for the Rand School by Randolph's associate W.A. Domingo, Blacks were declared to be an incipient "lumpen proletariat," and an ignorant "Black Guard" ready to be used by the capitalists to divide and wreck the labor movement and radicalism in general. Domingo demanded increased efforts be made to recruit Blacks into the socialist struggle, and in a sense was arguing that this was necessary to turn the liability of being Black into something worthwhile.[37] One would have to expect the development of strained relations between the Randolph group and Marcus Garvey.

In its inception, the Harlem New Negro Movement was composed of two loosely defined groups, friendship circles more than ideological alignments. In one there was, among others, Marcus Garvey, John E. "Grit" Bruce, Arthur A. Schomburg, Hubert H. Harrison, Richard B. Moore, Rabbi J. Arnold Ford, Henrietta Vinton Davis, Andrea Razakeriefo, and Cyril V. Briggs.[38] These people shared a deep interest in Afro-American and African history; most of them were involved in Bruce and Schomburg's Negro Society for Historical Research. The group was primarily composed of immigrants from the West Indies. All shared a deep interest in international affairs. Many were associated with Duse Mohammed, and contributors to or agents for his London based monthly magazine. Through correspondence, there were ties between this fraternity in Harlem and political leaders in the Black Republic of Liberia. Schomburg had served five years as secretary of the Las Dos Antillas Cuban Revolutionary Party, and had been a member of the Puerto Rico Revolutionary Party.[39] From this social group, Garvey would take many of his most capable lieutenants in the building of the UNIA. There were yet others who were not actually Garveyites but were involved in activities in and around the Garvey movement. There was J. Griffith, head of the Art Publishing Company, which did a large business selling the work of Black artists to Garveyites. There was Hodge Kirnon of the *Promoter* magazine, which was heartily endorsed by the Garveyites.[40] Cyril Briggs's *Crusader* was considered by the *Negro World* to be good reading for Garveyites.[41] Briggs created his African Blood Brotherhood early in 1919 and encouraged its members to join the UNIA; two members became Black Star Line officials, and in some local areas the head of the UNIA was also the head of the ABB. In addition, Briggs and his Brotherhood were deeply involved in organizations loosely affiliated with the UNIA, such as the Liberty League, the Negro Society for Historical Research, the Hamitic League of the World—a cultural organization headed by George Wells Parker, and the Bahamian Rejuvenation League of Fred Toote.[42]

The second social group was composed of Randolph, Owen, Lovet Fort-Whiteman, Walter A. Domingo, Frank Crosswaith, Louis George, Rev. George Frazier Miller, and Madame C.J. Walker the wealthy inventor of the hair straightening process.[43] Many in this fraternity had studied socialism together at the Rand School. All but Domingo and Crosswaith were born in the U.S. Randolph, Owen and Crosswaith had been active in trade union organizing. Fort-Whiteman shared with Randolph an interest in the theater.

The attitude of the socialists toward the UNIA was first to ignore it. However, as the Garveyites developed their massive organization Randolph's group tried infiltrating the UNIA to direct it toward socialism. This was at first not hard to accomplish; Garvey, on his part, started with no animosity toward Randolph. At the end of the World War Garvey selected Randolph to be the UNIA representative of the Negro Peoples of the World to the Versailles Peace Conference. "Needless to say, I never went," Randolph would later write sarcastically.[44] The infiltration of the UNIA came with Domingo, Randolph's Rand School associate, who took the post of first editor of the *Negro World*. Domingo worked there eleven months, being removed after his secret Rand School anti-Negro report was made public in the Summer of 1919.[45]

Another tactic of the socialists was to try and wean away those individuals loosely connected with the Garvey movement; in particular Randolph was interested in winning the left-wing individuals in and around the UNIA. A case in point was the poet Claude McKay, who in 1919 had been a reporter for the *Negro World*. McKay would write in his autobiography that he stopped contributing to the *Negro World* because it did not pay for his articles. Since radical periodicals rarely pay for contributions, this rather trite explanation by McKay seems to have been an attempt to cover up other reasons, and his autobiography reveals how he was captivated by the white intellectuals of the left, such as Max Eastman.

The *Messenger* socialists also worked with Cyril Briggs and the ABB. With its inside connections to the UNIA, an ABB in opposition to Garvey could be a most disruptive force. Domingo became a member of the Brotherhood and rose to a position on its Supreme Executive Council. Randolph endorsed the *Crusader*; and he exchanged mailing lists of the *Messenger* with Briggs's magazine.[46] The attempts to win Briggs had apparently borne some fruit by the Fall of 1919 when the *Crusader* began carrying ads for the Rand School.

The Conflict

As the New Negro era unfolded there developed a complex intertanglement of political forces. One of the more interesting cases involved the Liberal Party of 1920, which appears to have been the first all-Black political party in the United States. The creation of the Party was the brainchild of William Bridges, editor of the *Challenge* magazine, which publicly endorsed the Bolshevik Revolution, the I.W.W. and the Socialist Party, and was secretly funded by Tammany Hall Democrats.[47] Bridges' idea was to use the party for a single dramatic purpose, to run a Black man for president of the United States; he hoped to drum up interest in the Party over the Presidential issue and then have it endorse his Democrats in the local elections. Bridges found immediate support for the Liberal Party from the Socialist backed weekly *Emancipator*.[48] He also received encouragement from Garvey's *Negro World,* in which Hubert Harrison declared that, while many might laugh at the idea of a Black running for President, the act would nonetheless "come to be ultimately accepted as one of the finest contributions to Negro statesmanship... It would be carrying 'Race First' with a vengeance into the arena of domestic politics. It would take the Negro out of the ranks of the Republican, Democratic and Socialist parties and would enable their leader to trade the votes of their followers, openly and above board, for those things for which masses of men largely exchange their votes."[49]

Garveyites took over the Liberal Party and picked as their presidential candidate, Rev. James Walker Hood Eason, UNIA Leader of American Negroes. The SP no longer looked with favor; and Bridges apparently lost interest in the project when he failed to win it over to endorsing his favored candidates in local elections. Eason's name failed to appear on the ballot, because Bridges had neglected to file the proper papers.[50] The pre-election issue of the *Messenger* carried a scathing condemnation of the Garveyites in general and of the whole idea of an all-Black political party.[51] This was the first open assault of the *Messenger* on the UNIA. Perhaps it was more than coincidence that no sooner did this *Messenger* reach the street than Randolph and Owen were expelled from the Harlem branch of the Socialist Party for financial mis-management. This SP branch contained at the time a number of Garveyites. The Liberal Party episode is one of the few intrigues of this period on which there is a generally consistent picture of what had actually happened.

Cyril Briggs appears repeatedly to have been ingratiating himself into Garvey and the UNIA, and simultaneously knifing Garvey in the back. Briggs supported the Black Star Line in an article in the December 1919 *Crusader*. He then presented a strong endorsement of the coming UNIA International Convention in a March 1920 *Crusader* article titled "A Paramount Chief for the Negro Race." Garvey was so impressed with this article that he wrote Briggs a personal letter inviting him to the Convention and terming the article "the most intelligent explanation of the real purpose of our Convention that I have read from the pen of a contemporary journalist..." The letter was dated March 9, 1920. On March 14, the first issue of the weekly *Emancipator* appeared. Edited by Domingo, its contributing editors list included Briggs, others of the ABB, and A. Philip Randolph as well. The March 27, 1920 issue put two faces in juxtaposition on page one. On the left there was a pro-Garvey article condemning the witch-hunt of U.S. Attorney General Mitchel A. Palmer against the *Negro World*. On the right side was the large headline, "B.S.L. Exposed: Document Shows Yarmouth Owned by White Company." Below was a photostat of a letter from a British shipping official replying to an inquiry of Cyril Briggs about the alleged BSL ownership of the *Yarmouth*. The article went on to praise Briggs for initiating the investigation. About the same time that this reached the news stands, so did the April issue of the *Crusader*. There, on the first page was Garvey's glowing letter of praise to Briggs. Thereafter followed a lengthy verbal dispute between the socialists and Hubert Harrison, then editor of the *Negro World*, who remained with the paper through 1922 and never seriously broke with Garvey.

Harrison had had long experience with the political left of the United States, dating back to at least 1912 when he had worked with John Reed and Max Eastman. Harrison's ability to argue with the left was gradually learned by Garvey. But it must be said that in the immediate post-War years Garvey repeatedly made statements which could easily be misconstrued as reverse racism; statements which confused the left and helped push people like Randolph into the lap of the NAACP. For instance, Garvey was quoted as saying,

> The Universal Negro Improvement Association stands in opposition to the Pan-African Congress and to the leadership of Dr. DuBois because they seek to bring about a destruction of the Black and white races by the social amalgamation of both. The Dr. DuBois group believe that Negroes should settle down in communities of whites and by social contact and miscegenation bring about a new type. The Universal Negro Improvement Association believes that both races have separate and distinct social destinies...[52]

In the opinion of NAACP National Secretary James Weldon Johnson, this statement of Garvey "consciously or unconsciously plays to the most deep seated prejudices of the white man in America. It is the very sort of a thing that Vardaman, Cole Blease and the rest of that ilk say and wish to have accepted." According to Johnson, Garvey was here abandoning the whole struggle for "social equality."[53] In a *Negro World* reply, Garvey stated, "Mr. Johnson and his associates ... hanker after social equality with white people. I demand social justice."[54] But leftists considered people who talked of justice while criticizing equality conservative supporters of the status quo. For Garvey, however, these terms had a different connotation, as he tried to explain in his reply to Johnson. For Garvey, to achieve social equality was to be bought off with identity with the slave masters, and a slave who identified with the master was no help to the cause of the slaves. "You are not going to expect the race of slave master to yield up to the race of slaves, equality in everything," Garvey declared. "If the Negroes will stop making all this noise about social equality, giving white people the idea that we are hankering after their company, and get down to business and build up a strong race, industrially, commercially, educationally and politically, everything social will come afterward." Garvey added that in working toward these ends, "I demand from every man in the name of and by the law my constitutional right to go anywhere in the country of which I am a citizen."[55]

Those radicals who did read Garvey's entire article would still probably end up confused on at least one very important point. How could one be assured that the Garvey separate and "superior" society would really be "superior." There was already in the U.S. a separate and inferior Black society. Garvey believed that race conscious Blacks would make the personal sacrifices necessary to remold their society. However, to be convincing on this point he would have had to show that he was indeed superimposing race on what was basically a class analysis, that the sacrifices he talked about involved a commitment to some type of communal society in which all Blacks pooled their wealth for the enrichment of all. Garvey built economic cooperatives, and condemned the greedy among Black capitalists, but he never sufficiently clarified himself to the left. Ironically, his poorly educated working-class followers seem to have understood, for in the 1930s, after the UNIA was crushed, Garveyites by the many thousands flocked to the most rigorously communal movement of the century, that of Father Divine. And after the *Negro World* was discontinued in 1933 its editor, M.L.T. DeMena, put it together again in 1934 and renamed it the *World Peace Echo,* the organ of Father Divine.[56]

An Alliance is Attempted

Arising out of Garvey's ideological imprecisions, Harrison had, early in 1921, contacted the white Communist liaison with Blacks, Robert Minor, and asked him to help arrange a meeting of radical Blacks for the purpose of discussing, as Claude McKay described it, "the possibility of making the Garvey movement more class-conscious." The meeting was held in the Greenwich village office of the *Liberator* magazine, and in attendance, in addition to Harrison and Minor, were Briggs, Domingo, McKay, Richard Moore, Otto Huiswood, Grace Campbell, and a Mr. Fanning. Present was the leadership of the African Blood Brotherhood. Of those attending, all but Harrison and Domingo would become members of the Communist Party.[57]

After the meeting at the *Liberator* the ABB set out to infiltrate the coming 1921 International Convention of the UNIA and convince its delegates to vote for an alliance with the Communist International. In addition, Briggs sent a personal letter to Garvey requesting that the ABB be made the secret military arm of the UNIA.[58] At the Convention, ABB representatives passed out leaflets outlining a proposed alliance with the Communist International. The Brotherhood also arranged to have the white Anarchist-Communist Rose Pastor Stokes speak to the Convention on behalf of the Communist

International. As reported in the 27 August 1921 *Negro World* her attendance at the Convention was a memorable occasion. That day had been devoted to the subject of liberation struggles in the Third World, and Mrs. Stokes was preceded by speakers praising the guerrilla warriors then fighting a struggle for independence in Spanish Morocco. When her turn came she was introduced by Marcus Garvey, whose remarks covered much of his position at that time on Communism.

> "We have with us tonight," said Garvey, "a lady visitor who has been widely made known... the world over as belonging to that class of agitators who are endeavoring to free struggling white humanity... It is for me to explain that Liberty Hall welcomes all friends of Liberty (applause). We welcome the Irish, we welcome the Jews, the Egyptians, the Hindus, and all peoples struggling for liberty, because we are in sympathy with suffering humanity everywhere. But that does not mean to say that we support every program, every method that is being used. We are in sympathy with the cause of freedom everywhere and this lady in her own way has linked up herself with the cause of bleeding Russia... So we welcome this friend of Soviet Russia to tell us a little of what her people are doing to get liberty, and if we can find any good in what she says we shall certainly be quick to seize upon it and adopt it for our own benefit..."

Mrs. Stokes proceeded to discuss only briefly the issue of what the Communists were doing in the Soviet Union. She was primarily interested in pointing out that the Soviet Union "seeks not only to free herself from economic and social oppression and inequality, but it seeks to free also every people, every nation, every race upon the face of the earth." The Communists "give aid, they give unstinted help to the weaker peoples, to the darker races of the East. Wherever men are oppressed we say there is neither color, nor creed, nor nation. We stand together against all oppressors... In the Soviet Union they have decided that Persia shall be free; that India shall be free (applause) that Africa shall be free (great applause)...." In general Mrs. Stokes was quite well received. When she had finished, the *Negro World* report noted, "The President-General thanked Mrs. Stokes for her address..." and added humorously, that Liberty Hall would give her a fair trial in judging her opinion as gathered from her speech "after we have heard the other fellow." The audience roared their appreciation of the joke, and Mrs. Stokes laughed and took it good naturedly too. Garvey's rather tolerant attitude toward the white left was also displayed in a speech reported in the 12 February 1921 *Negro World* in which he stated, "Please understand that Marcus Garvey is no I.W.W.; he doesn't even know what it means; he is no anarchist, as far as Western civilization is concerned; but if anarchism means that you have to drive out somebody and sometimes kill somebody, to get that which belongs to you, then when I get to Africa I am going to be an anarchist."

But African Blood Brotherhood had been quite serious in its intention of getting the UNIA to accept Mrs. Stokes' offer of an alliance with the Soviet Union. A Convention struggle over this issue resulted in the Brotherhood being formally expelled from the Convention and the UNIA.[59] The ABB now went into open opposition to the Garvey movement (although remaining separate from the Randolph opposition to Garvey). In return, the *Negro World* launched a vigorous attack on the ABB. On the one hand, Briggs argued in the *Crusader* that the ABB had been thrown out of the UNIA Convention because Garvey saw the Brotherhood program "gaining favor in the eyes of most of the delegates" and Garvey feared to make an alliance with revolutionaries.[60] The *Negro World*, on the other hand, saw the confrontation in a quite different light.

In the beginning of the fight Briggs picked up the support of some prominent Garveyites: former Chaplain General George Alexander McGuire, former UNIA representative to Liberia Cyril Crichlow, and former Assistant President-General J.D. Gordon.[61] In the long run, the attack of the *Negro World* proved disastrous for Briggs. Whatever popular support he had had for his championing of armed self-defense and radicalism in general was now cut out from under him. The *Crusader* readers had been largely Garveyites. Without them the *Crusader* was quickly reduced to an irregular *Crusader Bulletin*, and by 1923 only a "Crusader News Service" remained.

The Alliance Breaks Up

Faced with dwindling mass support, both the Briggs crowd and the *Messenger* followings resorted to desperate measures. Briggs, with his inside information, launched another investigation into the Black Star Line. He later boasted that the published findings of this investigation had prompted Black Star Line stockholders to write letters of inquiry to the U.S. Government, letters which helped to initiate the Garvey mail-fraud trial of 1923.[62] The *Messenger* group, learning of the impending Government indictment, sought to speed up the proceedings with a "Garvey Must Go" campaign. Chandler Owen put together a lengthy letter of alleged criminal actions of Garvey and demanded the authorities take action. Owen had it signed by a half dozen supposedly prominent Blacks, and mailed it to the U.S. Attorney General. Owen sent a follow up letter to make sure the Attorney General was going to take prompt action.[63]

Until the "Garvey Must Go" campaign, Garvey displayed an almost blasé attitude toward the leftists. Now, this was replaced with bitterness. When Chandler Owen retired to Los Angeles in 1923 to become a "capitalist," Garvey wondered aloud in the *Negro World* what had happened to

> the Chandler Owen who advised Negroes under the direction of white Socialists to discard property and capitalism?... When did Owen change heart? Was it before or after he wrote the letter to the Attorney-General? Was it before or after he campaigned on the slogan, 'Garvey Must Go!'? How much did Owen get for writing the letter against Garvey? How much did he get for the campaign against Garvey? If he got anything, where did it come from? And if it was a large amount, is it the reason he has become a capitalist immediately after Garvey has been convicted?"[64]

Randolph's and Owen's "Garvey Must Go!" campaign was waged with help from the NAACP; and in addition to fighting Garvey the campaign involved applying pressure upon independent Blacks to repudiate the UNIA—in effect, to polarize Black society. Anyone who argued for calm and reason was considered an enemy. A case in point involved *Messenger* columnist Floyd Calvin. He was a writer of social satire and not much interested in socialism. In the 21 February 1923 issue of the New York *Amsterdam News* there appeared an article by Calvin in which he declared that the feud between the NAACP and the UNIA had gotten out of hand, and that there was both good and bad in each organization and neither deserved to be ruined. Calvin was promptly fired from his job with the *Messenger*. The *Negro World* provided him the opportunity to write an explanation of why he had been fired.[65]

Briggs would not cooperate in the NAACP attack on Garvey. He was not out to destroy the UNIA but wanted to take it over. His complaint was with Garvey's alleged lack of revolutionary nerve. A related point was made by the Blood Brotherhood official, Harry Haywood, who said, "I could never see Garvey's program. It was not that he was too bourgeois. It was that he was wrong to think twelve million Negroes could obtain freedom on their own, when they were such a minority in the nation as a whole."[66] In the battle against

Garvey, the ABB and the *Messenger* socialists were driven farther apart. Involved here was a surfacing of tension between Afro-Americans and West Indian immigrants. The ABB's Domingo expressed concern that the *Messenger* fight against Garvey was becoming a fight against West Indian Blacks in general; and that instead of trying to win over Garveyites the "Garvey Must Go" campaign was simply out to destroy them. Chandler Owen replied that the new Black organization for socialists, the Friends of Negro Freedom, only "in rare instances" solicited support from UNIA members, because Garveyites were either "too ignorant for the FNF" or "too venal, since they could only have had in mind fleecing the uninitiated."[67] It should be remembered that the Messenger group, now the Friends of Negro Freedom, was largely of a middle-class and intellectual composition. In the battle against the predominantly working-class UNIA the bias of the Randolph supporters came into the open. In the October 1922 *Messenger* Randolph expressed horror at a Section of the UNIA Constitution which seemed to invite criminality, and allow certain felons membership in the organization. That one could hardly have a Black working-class movement that excluded all felons in a country with a racist police force and racist courts was a point that escaped Randolph's logic. There was another point that Randolph, an alleged radical, should have noticed in this section of the UNIA Constitution, which read, "No one shall be received by the Potentate and his consort who has been convicted of crime or felony, except such crime or felony was committed in the interest of the Universal Negro Improvement Association and the African Communities League." Here an obvious distinction was drawn, which is basic to revolutionary movements, that there is a difference between illegal acts taken in the cause of justice and common anti-social behavior.

Randolph no longer talked of revolution as he once had during the First World War. As a member of the Socialist Party he had come to think of Communists as "irrational," and declared in the August 1923 *Messenger* that "Negro Communists are a menace," they "seek to wreck all constructive, progressive, non-Communist programs." For Randolph, legitimate New Negro radicalism had come to be relegated almost entirely to trade unionism. From 1926 on he would be president of the Brotherhood of Sleeping Car Porters. Randolph had been involved in the trade union movement since early in 1917. It appears that it was Garvey's opposition to American trade unions as much as anything else which first set Randolph in opposition to the UNIA. In Jamaica the head of the Federation of Labour was a staunch Garveyite and unions in Jamaica and elsewhere in the Caribbean were supported by Garvey.[68] But in the United States trade unions were quite often little more than associations for the practice of nepotism among the native white skilled craftsmen. Not only was there Black exclusion, but exclusion of Mexicans, Orientals and immigrant whites. One can note for instance, the trade union situation in the two U.S. industries that would be of most importance to the Garvey movement, in the shipping industry, which would affect the Black Star Line, and in printing, which would affect the *Negro World*, *Negro Times* and Universal Publishing Company. Blacks were excluded from membership of the Iron Shipbuilders and Helpers, and Boilermakers unions. Of more than a dozen different aboard ship seamen's unions, Blacks were not admitted to a single one involved in deck work or in the engine room. The one seaman's union with a sizable number of Blacks was the East and Gulf Coast Marine Cooks and Stewards Union. In the printing trade, union exclusion had made it almost impossible for Blacks to find work, and by 1920 there were hardly 2,000 Black printers and compositors in the U.S.[69] Randolph would urge Blacks to join unions they could not join. What is more, during the New Negro era the unions affecting the UNIA showed little change of heart. The *Topographical Journal* of the topographers union had not a single article on the Black worker from 1917 to 1927; the *Seaman's Journal*, organ of eleven seamen's unions was likewise silent. However, this latter magazine waged a vigorous campaign for exclusion of immigrants to the United States, and against the employment of Orientals on U.S. ships.

One of the more thought-provoking aspects of the New Negro era was the way people who had broken away from Garvey and the UNIA would later come back into the fold. It happened with Duse Mohammed and with William Ferris. William Bridges made his amends after his *Challenge* folded; he became a periodic contributor to the *Negro World*. Bishop McGuire and J.D. Gordon came back from the ABB. Perhaps it was Briggs' break with the Socialists and refusal to be involved in the "Garvey Must Go" campaign that convinced Garvey that Briggs, despite his previous disruptive conniving, still deserved another chance at working with the UNIA. Early in 1924 an arrangement was made whereby Briggs, who had twice tried to sabotage the Black Star Line, would now pass as a white man to purchase a steamship for the Line. This purchase, the *"General Goethals,"* was the only fairly priced ship ever obtained by the Garvey line.[70]

In 1924 the Communist Party had decided that increased attention should be given to Blacks, and to that end there should be formed an American Negro Labor Congress to coordinate trade union and civil rights struggles. Good relations with Garvey would be useful in enabling Communist organizers for the ANLC to approach the rank and file of the UNIA. A Communist Party memo to Black organizers, written early in that year, carried the instruction, "Toward the existing (non-church) organizations of Negroes other than labor unions but generally working-class composition, we shall throughout pursue the policy of friendly invitation to cooperate. This shall apply to the Universal Negro Improvement Association's local bodies in each town."[71] The Communists also hoped to bring to the 1924 UNIA Convention a strong contingent that would push through a strong condemnation of Ku Klux Klan violence. The Klan had been the subject of much discussion during the 1922 Convention, and it appeared then that the most prevalent attitude of the Garveyites was that the only effective method of stopping the Klan lyncher was with self-defense. But for the UNIA to make this view official policy would have been suicide for southern Garveyites, in either 1922 or 1924. A rather mild resolution on the KKK was passed at the 1924 Convention; and even many loyal Garveyites felt there could have been stronger language, and that it was unnecessary to qualify the condemnation of the Klan by referring to its "alleged" atrocities. The Communists were irate, and a *Daily Worker* banner headline read, "Garvey Movement Bows to Ku Klux Klan."[72] It should be understood that at this time Garvey was in a very tenuous position; arrangements for the UNIA colony in Liberia were falling through; the Association was faced with a number of law suits; Garvey was fighting appeals to his mail fraud conviction, and he was also being threatened with a new indictment.

Garvey in Jail

His appeals failed, and early in 1925 Marcus Garvey entered the Federal Penitentiary in Atlanta. Of the left which had contributed to his downfall, the erstwhile socialists who had aligned themselves with the NAACP became in Garvey's mind yet another appendage to the forces in Black America that identified with whites, and hardly deserved independent consideration. But among the Communists of the ABB were much more disturbing and personal enemies since many in the Brotherhood had come out of the same race-conscious social circle which had initially launched Garvey in the United States. These were friends turned enemies. Domingo, who went from Randolph's group to the ABB, had actually been a boyhood friend of Garvey. From the surroundings of prison Garvey would write, "Communism among Negroes in 1920-21 was represented in New

York by such Negroes as Cyril Briggs and W.A. Domingo, and my contact and experience of them and their methods are enough to keep me shy of that kind of communism for the balance of my natural life... The American Negro is warned to keep away from communism, as it is taught in this country...."[73]

But what of Communism in other countries? Marcus Garvey respected the achievements of the Communists in modernizing Russia. Amy J. Garvey writes in *Garvey and Garveyism;* "On the death of Lenin in 1924, Garvey sent a cable to Moscow, on behalf of the Negroes of the world expressing sorrow at his passing. For despite the fact that he felt convinced that his race should not participate in Communists' activities in the U.S.A. or be used by that Party, yet Nikolai Lenin, as leader of the masses of Russia deserved respect for what, in all sincerity, he tried to do for them. Said he, "the masses need peace, bread, liberty and land."[74] Marcus Garvey never really condemned the system as it might be applied in an all Black country, by Blacks and for Blacks. Where Garvey had acted against the radical left, it had been in reaction to their disruptive activities, for example, in 1920 when he had had the UNIA police force "arrest" Domingo after the publication in the *Emancipator* of the article on the Black Star Line, and in 1921 when he had expelled the ABB from the Convention.[75]

The division between Black nationalists, communists and socialists was well established by the time Garvey went to jail. And it is only by way of a post script that the discussion is carried up to 1933—the year the Communist International declared its policy of a United Front, the joining of Communists with all non-fascist forces, Garveyites included. From 1929 to 1933 however, a quite different policy had been followed, one that would cement the bitter feelings between nationalists and the left.

When the world depression hit in '29 the Communists seized their first real opportunity to openly build a Communist mass movement. Around the issues of starvation wages and unemployment Communists could engage in militant public actions and win followers from the desperate poor. The Communist Party now drew a distinction and placed on one hand the "Garvey rank and file" who were seen as "potentially.... good fighters, willing and ready to wage a relentless struggle," and on the other the Garveyite leaders who "show political weaknesses, petty bourgeois wavering and helplessness."[76] The Communist Party now sought to wean away the rank and file Garveyites to Communism, much as the Socialist Party had tried in the early New Negro era. Yet by 1938 the Party would report that there had been over the previous five years a virtual one hundred percent turnover in Harlem Communist Party membership.[77] But earlier, in the depression years, the Communist prospects looked better since the Garvey movement was in decline. In addition, the Communists had adopted an apparently nationalistic goal of self-determination for American Blacks in a Black Belt Republic, to be created in the southern United States. Armed with this plan the Communists argued that nationalism had now been usurped from Garvey. There was no excuse for the existence of Garveyism. So when the California UNIA leader Arthur S. Gray endorsed Communism in 1931, his endorsement was caustically rejected by Party spokesman George Padmore who stated,

> Despite all of his "left" phrases... Mr. Gray still supports Marcus Garvey, who has been exposed over and over again as one of the greatest lackeys and defenders of capitalism... We want to say to Mr. Gray and other "left" Negro politicians inside and outside of the Garvey Movement that the only way that they can prove their sincerity and loyalty to the oppressed millions of their race is by breaking away from Garveyism and all other brands of Negro petty-bourgeois reformism, and actively supporting the revolutionary class struggle of the Negro workers.[78]

Just as Marcus Garvey had at first seen little reason to be opposed to Communists, so too in the depression period many a young Garveyite looked favorably on the radicalism of the Communists and expressed bewilderment at the attacks on Garvey. Garveyite Henry H. Kendal of Guyana wrote to Padmore's *Negro Worker* asking to be made an agent for the magazine. And Kendal added the query,

> Now I, as an African born in British Guiana cannot understand how you can talk that way of the Hon. Gentleman Marcus Garvey. For I say with no apology that when he came forward and told us of a free Africa, and nationalism for the Africans at home and abroad,—that caused the other races to respect us as a people... Why should you as a leader of the race count a man like Garvey among the crooks of the world? I say we of British Guiana do not like it and if you attack Garvey your work will not get as much hearing as it ought to get. I say stop criticizing Garvey and strike your blows on the one side and leave Garvey on the other.[79]

Padmore replied, "We make no apologies for our uncompromising exposure of the reformist politician Garvey, especially his capitalist utopian scheme of "Back to Africa".... Don't wait until you go to

Africa to begin the fight against your exploiters, for you might never get over there." Padmore would have Kendal forget Garvey, for "he lives in ease and comfort, out of the millions of dollars which you and other misled workers have given to him... You must not permit yourself to be misled by Garvey's 'radical' talk. That is exactly what he depends upon to fool the Negro masses."[80]

The race issue brought about other casualties among the left-wing race-conscious vanguard. One of these was Cyril Briggs, editor of the *Harlem Liberator*, weekly organ of the Harlem Communist Party, in the early years of the great depression. In 1934 however he was removed from this post. For although he appeared to follow the Party line, and to contribute his share of attacks on Garvey, he was losing his place as the leading Black Communist. Many newer members, vigilantly following the Party line, came to look with suspicion on the older ABB associates. Brotherhood people like Briggs, Richard B. Moore and Harry Haywood seemed incessantly to talk of racial issues, particularly of white racism in the Communist Party itself. One of the new Party members, MacKawain, wrote in 1934 that when he had joined up four years earlier, "the situation within the Party in Harlem was rotten. Petty-bourgeois nationalist tendencies were very rampant among our Negro comrades. Nearly every white comrade was charged with the crime of white-chauvinism, a vast majority of these charges had no foundation whatsoever. At this time, as a new member, it appeared to me that the duty of a Negro worker in the Party was to accuse a white worker of white chauvinism..."[81]

In MacKawain one could see a new generation of the left about to repeat the error of old socialists and the old African Blood Brotherhood in badgering those who didn't quite show enough militancy. On the other hand, within the Garvey movement there was a tendency to correlate alliances between Blacks and left-wing white and anti-Black behavior. In the long run, the biggest loser in the historic Black nationalist/communist-socialist split has been the laboring Black man the world over. The Black man will not win his freedom without nationalism; and nationalism will not liberate the Black unless it is thoroughly socialistic.

Notes

1. In arriving at the one million figure, membership of the small town UNIA Divisions was assumed to be no more than the required one hundred person minimum. However, among the public documents in the U.S. Department of Justice "Marcus Garvey" file there are some two hundred telegrams from small town Divisions, protesting

Garvey's imprisonment; each telegram was the product of a local mass meeting, and the telegrams declared the size of these small town gatherings— the average was one thousand people. The low was one hundred and the high, five thousand, in Natchitoches, Louisiana and in Blytheville, Arkansas respectively.

2. *Negro World*, 25 March, 8 May, 9 and 26 June, 21 August, 6 November 1920.
3. *Negro World*, 6 November 1920; *Messenger*, November 1920.
4. Theodore G. Vincent, *Black Power and the Garvey Movement* (Ramparts Press, Berkeley, 1971) pp. 157, 214, 219.
5. *Veteran*, quoted in Mitchell A. Palmer, "Radicalism and Sedition among the Negroes as Reflected in their Publications," Report of the United States Department of Justice, Vol. 12 of Senate Documents, No. 153, 66th Congress, 1st Session 1919, pp. 161-187.
6. R.R. Wright Jr. quoted in Robert T. Kerlin, *The Voice of the Negro* (E.P. Dutton and Company, N.Y., 1919) p. 22; Marcus Garvey in *Negro World*, 11 October 1919.
7. In Kerlin, *op. cit.*, pp. 63-65.
8. Vincent, *op. cit.*, pp. 197-198, 209-211; New York *World*, 13 August 1922.
9. *Crisis*, May 1919.
10. *Challenge*, August 1919, quoted in Palmer, *op. cit.*
11. *Crisis*, July 1918.
12. Quoted in Jervis Anderson, "From Florida to Harlem," *New Yorker*, 2 December 1972.
13. Cyril V. Briggs, "Notes for an Autobiography," in Cyril Briggs' papers, Los Angeles; interview with Richard B. Moore, May 1968; *Messenger*, August 1922, *Negro Digest*, September 1961 and March 1967.
14. *Negro Worker*, December 1936; 15 August 1932.
15. Los Angeles *California Eagle*, 6 May; 3 and 10 June; 29 July, 1922.
16. *Negro World*, 19 February 1921.
17. Amy J. Garvey, editor, *Philosophy and Opinions of Marcus Garvey* (Cass & Co., London, 1967), Vol. II, p. 126; Edmund David Cronon, *Black Moses, The Story of Marcus Garvey and the Universal Negro Improvement Association* (University of Wisconsin Press, Madison, 1955), p. 17.
18. Marcus Garvey to Major R. Moton, 29 February 1916, copy in Tuskegee Institute, reprinted in Daniel T. Williams, *Eight Negro Bibliographies* (Kraus Reprint Co., N.Y., 1970).
19. John Rex, "The Plural Society: The South African Case," *Race* XII 4, 1971.
20. Shawna Maglangbayan, *Garvey, Lumumba, Malcolm: Black nationalist separatists* (Third World Press, Chicago, 1972, p. 34).
21. Quoted in *Daily Worker*, 12 August 1924.
22. Personal background of Briggs taken from "Notes for an Autobiography," *op cit.*; *Who's Who of the Colored Race* 1915; Interviews with Harry Haywood, June 1966, and Richard B. Moore, May 1968.

23. Louis B. Bryan, "Brief History of the Life and Work of Hubert Harrison," MS (New York Federal Writers Project 1937) copy in Schomburg Library.
24. *Colored American Review,* 15 September 1915; 15 October 1915.
25. Briggs, "Notes..." *op. cit.*
26. Cyril Briggs to Sheridan W. Johns III, 7 June 1961; Cyril Briggs to Theodore Draper, 17 March 1958, in Cyril Briggs papers.
27. "Programme of the African Blood Brotherhood," *Communist Review* (London) April 1922.
28. *Crusader,* November 1919.
29. *Crusader,* September 1919.
30. Briggs, "Notes..." *op. cit.*
31. Ceremony explained in *Crusader,* November 1921.
32. Quoted from *Crusader* in *Negro Yearbook* 1918-1919 (Negro Yearbook Publishing Company, Tuskegee, Alabama, 1919); Vincent, op. cit., pp. 46-47.
33. See *Communist Review,* (London) April 1922; *Worker,* 5 August 1922.
34. Jervis Anderson, *op. cit.*
35. *Ibid.*
36. Spero and Harris, *The Black Worker,* (Atheneum, N.Y., 1968) p. 390.
37. Domingo's report was reprinted in "Revolutionary Radicalism: A Report of the Joint Legislative Committee of New York Investigating Seditious Activities," Vol. 2 (J.B. Lyon, Albany, New York, 1920).
38. The composition of this group is evidenced in the extensive correspondence of John E. Bruce, in Bruce papers — Schomburg Library, in the listings of *Who's Who of the Colored Race,* 1915, in the *Negro World,* 6 November 1920; 2 April 1921; 22 April 1922; the *Crusader,* November 1918; April 1919.
39. Background on A.A. Schomburg in *Who's Who of the Colored Race,* 1915.
40. *Negro World,* 21 August 1920.
41. *Negro World* endorsement carried in *Crusader,* August 1919.
42. ABB members urged to join UNIA, *Crusader,* December 1919; UNIA and ABB local branches, Briggs "Notes..." *op. cit., Crusader,* November 1921; ABB members in Liberty League, *Negro World,* 2 July 1921; on Hamitic League, *Negro World,* 6 November 1920; *Crusader,* November 1918; September 1919; on Bahamian Rejuvenation League, *Crusader,* April 1921.
43. Jervis Anderson, op. cit., various issues of *Messenger,* 1917–1919.
44. *Messenger,* August 1922.
45. Portions of the report were printed in the New York *Age,* 5 July 1919, at the time Marcus Garvey was on tour. Domingo left the *Negro World* early in September 1919.
46. *Crusader,* August 1919; *Messenger,* December 1919.
47. *Challenge,* May 1920; Bridges' connections with Tammany disclosed in *Negro World,* 6 November 1920.
48. *Emancipator,* 10 and 17 April 1920.
49. *Negro World,* 26 June 1920.

50. *Negro World,* 6 November 1920.

51. *Messenger,* November 1920.

52. New York *Age,* 24 September 1921.

53. New York *Age,* 24 September 1921.

54. *Negro World,* 1 October 1921; in this issue Johnson's article was reprinted next to Garvey's reply.

55. *Ibid .*

56. On Garveyites in the Divine movement see, *Negro World,* 15 April and 6 May 1933; Amy J. Garvey, *Garvey and Garveyism* (published by author, Kingston, Jamaica, 1963) p. 213 ; the last *Negro World* was published 17 October 1933, Vol. 32, No. 11. The *World Peace Echo* started publication 6 January 1934, New Series Vol. 1, No. 1, Old Series, Vol. 32, No. 12. This issue contained an explanation of the name change and new policy.

57. McKay, *A Long Way from Home,* (New York 1937) p. 109.

58. *Crusader,* November 1921; Washington *Bee,* 29 October 1921.

59. Vincent, op. cit., pp. 79-80; *Crusader,* November 1921; Amy J. Garvey, op. cit., pp. 64-65.

60. *Crusader,* November 1921.

61. Connections of these former UNIA leaders to the ABB revealed in *Negro World,* 31 December 1921; 14 January 1922.

62. *Pittsburgh Courier,* 30 June 1923.

63. See *Philosophy and Opinions of Marcus Garvey,* Vol. II, pp. 293308; correspondence between Chandler Owen and the Department of Justice, in Justice Department "Marcus Garvey" file, National Archives, Washington.

64. *Negro World,* 1 September, 1923.

65. *Negro World,* 10 March 1923.

66. Interview with Harry Haywood June 1966.

67. *Messenger,* March 1923.

68. Vincent, *op. cit.,* pp. 159, 172-174.

69. Spero and Harris, *op. cit.,* pp. 21, 57.

70. Briggs, "Notes..." *op. cit.*

71. Copy of Memo of Robert Minor in possession of Professor Stanley Coben, UCLA; original in Robert Minor papers, Columbia University.

72. *Daily Worker,* 9 August 1924.

73. *Philosophy and Opinions of Marcus Garvey,* Vol. II, pp .333-334.

74. Amy J. Garvey, *op. cit.,* p. 90.

75. *Messenger,* March 1923.

76. Cyril Briggs in *Harlem Liberator,* 23 September, 1933.

77. *Party Organizer,* June 1938.

78. *Negro World,* 25 July 1931; *Negro Worker,* July 1931.

79. Henry H. Kendal to George Padmore, Georgetown, 4 June 1932, reprinted in *Negro Worker,* 15 August 1932.

80. *Negro Worker,* 15 August 1932.

81. *Party Organizer,* April 1934

MWALIMU MARCUS GARVEY

E. U. Essien-Udom

T he influence of Garvey's ideas on recent Black nationalist movements in the United States has often been acknowledged. For example, his influence on leaders such as the late Honorable Elijah Muhammad, one-time uniformed officer of the U.N.I.A. and head of the "Nation of Islam," an Islamic movement among Black Americans. In Africa we know also that the late Ghanaian President, Osagyefo Kwame Nkrumah, one of Africa's greatest leaders, acknowledged Garvey's influence as the most important during his years as a student in the United States. "I think," he wrote, "that of all the literature that I studied, the book that did more than any other to fire my enthusiasm was *The Philosophy and Opinions of Marcus Garvey...*"[1] Unfortunately, we do not know which of Garvey's ideas influenced him most. However, it can be said that probably the most influential ideas which Nkrumah inherited from Garvey are embodied in the twin aspirations: "Africa Must be Free," and "Africa Must Unite"— both expressions are also titles of Nkrumah's books. To both Garvey and Nkrumah these aspirations meant the liberation of Africa and the African Diaspora, and cooperation between them, not only for their advancement, but for the advancement of mankind as a whole. But quite often, Garvey is remembered not for these or other fundamental ideas but for his "Back to Africa" scheme. Consequently, because of the prominence given to this misleading slogan, Garvey's ideas have suffered from gross over-simplifications or outright prejudice.

Undoubtedly, it is possible to interpret Garvey's ideas in a variety of ways, but I believe that any serious assessment of his ideas must take into account the full range of his utterances and writings, and the ideas implicit in his activities. Because of long-held prejudices and the tendency to oversimplify his ideas, the other Garvey, an extremely sensitive, reflective and humane man is yet to be fully analyzed and understood. Although Garvey's private papers are not available, and we have no way of directly assessing his innermost thoughts, I believe that a study of his published writings and speeches and the commentaries of those who knew him warrant the conclusion that he was highly sensitive to broad humane problems, that he suffered from personal dilemmas and intellectual agonies resulting from the effort to be both a virtuous man and leader of a downtrodden race.

This seminar can be regarded by scholars as a beginning of the critical examination of the whole range of Garvey's ideas and the reevaluation of their relevance for contemporary problems confronting African peoples and the world at large. However, I do not pretend to and cannot undertake this task here. Rather, I wish to suggest that hitherto, with few exceptions, the study of Garvey has been confined to his activities as leader of a political movement and to a few quite often over-simplified and flamboyant ideas associated with his African colonization scheme. Having made this suggestion, I wish to plead that attention ought to be given to Garvey as "Mwalimu," a teacher.

Garvey the Man

Of course, Garvey was a man of many parts; he was master of flamboyant oratory; but he was also Mwalimu, and this, I believe, distinguished him from the general run of leaders of recent political movements in Africa and the African Diaspora. Why do I call him Mwalimu? Why should I not call him 'philosopher'? The reason is simple. First, because in European conception a philosopher is a chap who talks or writes a lot about justice, equality, et cetera, but rarely gets involved in action against social injustice and inequality. Second, Garvey was not a philosopher in the formal sense. Although his ideas can be systematized, he did not devote the major part of his working life exclusively to elaborating and systematizing his ideas. He was a man of action as well. Nevertheless, he developed a coherent body of ideas about the world which he sought to impart to others, especially the "Africans at home and abroad." To me the word 'Mwalimu', in the sense approximately represented by the late

Osagyefo Kwame Nkrumah and by Julius Nyerere, Tanzania's President, seems to convey this meaning of leader and teacher. Exceptionally few political leaders attempt to develop and articulate a "world view," to impart it to others or to implement it. Thirdly, Garvey thought of himself as leader and teacher. To his followers he was a teacher in the sense Mahatma Gandhi or Mao Tse Tung can be considered teachers.

Garvey's role as a leader is well known. But the conception of him as Mwalimu, which is the way his devotees regarded him, is not often acknowledged. Yet, he referred to himself frequently as a teacher, especially but not exclusively to the African Diaspora. He believed that the New World Blacks had suffered much because their "outlook and philosophy were wrong." They were victims of an environment "that we ourselves did not create... Our habits, our manners, our everything has been shaped just by what plan was fixed up for us to fall into, in the respective places which we have come from." The U.N.I.A. program, he said, was therefore to bring to the Blacks "something positive out of which will rise a new race, a new dream." (pp. 48–50).[2] Garvey repeated in several places and contexts that his writings and speeches were intended to educate and inspire the African peoples. (p. 20) Elsewhere he observed:

> I am a public lecturer, but I am President-General of the Universal Negro Improvement Association. As a public Lecturer I endeavour to help educate the public, particularly of the race, as I meet that public... I do not speak carelessly or recklessly but with a definite object of helping the people, especially those of my race, to know, to understand, to realize themselves. Whether that audience is one or two or a hundred it wouldn't matter at all, because I am ... desirous of helping even one man to discover himself, to be himself... (pp. 20-21).

Still in another context Garvey came close to identifying himself as a philosopher: "I am a sort of philosopher, I can always sympathize with a man and reason with him, instead of using the strong arm, but there are others who are not so disposed." (p. 309) As Mwalimu, Garvey had much faith in the efficacy of reason and judgment. Consequently in the resolution of social conflict he believed in persuasion and probably would have endorsed violence as a last resort. In brief, he accepted the ethical values embodied in the teachings of Christ: "... We believe in Him. We believe He is the God of love, of mercy, of justice. We have adopted that fine philosophy of approaching Him and all things human through reason, through judgment, and through brotherly and fatherly love." (pp. 100-101) He ranked

Christ's Sermon on the Mount as "a wonderful bit of philosophy, probably the greatest statement of political and social economy ever delivered by man since Creation." (p. 219) For him Christ was a model of life, morality and ethics. Christ was the embodiment of all humanity and had as much Negro in Him as Anglo-Saxon, as much European as Ethiopian (pp. 222-223). Of course, it may be argued that Garvey also made speeches which were threatening and violent. This is true. But on balance, the evidence is strong that he disavowed violence except as a last resort in the resolution of social conflict.

Garvey attached much importance to the acquisition of knowledge, but knowledge was not to be sought for its own sake. He saw clearly the relationship between theory and practice. Thus while he considered it the "duty of man to learn all of nature's ways if he is to boss nature and to be sovereign of the world," he noted the need to fashion a theory that explains nature and the world. Arguing by analogy, he observed: "There can be no king without the thought of being king, there is no sovereign or dictator without the thought in that direction. As a man thinketh so is he ... the man must first think before the thing becomes a reality." (p. 25)

Mwalimu Garvey was not content performing the function of teacher mainly by speeches, writings and public lectures. Thus, about three years before his death, in September 1937, Garvey made the significant move of establishing formally the School of African Philosophy for the training of U.N.I.A. cadres. He designated the course "African Philosophy." He claimed that it was "African philosophy not Platonic philosophy" which would save "this perishing race of ours." (p. 187) "African Philosophy," he said, was "the peculiar and particular philosophy that is to emancipate" the Blacks from "the thraldom of other philosophers." He envisaged that the U.N.I.A. cadres so trained would "go out and teach that philosophy as probably Socrates and Plato and Aristotle and more recent philosophers have taught." (pp. 178-179) Unfortunately, I am not aware of records describing the *content* of the course on "African Philosophy," although Garvey mentioned that forty-two different subjects were taught. However, it is likely that "African Philosophy" encompassed ideas which Garvey had developed and expressed in his speeches and writings during the preceding decades.

In our view Garvey was a much bigger man than the "buffoon" his detractors sought to make him. He was bigger than a mere political agitator, anti-colonialist or anti-this or that. He was a man with positive ideas as well. He was a teacher, and thought of himself as such. In many ways he was a gifted man whose thoughts covered wide fields. Thus his ideas no less than his activities deserve closer critical analysis. I suspect that such a study would include, for example, the sources of various strands of his ideas. In all probability the study would reveal that underlying his social ideas is his conception of God, and man's relationship to Him through man's participation in what he called "universal intelligence."

Religion and Garvey

We may discover that he had a rather peculiar conception of God; that although his conception of God resembles the Christian concept, his is nevertheless different. Briefly, Garvey believed, as I suspect many do, that God created the universe once and for all times. From that moment on man is left entirely on his own, having been endowed with intelligence by his creator. Hence, there is no use blaming God for his misfortunes or turning to Him for help by prayers. I believe that it is from this premise that we begin to understand Garvey's insistence on the notion of self-reliance, self-determination, and responsibility for individuals and groups. Again, from this basic conception of God and man, Garveyism emerges as a powerful, meaningful, and appealing social philosophy. It explains Garvey's firm and fervent belief in human equality, his belief in human freedom and creativity, his belief in social justice, his belief in self-reliance and industry, individual responsibility and accountability to man and to God, and his doctrine of human destiny. What emerges from a close analysis of his ideas throws a different light on the Garvey and Garveyism of journalists, detractors, of many Garvey scholars, and of course, some of his own followers.

There are, of course, many difficulties in studying Garvey's ideas. One such difficulty among others is the fact that his ideas were very much interwoven with the grave and urgent problem of racial emancipation. Because of this, his incisive insights into human and social affairs are often lost to many who claim to understand him. In turn, this gives rise to such appallingly ignorant conclusions as that he was a "fascist." But I am convinced that his thoughts issued from a profound philosophical frame of reference and an unparalleled faith in man as man. Furthermore, Garveyism is a disciplined philosophy and I suspect that his method of protest was probably determined and limited by it.

However, it can be said that Mwalimu Marcus Garvey was an optimist. He had an undying faith in the infinite possibilities of human intelligence for the highest possible achievements. He wrote, "Nature's endowment is prolific and grand. The assumption and firm belief is that there is no human limit. The only limit is transgression of Divinity." (p 130) He believed unswervingly that intellectual capabilities are common to all men: "The creative source of life made common intelligence, something that is the possession of every man." (p. 133) Human freedom issues from this "unique sovereignty" in man, the capacity to think and reason—the bulwark against tyranny. His optimism and belief in reason is revealed in his assessment of the future of tyrannical rule in the apartheid Republic of South Africa: "Fools that they are, who know not that prison bars cannot deaden or kill the souls and minds of men; fools that they are, who do not realize that there is no power on earth to suppress the hopes of man." (p. 104)

Obviously this essay is not an analysis of Garveyism. Rather, it is a plea that his ideas ought to be studied on their own merit. To me Mwalimu Mosiah Garvey was a great teacher and inspiring leader of a downtrodden race. It is a measure of his greatness that one can relate to his ideas according to one's understanding and needs and that many of his essential ideas are just as valid today for Africa and the African Diaspora.

Notes

1. *Ghana: Autobiography of Kwame Nkrumah,* Thomas Nelson and Sons, 1957, New York, 1957, p. 45.

2. All quotations and paginations in this essay refer to *More Philosophy and Opinions of Marcus Garvey,* Vol. III, eds. E.U. Essien-Udom & Amy Jacques Garvey, Frank Cass & Co. Ltd., London & New Jersey, 1977.

NOTES ON CONTRIBUTORS

John Henrik Clarke
Associate Professor, Dept. of Black and Puerto Rican Studies, Hunter College, New York City, USA.
Distinguished Visiting Professor of African History, Africana Studies and Research Center, Cornell University, USA.
Editor, *Harlem: Voices from the Soul of Black America; Marcus Garvey and the Vision of Africa.*

William Elkins
Author, *Black Nationalism in the British Caribbean, 1918–1920.*

Essien-Udom Essien-Udom
Former Vice-Chancellor, University of Maidguri, Nigeria.
Professor, Dept. of Political Science, University of Ibadan, Nigeria.
Author, *Black Nationalism: a Search for an Identity in America.*
Co-editor (with Amy Jacques Garvey), *More Philosophy and Opinions of Marcus Garvey,* Vol. 111.

Amy Jacques Garvey
Author, *Garvey and Garveyism: Black Power in Jamaica.* Editor, Philosophy and Opinions of Marcus Garvey, *Vols. I and II.*
Co-editor (with E.U. Essien-Udom), *More Philosophy and Opinions of Marcus Garvey,* Vol. III.

George Huggins
Programme Officer for the Caribbean Area of the United Nations Food and Agriculture Organization, Action for Development/Freedom From Hunger Campaign.

Arnold Hughes
Lecturer in Political Science, Centre of West African Studies, University of Birmingham, England.

Rupert Lewis
Lecturer, Dept. of Government, University of the West Indies Jamaica.
Editor (with Trevor Munroe), *Readings in Government and Politics of the West Indies; Bongo Man, Abeng, Struggle* radical newspapers.

Tony Martin
Professor, Black Studies and History, Wellesley College, Massachusetts, USA.
Author, *Race First: the Ideological and Organizational Struggles of Marcus Garvey and the Universal Negro Improvement Association.*

Gabriel Olakunle Olusanya
Professor of History, University of Lagos, Nigeria.
Author, *The Second World War and Politics in Nigeria, 1939-1953; The Evolution of the Nigerian Civil Service, 1861-1960: the Problems of Nigerianization.*

Emory Tolbert
Assistant Professor, Dept. of History, University of California at San Diego, USA.
Author, *The UNIA and Black Los Angeles: Ideology and Community in the American Garvey Mouement.*

Theodore Vincent
Author, *Black Power and the Garvey Movement; Voices of a Black Nation: Political Journalism in the Harlem Renaissance.*

INDEX